MUSIC OF OUR TIME

MUSIC OF OUR TIME

*An Anthology of Works of Selected
Contemporary Composers of the 20th Century*

By

NICK ROSSI
Los Angeles City School Districts

AND

ROBERT A. CHOATE
School of Fine and Applied Arts, Boston University

CRESCENDO PUBLISHING COMPANY

BOSTON

Standard Book Number 87597—005—2
Library of Congress Card Number 69—16933
Printed in the United States of America
Copyright ©1969 by Nick Rossi and Robert A. Choate

PREFACE

With the possible exception of the Baroque era, no period in the history of Western civilization has witnessed so many vital changes in music as the 20th century has seen. The changes have been drastic and rapid. Spawned by scientific and technological developments, a new aesthetic and a not-so-silent revolution have been restructuring and reshaping our intellectual, artistic and social spheres. Traditional definitions of music have been challenged or radically changed. Innovation, new sounds, and altered forms or formlessness are the order of the times. While resistance to the new is hardly peculiar to this age, heated controversy or outright hostility on the part of traditionalists maintains a seemingly unbridgeable gap. Yet, this music of our time exists — or more correctly, co-exists with the acknowledged musical tradition. In this book, some of these developments and expressions are presented. In many instances, viewpoints and the aesthetic of the composer are included to enlighten and broaden the understanding of their musical intent.

The authors have begun *Music of Our Time* at the turn of the century, with the works of Claude Debussy who, in his own words, sought "a new type of music, a kind free from themes and motives, or formed on a single continuous theme, which nothing interrupts and which never returns upon itself. I want to see this creation; I myself shall achieve it."

The authors have divided the book into two sections: the first is devoted to composers from Europe and Latin America; the second section deals with composers of the United States. Within each section the composers are considered in chronological order by year of birth. Such a procedure presents an exciting panorama of the simultaneous development of diverse compositional styles, the search for new sounds, and individual expressiveness; it also avoids inappropriate or inept grouping by nationality or style.

Without attempting value judgments (leaving that up to the individual auditor of the music itself), the authors have presented the universally acknowledged master composers of our time: Debussy, Schoenberg, Stravinsky, Bartók, Berg and Webern. They have also included lesser figures whose works have affected the style of others: Satie, Varése and Cowell. The radical new trends are recognized: *musique concréte,* aleatoric music, electronic music, and music involving computers and synthesizers. Included along with the revolutionary figures and their "way out" music are traditionalists who have built on idioms of the past: neo-Baroque

i

composers such as Hindemith, neo-classicists such as Piston and neo-Romantics such as Hanson and Rorem. Included are a score of composers whose music is among that most frequently heard in opera houses and concert halls — men such as Britten, Thomson, Prokofiev and Copland. Figures unique in the annals of music history, Charles Ives and George Gershwin, are to be found in *Music of Our Time.*

The authors are very much aware that because of the limitations of space, an impressive list could be drawn up of fine composers who, unfortunately, had to be omitted: Sessions, Carter, Imbrie, Pousseur, Penderecki, Lutoslawski, Dallipiccolo, Bernstein, Schuman, Menotti and countless others. Likewise, in trying to select musical compositions which represent the major forms — opera, choral music, art song, ballet, solo sonata, chamber music and the major orchestral forms — the authors have had to omit some of the great masterpieces of the century: *La Mer, Daphnis et Chloé, Wozzeck, Petrouchka. L'Oiseau de feu,* and *Appalachian Spring.*

Since the distinguishing characteristic of music is tone, and tone is perceived through the ear, listening to the music described and discussed in this book is an indispensable activity. Furthermore, it is not enough merely to hear the music. One must listen to it with a focus of attention upon its most significant characteristics, rehearing it again and again so that — with exposure — the meaning of the music (in music's own terms) becomes clearer and clearer.

The listener needs help in knowing what to listen for. The authors have tried to point out in their verbal explanations the significant musical characteristics of the compositions. They have tried to help the listener investigate the elements of music and the relationships which exist among them, thus leading — it is hoped — to an understanding of the nature, structure and meaning of this music of our time.

ACKNOWLEDGMENTS

The authors would like to express their appreciation and gratitude to Louis "Satchmo" Armstrong, Milton Babbitt, Samuel Barber, Luciano Berio, Ira Gershwin, Howard Hanson, Roy Harris, Otto Luening, Darius Milhaud, Walter Piston, Ned Rorem, William Grant Still, Morton Subotnick and Charles Wuorinen who have assisted with biographical sketches and/or analyses.

The authors also would like to express their thanks to Miss Stella Herman, an outstanding musician in her own right, who graciously typed the manuscript. For assistance in setting the many musical examples in contemporary notation, appreciation is expressed to Mrs. Viola Joros.

For permission to quote copyrighted material, the following acknowledgements are made:

George Antheil: *Ballet mécanique*, copyright MCMLIX, Templeton Publishing Co., Inc. International Copyright Secured. All Rights Reserved. Sole Agent: Shawnee Press, Inc., Delaware Water Gap, Pa. 18327.

Samuel Barber: *Adagio for Strings*, copyright 1939 by G. Schirmer, Inc. International copyright secured.

Béla Bartók: *Roumanian Folk Dances*, copyright 1918 by Universal Editions A.G.; renewed 1945. Copyright and renewal assigned to Boosey & Hawkes, Inc. for U.S.A. Reprinted by permission. *Concerto for Orchestra*, copyright 1946 by Hawkes and Son (London) Ltd. Reprinted by permission of Boosey & Hawkes.

Alban Berg: *Violinkonzert*, copyright 1936 by Universal Editions; sole agents Theodore Presser Co., Bryn Mawr, Pa.

Luciano Berio: *Sinfonia*, copyright 1968 by the composer; permission to quote granted by the composer.

Pierre Boulez: *Le Soleil des eaux*, copyright 1964 by Universal Editions; sole agents. Theodore Presser Co., Bryn Mawr, Pa.

Benjamin Britten: *Peter Grimes*, copyright 1945 by Boosey & Hawkes Ltd. Reprinted by permission of Boosey & Hawkes, Inc.

Carlos Chávez: *Toccata*, copyright 1954 by Mills Music, Inc. Used by Permission

Aaron Copland: *Sonata for Violin and Piano*, copyright 1944 by Aaron Copland. Reprinted by permission of Aaron Copland, Copyright Owner, and Boosey & Hawkes, Inc. Sole Publishers.

Henry Cowell: *The Banshee*, copyright 1930 by Associated Music Publishers, Inc. used by permission.

George Gershwin: *Rhapsody in Blue*, copyright 1924 by New World Music Corp. Reprinted by Permission.

Alberto Ginastera: *Estancia*, copyright 1953 by Barry & Cia. Reprinted by permission of Boosey & Hawkes, Inc.

Howard Hanson: *Lament for Beowulf*, copyright MCMXXV by C.C. Birchard & Company. International Copyright Secured. Reprinted by permission of the composer.

iii

For providing photographic portraits of the composers represented in MUSIC OF OUR TIME, the following acknowledgements are made:

Isabella Arnstam, Muedon (France) for the portrait of Luciano Berio.

Associated Music Publishers for the portrait of Paul Hindemith.

Berko (Aspen, Colorado) for the portrait of Benjamin Britten.

The Bettmann Archive for the portrait of George Antheil and the photograph of Debussy visiting Stravinsky.

BMI for portraits of Alban Berg, Henry Cowell, Hans Werner Henze, Carl Orff, Gunther Schuller and Karlheinz Stockhausen.

Boosey & Hawkes for portraits of Aaron Copland (photograph by Paul Moor) and Ned Rorem (photograph by William Claxton).

Columbia University for the portraits of Vladimir Ussachevsky and Otto Luening.

Curtis Institute of Music for the photograph of Samuel Barber and Gian-Carlo Menotti in Italy.

Ira Gershwin for the portrait of George Gershwin.

Howard Hanson for the portrait of himself (photograph by J. Sam Smith).

MCA Music for the portrait of Morton Subotnick.

Darius Milhaud for the portrait of himself.

The Moldenhauer Archives, Spokane, Washington, for the two photographs of Anton Webern.

Walter Piston for the portrait of himself.

Ricardo Salazar for the portrait of Carlos Chávez.

G. Schirmer, Inc. for the portrait of Samuel Barber.

Evan Senior, copyright owner of the photograph of Paul McCartney with composer Luciano Berio.

William Grant Still for the portrait of himself.

Virgil Thomson for the portrait of himself.

The White House, J. Bruce Whelihan, Staff Assistant, for the photograph of President Nixon playing the piano for his dinner in honor of Duke Ellington.

For permission to reproduce various works of art and special photographs, the following acknowledgments are made:

Academia Republicii Socialiste România, Institutul de Etnografic şi folclor (Bucharest) for photograph of *Joc cu bâtă* dance.

BBC, London, for the copyrighted photograph of Act II from their production of *Peter Grimes.*

Curtis Institute of Music, Philadelphia, for the photograph of Samuel Barber and Gian-Carlo Menotti with their teacher in Italy.

Howard Hanson for the photograph of his island retreat off the coast of Maine.

Musée Marmottan, Paris (Photographie Giraudon) for the photograph of Monet's painting, *Impression: Soleil levant.*

Museum of Modern Art, New York, for the photograph of Paul Klee's *The Twittering Machine* (Zwitscher-Maschine).

New York Public Library, The Library and Museum of the Performing Arts, Lincoln Center, for the photograph of the Balanchine production of *Le Sacre du printemps* at La Scala (Italy).

Nonesuch Records, New York, for permission to reprint the composer's notes on *Silver Apples of the Moon.*

Philadelphia Museum of Art for permission to reproduce Fernand Leger's *The City* (photograph by A.J. Wyatt, staff photographer).

San Francisco Opera Company for the two scenes from Orff's *Carmina Burana,* Carolyn Mason Jones, photographer.

Walter Piston for the photograph of his home at Belmont, Massachusetts.

Tony Ray-Jones for his copyrighted photograph of the "front" of Aldeburgh.

Virgil Thomson for the photograph of the Prologue to *Four Saints in Three Acts* (by White Studios).

Universal Editions for the copyrighted quotations from Karlheinz Stockhausen's *Nr. 11 Refrain* and *Studie II*.

Wadsworth Atheneum, Hartford, for Leon Bakst's costume design, "Nijinsky in *L'Après-midi d'un faune.*"

CONTENTS

Claude Debussy and Igor Stravinsky about 1910. The musical creations of these two men span more than seven decades and involve the major compositional styles of our time.

PART I

MUSIC OF EUROPE AND LATIN AMERICA

The creative musicians of the 20th century have been an active group. Perhaps never before in history have composers lashed out in so many directions, seeking new sounds, new techniques and new systems. Some of these systems have evolved naturally out of the styles of earlier periods as composers sought an idiom that would best express their musical ideas. In other cases, there has been a conscious revolt by the composer against the past and all its sounds, forms and rules.

The greatly accelerated pace of the 20th century — starting with the machine age, moving on to the atomic era, and continuing with space explorations — has speeded the tempo of life, raised the threshold of noise and human tolerance, and made world-wide communication almost instantaneous. All forms of art, including music, have become easily accessible to most of western civilization through modern reproductions: art prints and slides, books and magazines, phonograph records and tape recordings. New forms of art have been developed including still photography and motion pictures. The composer of the 20th century has attempted to assimilate these changes, reflect the accelerating pace and give artistic meaning to the noise and confusion of the times.

At present we are too close to the confusion to properly judge what innovations will be lasting, almost too close to make value judgments concerning the artistic merits of the more revolutionary compositions. The best that we can do is to make an honest attempt to study and understand the style, technique — even the dogma of the composer — and then listen to his music. From such a survey, certain compositions will remain in our memory, works that we would like to hear again. For the individual, these are the important compositions of our time.

How does this music of our time differ from that of earlier eras? In many ways, to be sure, but certain fundamental changes permeate much of this new music. These changes can be related to the basic elements of music — melody, rhythm, harmony, form,

1

and the associative elements of expression — tempo, dynamics, and timbre (tone "color"). In the 20th century, musicians have sought a wider interpretation of what is considered as *melody,* trying to escape from the confines of the major and minor scales and even the semi-tone division of the octave. Composers have looked for a rhythm that was not a stereotyped repetition *ad infinitum* of duple or triple meter (two or three pulses to the measure) or the compound forms of these (four and six pulses per measure, for example). These modern creators have attempted to escape from the traditional idea of harmony of the 18th and 19th centuries, of major and minor triads and "logical" chord progressions. *Form* itself has perhaps undergone the most careful scrutiny. Concerning the expressive elements, music historians have told us that tempos have increased in modern performance, and we know from what we hear ourselves in everyday life that the dynamic levels are building higher and higher through the use of electronic circuitry in radios, hi-fi's and phonographs. And last, and very far from least, new concepts of musical timbres have permeated much of the writing, such as the use of instruments from India and the Orient, electronic instruments and devices, and modern adaptations of traditional instruments.

We unfortunately do not have an accepted word yet that describes the era and type of music about which we have been talking. To call it *Twentieth-century Music* or *Contemporary Music* would be to identify the dates but not the style, since such late-Romantic composers as Richard Strauss (1864-1949), Jan Sibelius (1865-1957) and Serge Rachmaninoff (1873-1943) all lived and worked creatively in the 20th century. To refer to it as *New Music* may easily confuse it with two earlier epochs: the *ars nova,* the "New Art" around 1300 when progressive composers attempted to produce new rhythmic and harmonic principles; and the *nuove musiche,* "The New Music" of the 1600's in Italy, in which Monteverdi and his contemporaries tried composing expressive melodies, and developed the dramatic concept of opera which challenged the tradition of religious choral music.

Actually, all labels are poor, whether they be "Romanticism," "Impressionism" or something else, for they imply pigeon-holes, a desire on the part of the academic historian to fit everything into neat little compartments, all easily identifiable by their label. But, music can not be pigeon-holed. It is an art, an art that has evolved out of use, and it is constantly changing, even within the works of a single composer. For convenience however, in this book we shall use the more accepted labels, inaccurate though they may be. Society and the musical public have accepted them, and they will at least serve as a point of departure for our musical discussions.

. The break with the past first occurred in the music of Claude Debussy. He had opened his ears to the sounds around him. Although he abhorred the term *impressionism,* contemporary writers started using it to refer to his "style". (It was a term borrowed from the painter's art.) We generally acknowledge as followers of Debussy's "impressionist style" the Frenchmen Albert Roussel (1869-1937), Maurice Ravel (1875-1937) and Jacques Ibert (1890-1962); the Englishmen Frederick Delius (1862-1934) and Cyril Scott (1879-   ); Manuel de Falla (1876-1946), a Spaniard, and Ottorino Respighi (1879-1936), an Italian; and, in the United States, Charles Tomlinson Griffes (1884-1920) and John Alden Carpenter (1876-1951).

I

CLAUDE ACHILLE DEBUSSY (1862-1918) was greatly impressed by the Paris World Exhibition of 1889. To celebrate this centennial of the French Revolution, a huge steel structure, the Eiffel Tower, was erected on the *Champs des Mars.* In addition to Gustave Eiffel's great feat of engineering, the Exhibition included many exotic displays from the near and far east. The pavilions of China and the Dutch East Indies included performances of native folk music. Debussy was deeply affected by what he heard; he incorporated into his *Quartet* a suggestion of the *gamelang,* an orchestra made up of peculiarly Javanese instruments. His piano piece, *Pagodas,* was based on the pentatonic scale, which hints of the Orient.

"Autumn Print", created in 1898 by the French artist Alphons Mucha, illustrates the decorative motive of the *Art Nouveau* movement.

"The Peacock Skirt" by Aubrey Beardsley. Used in Oscar Wilde's *Salome.*

"Impression: Soleil Levant" (A Sunrise) painted in 1872 by Claude Monet provided a name for the stylistic movement of the turn-of-the-century.

Debussy learned from *all* the world of music. In addition to the influences of the *art nouveau* style and jazz as imported from the United States, he was impressed by the unschooled writing of the Russian composer Modest Mussorgsky (1839-1881), "the art," according to Debussy, "of an inquisitive savage who discovered music at every step made by his emotions." Gregorian chant and Renaissance polyphony always greatly interested Debussy.

Although the composer was schooled in the 19th-century traditions of French music, he showed a rebellious nature early in life. One evening, when he was about 20 and studying at the Paris Conservatory, he went to the piano "to imitate the sound of buses in the street" according to a fellow student. "He played a sort of chromatic groaning, to which his friends and a few people who had stayed on from other classes listened mockingly. 'Look at them,' Debussy said, turning around. 'Can't you listen to chords without knowing their names?' . . . chords of the ninth on all degrees of the scale, chords of the 11th and 13th; all the notes of the diatonic scale heard at once in fantastic arrangements. . . And all this Claude called . . . 'a feast for the ear.' He was asked, 'what rule do you follow?' Debussy answered, *'Mon plaisir!'* "

Born of poor parents in a little second floor apartment above his father's china shop in St. Germain-en-Laye, a suburb about a half-hour's drive from Paris, the boy at first showed no interest in music. His godmother arranged for his first piano lessons; the teacher claimed the lad had "no ear for music" since he banged away at the piano, caring little for tone quality or subtlety in the musical interpretation. By the time Claude was 11 he was enrolled at the Paris Conservatory where he studied piano, 18th-century harmony, early 19th-century form, classical counterpoint, and other related traditions. He was the problem child of the Conservatory, and had an erratic record because he objected to the accepted theories of harmony and composition. His fellow students found him both uncouth and sarcastic.

The Conservatory's highest award was the *Prix de Rome* given annually to a student for the best composition of the year. The winner was entitled to three years of study, free of charge, at the French Academy in Rome. In three years of submitting compositions for consideration, Debussy netted, in order, a *no mention*, a *fourth place* and a *second place*. He finally decided to write a work in a more conventional form to please the judges. It won the first prize for him!

Debussy was not favorably impressed by the Academy in Rome. "It would be idle to imagine that new theories of art could evolve here," he wrote home. "This is the home of mediocre art. I have tried to work, but haven't been able to. This just isn't the place for me! " Before his three years of study were up, he quit the Academy in disgust and returned to Paris. "I could no longer drag out a monstrous, easy life. In Rome, I could come to nothing, my musical mind was dead."

Back home in Paris, Debussy listened to the world of music around him, searching for his own idiom of expression. "Music until the present day," he said, "has rested on a false principle. There is too much *writing* of music. Music is made for its effect on paper although it is intended for the ear. Too much importance is attached to the writing of music, the formula, the craft. Composers seek their ideas within themselves when they should look around for them." At another time he said, "I am all for liberty. Music is by its very nature free. Every sound you hear around you can be reproduced. Everything that a keen ear perceives in the rhythm of the surrounding world can be represented musically. To some people rules are of primary importance, but my desire is to reproduce only what I hear."

And so Debussy, in his compositions, gave audible form to his theories. Of his better known works, the *Prélude à l'après-midi d'un faune* (Prelude to the Afternoon of a Faun) came first, written in 1894; then the *Nocturnes* for orchestra in 1899, followed by his opera *Pelléas et Mélisande* in 1902. His finest orchestral composition came next, in 1905, *La Mer,* (The Sea.) It was followed in 1912 by another major work for orchestra, *Images.* His two books of *Préludes* for the piano, written in 1910 and 1913, were based on J. S. Bach's original idea of a cycle of preludes; the *Études* (Studies) of 1915 perhaps were inspired by Chopin's example. In addition Debussy wrote many fine songs throughout his creative career.

In these works one discovers Debussy's idiom. His technical innovations — his new freedom in using dissonant sounds, his use of different scales and modes, his violation of the traditional rules of harmony and counterpoint — all evolved from late-Romantic ideas. His abandonment of the age-old forms of music was not complete, for by training he was too steeped in the 19th-century traditions. The competent student can discover, for example, that the *Prélude à l'après-midi d'un faune* is cast basically in a variant of ternary form. In the larger works such as *La Mer* the contrasting movements, despite their programmatic titles, correspond to the traditional movements of a symphony.

Debussy's contemporaries questioned his free use of chords. To them he replied: "A chord in a structure of sound is like a stone in a building. Its true value depends on the place it occupies and the support it lends to the flexible curve of the melodic line." Concerning tonality the composer told his contemporaries: "Music is neither major nor minor, or rather, it is both at once. What keeps it fresh and supple is a continuous fluctuating between major and minor thirds. . . . Mode is what the musician thinks of at a given moment; it is unstable."

In defense of these theories, Debussy wrote his publisher in 1908: "I am trying to make something new — *realities,* as it were; what imbeciles call *impressionism.*" That term, "impressionism," had plagued him ever since he completed his *Prélude à l'après-midi d'un faune.* The music critics had borrowed the word from the painter's art to try to "label" Debussy's new style. The critics would have been better advised to substitute a term used to identify the poetry of the era, *symbolism*, for Debussy felt much more akin in spirit to the symbolist poets. He created vocal and choral settings of a number of symbolist poems.

As a term, *impressionism* was originally used in a derogatory sense to identify a style of late 19th-century French painting. The word was first employed by Claude Monet (1840-1926) in a title for one of his works in the Paris exhibit of 1863 — *Impression: Soleil levant* (Sunrise, an impression). Rather than using photographic realism, he attempted to give the "impression" of a sunrise, what might be seen in a quick glance, thus lacking definite detail of form and line. Monet's colleagues — Edouard Manet (1832-1883), Edgar Degas (1834-1917) and Auguste Renoir (1841-1919) — joined him in the revolt against Romantic realism; they tried to concern themselves with fleeting glimpses and first impressions. They preferred common subjects: still life, dancing girls, nudes, scenes of middle-class life such as picnics, boating parties and cafe scenes, as opposed to the grandiose and drama-packed scenes of their predecessors. These *impressionists* were concerned with color and light and shade; the actual subject of the painting was of secondary importance. The public at first was offended by this lack of definition of line and form, and it objected to "grass that was pink, yellow or blue."

A similar revolt against realism occurred in the 1880's among the French poets. Known as *symbolists*, they attempted to suggest a fantasy of imagination rather than describe in detail; they abandoned rhyme and the traditional forms; they used a word for its "color" or "flavor" rather than for its specific meaning. They preferred to present the *symbol* rather than to state the thing, to experiment with new sounds and sonorities. Important poets of the Symbolist school, all of whom were close personal friends of Debussy, included Charles Baudelaire (1821-1867), Stéphane Mallarmé (1842-1898), Paul Verlaine (1844-1896), and the Belgian poet Maurice Maeterlinck (1862-1949).

As has been stated before, Debussy's break with the Romantic tradition, the start of the so-called *impressionistic* movement, occurred in 1892 with his *Prélude à l'après-midi d'un faune* inspired by the symbolist poem or ecologue of Stéphane Mallarmé. This is music that hints rather than states; music in which a succession of colors takes the place of dynamic development; music that is vague and intangible.

PRÉLUDE À L'APRÈS-MIDI D'UN FAUNE

Claude Debussy was a frequent guest in the home of Stéphane Mallarmé, for he was impressed and inspired by the writings of this symbolist poet. One of his poems fascinated Debussy, *The Afternoon of a Faun.* The composer at first planned a major work in three movements based on this ecologue. He would call his new composition "Prelude, Interlude and Final Paraphrase on the Afternoon of a Faun." Although he made sketches for all three movements, Debussy changed his mind and wrote only a single movement. The completed work he called, quite simply, *Prélude à l'après-midi d'un faune,* the "Prelude to the Afternoon of a Faun." The composer attached a note to the completed score, saying that the music "evokes the successive echoes of the Faun's desires and dreams on a hot afternoon."

"A Faun's Costume" was designed in the *Art Nouveau* style by Leon Bakst for Nijinsky, the famous dancer, who in 1912 produced a ballet based on Debussy's *Prélude à l'après-midi d'un faune.* The flowing lines and oriental influence of the *Art Nouveau* can be seen in this stylized representation of a faun, that creature of Greek mythology with the ears, horns, hind legs and tail of a goat, and head and body of a human.

Edmund Gosse, writing in *Questions at Issue* in 1893, shows that Mallarmé, in the poem, rejected the old worn phrases in favor of odd, exotic and archaic terms. Mallarmé, according to Gosse, aimed to "use words in such harmonious combinations as will suggest to the reader a mood or condition which is not mentioned in the text but is nevertheless paramount in the poet's mind at the moment of composition."

Gosse continues with an excellent paraphrase in English of Mallarmé's poem:

A faun — a simple, sensuous, passionate being — wakens in the forest at daybreak and tries to recall his experience of the previous afternoon. Was he the fortunate recipient of an actual visit from nymphs, white and golden goddesses, divinely tender and indulgent? Or is the memory he seems to retain nothing but the shadow of a vision, no more substantial than the 'arid rain' of notes from his own flute? He cannot tell. Yet surely there was, surely there is, an animal whiteness among the brown reeds of the lake that shines out yonder. Were they, are they, swans? No! But Naiads plunging? Perhaps! Vaguer and vaguer grows the impression of this delicious experience. He would resign his woodland godship to retain it. . . . The delicious hour grows vaguer; experience or dream, he will never know which it was. The sun is warm, the grasses yielding; and he curls himself up again, . . . that he may pursue the dubious ecstasy into the more hopeful boskages of sleep. . .

Debussy scored the work for a small orchestra; neither trumpets nor trombones were used. The sound of the flute dominates; the work is full of melodic arabesques, languid but nervously fluctuating rhythms. Tonally it is vague, made so through the use of whole-tone scales, pentatonic scales, and free chromaticism. Underlying the whole is the suggestion of ternary form, in this case A A' B A".

Unaccompanied, a solo flute plays Example 1 — The Faun's "rain of notes from his own flute. . ."

Example 1

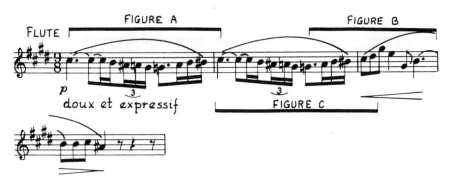

A harp glissando is heard, followed by a four-note French horn motive. The glissando is repeated, followed by two repetitions of the horn motive.

The flute plays Example 1 again, this time accompanied by soft woodwinds and a string tremolo.

The oboe enters on the last note of the flute solo with Example 2; the strings and other woodwinds double in octaves the melodic line starting with measure three.

Example 2

The clarinet repeats Figure D from Example 2. Three times the flute plays a variant of Figure A from Example 1; harp arpeggios are prominent in the accompaniment.

The clarinet introduces a melody derived from Example 1.

Example 3

The clarinet repeats Example 3 a third higher in pitch; the oboe then plays Example 4.

Example 4

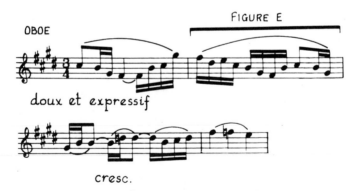

Figure E from Example 4 is played by flute and clarinet, and then by the violins. The first five notes, now in slightly altered form, are played by the flute and oboe, then by the violins.

Immediately the English horn and clarinets play a rhythmical variant of Figure B from Example 1; the violins repeat the figure. The French horns take up a melody, Example 5, whose beginning is derived from the third measure of Example 4.

Example 5

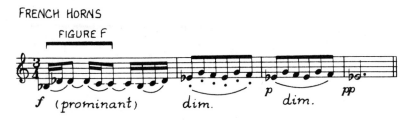

In a four-measure bridge, the clarinet is heard playing variants of Figure F from Example 5.

The second principal theme of the *Prélude,* Example 6, is introduced by the woodwinds.

Example 6

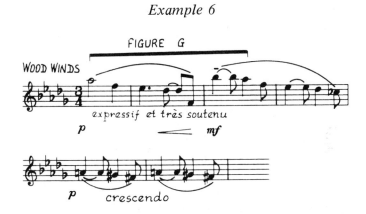

After a crescendo in which a descending triplet pattern is heard, the violins repeat the first four measures of Example 6 in octaves. As the crescendo continues in full orchestra, the violins twice play Figure F from Example 5, each time continuing the descending triplet pattern, the second time in a quite extended passage. The French horn plays Figure F; the clarinet repeats the descending triplet pattern.

Figure G from Example 6 appears in the solo violin as a counter-melody to further repetitions of the descending triplet pattern.

A return is made to figures from and variants of the first principal melody, Example 1. Accompanied by harp arpeggios and sustained strings, the flute plays Figure C in augmentation (its time values lengthened). Twice the oboe plays a rhythmic variant of Figure A; it is answered by descending, staccato chords in the woodwinds. The oboe then plays Figure C in augmentation. Twice the English horn is heard with a rhythmic variant of Figure A, each time answered by the descending, staccato chords.

Accompanied by a string tremolo, two flutes in unison play Example 1 "with great languor"; Figure F from Example 5 is played in octaves by two solo violins as an obbligato. One flute, doubled at the octave by a solo cello, repeats Example 1.

As the music fades away, muted French horns are heard in the closing measures playing Figure A.

IBERIA
3. Le Matin d'un jour de fête

Le Matin d'un jour de fête — (The Morning of a Festival Day) — is the third movement of *Iberia,* which in itself is the second of three works in the suite *Images pour orchestre.* If the *Prélude* had been Debussy's first faltering step away from tradition, an attempt to find his own style and idiom, *Iberia* — which followed 17 years later — represents the mature, established style of the composer. A greater sharpness of outline and brilliancy of color characterize this mature period. A tightening of structure is also evident.

With *Iberia,* Debussy joined a long list of French composers who drew inspiration from Spain and Spanish music, a group that included Saint-Saëns, Bizet, Lalo and Chabrier before him, and Ravel after him. Except for one afternoon spent in San Sebastian just a few miles south of the French border, Debussy never visited Spain. However, according to the Spanish composer Manuel de Falla, "Debussy created spontaneously . . . such Spanish music as might be envied him. . . by many others that knew [Spain] only too well."

Le Matin d'un jour de fête is scored for full orchestra. The instruments are treated soloistically and retain their individual

timbres throughout with the luminosity of texture so characteristic of Debussy. The score is marked *Dans un rhythme de marche lointaine, alerte et joyeuse* — "in the rhythm of a distant march, brisk and joyous." Except for this tempo indication and the title of the movement, there is no further guide as to its descriptive intent. To a program annotator who questioned Debussy on this point, the composer remarked impatiently: "It is useless to ask me for anecdotes about this work; there is no story attached to it, and I depend on the music alone to arouse the interest of the public."

Le Matin opens "with the rhythm of a distant march, brisk and joyous." It is scored for lower strings and tambourine.

Example 1

Immediately after Example 1, the sustained brass are heard *pianissimo*. Over this a solo flute plays Example 2, again "very distant."

Example 2

Example 1 returns in the lower strings. Now rapid figurations of 16th and 32nd notes in the upper woodwinds are heard over a variant of Example 1 in the strings.

Example 3 opens with oboes and piccolos in octaves. It continues with an important pattern in the trumpets. Example 3 is heard twice.

Example 3

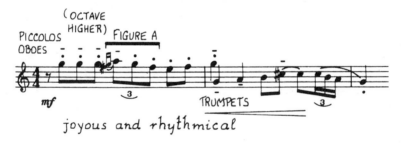

Figure A from Example 3 is repeated eight times in quick succession by the piccolos and oboe while trumpets repeat the last six notes of Example 3.

The music is now marked, "Tempo of a march movement, joyous and brisk." The violinists and violists are told to hold their instruments "in their arms to sound like a guitar." The melody and rhythm of this passage are derived from Example 1.

A bold melody, Example 4, reinforced by full chords is played by the strings, *pizzicato*. It is repeated.

Example 4

The march rhythm "gives way"; the rhythm and melody of Example 1 return "very freely."

Two shrill clarinets are heard in a "gay" theme of "exaggerated accents" — derived from the opening of Example 3 — over repetitions of the rhythmical string passage:

Example 5

The flutes, doubled by the bassoons two octaves lower, play Example 6 "a little mockingly." Example 6 is repeated by the violins.

Example 6

The woodwinds introduce a rhythmical variation of Example 1. A measure and a half later, the trumpets are heard with Example 7. They repeat it.

Example 7

As this section builds to a dynamic climax, the strings are heard in open fifths, almost as if they were tuning.

The tempo changes to *Moderato*. A solo violin is heard:

Example 8

The melody of Figure B from Example 8 is heard several times. It is played twice by the oboe, twice by the English horn, then twice more by the oboe.

The clarinets and bassoons introduce a rhythmical motive:

Example 9

   Figure B from Example 8 is played twice by the oboe. After two measures, the oboe again plays it twice, joined in the last measure by the English horn.

   The "guitar-effect" of the strings is heard again. The trumpets play a one-measure motive. The harp plays Example 4, accompanied by *pianissimo* trills in the woodwinds. Then the full string section repeats Example 4.

   Once again Figure B is played twice by the oboe. Two measures later it plays the figure twice more.

   After a four-measure bridge in which the xylophone is prominent, the trumpets take up a variant of Example 1 to open the *Coda* which is marked "lively and vigorous."

   The music builds to a final dynamic climax. In the full orchestral texture, bold interjections by the brass are heard: first the horns, then trumpets and, in the final measures, trombones with *glissandi*.

II

ERIK SATIE (1866-1925) is a composer about whose music much has been written, but whose works were seldom performed even in his own lifetime. A strange paradox, indeed! Only in the late 1960's and early '70's has the music itself become widely known, largely through the medium of phonograph recordings. These started a "cult" — as it were — quite similar to those caused by the recorded revivals of music by Gustav Mahler in the 1950's and Charles Ives in the 1960's.

Many composers have been affected by the stark, simplistic style of Satie's writing. He became the mentor for that group of Parisian composers known as the "Group of Six" which included Honegger, Auric and Poulenc. Debussy affectionately dedicated one of his works "to Erik Satie, the gentle medieval musician who strayed into this century for the happiness of his friend Claude Debussy." Satie said of Maurice Ravel: "Whenever I meet him, he assures me he owes me so much." Darius Milhaud calls Satie "my old friend and master." Virgil Thomson places "Satie's work among the major musical values of our century." Igor Stravinsky added the Waltz to his *Eight Easy Pieces* for piano "in homage to Erik Satie, a souvenir of a visit with him in Paris, . . . a very touching and attractive personality."

Who is this strange, enigmatic composer? Erik Satie was born on March 17, 1866, in the town of Honfleur in the Calvados region of France. The village organist gave him his first music lessons, acquainting the lad with the works of the old polyphonic masters and Gregorian chant probably before the boy ever had a chance to hear music harmonized in the more contemporary major and minor tonalities.

Erik's London-born mother (of Scottish descent) passed away when he was six; he then went to live with his grandparents as his father, who had been a ship-broker, left for Paris to establish

CLAUDE DEBUSSY   ERIK SATIE

himself as a music publisher. Later, at age 12, Erik rejoined his father who had by then remarried. The new Mme. Satie was a neighborhood piano teacher who also composed insipid salon music. The boy hated his step-mother and her music, but consented to attend concerts and enroll at the Paris Conservatory. He remembered the Conservatory to the end of his days as "that vast, uncomfortable building, a jail devoid of any attractive features either inside or out." He probably played the piano and completed exercises in harmony without ever accepting his parent's plan to make him a musician. "My harmony professor thought I had a gift for the piano," he said, "while my piano professor considered that I might be talented in composition!"

As a young man Satie earned his living by playing the piano in various Parisian cafés and cabarets, among the more famous of which were *Le Chat Noir* (The Black Cat) in Montmartre, and *Auberge de Clou* (Inn of the Prize Exhibit) where, in 1891, he first met Claude Debussy. They became the closest of friends. After Satie moved from his flat in Montmartre to a tiny, one-room apartment in the working-class Arcueil district of Paris, he returned weekly to visit Debussy, to use his piano and to chat with him. "If

I did not have Debussy," Satie confided, "I do not see how I should go about expressing my poor thoughts." He goes on to say:

> At that time [1891] I was writing *Le Fils des etoiles* [The Son of the Stars] . . . and I explained to Debussy that a Frenchman had to free himself from the Wagnerian adventure, which wasn't the answer to our national aspirations. I also pointed out that I was in no way anti-Wagnerian, but that we should have a music of our own — if possible, without any sauerkraut.
> Why should we not use the means that Claude Monet, Cezanne, Toulouse-Lautrec and others had made known? Why could we not transpose these means into music? Nothing simpler! [1]

In his philosophical outlook, Satie was as eccentric as he was in his music. Early in life he was attracted to the Rosicrucian sect which was oriented toward mystical ideas and medieval rites. Later he was active in the movement known as *Le Coeur* (The Heart); then, in 1895, he established his own "abbey of the church of Jesus the conductor." He wrote from Arcueil, "In this district one senses the mysterious presence of Our Lady of Lowliness." (He wrote a Mass for the Poor.) Satie was completely unworldly when it came to success and wealth. He was, in the words of one critic, "dedicated to music and poverty."

Just before his 40th birthday Satie went back to school! Dissatisfied with his technique, and determined to master formal theory and counterpoint, he enrolled at the Schola Cantorum. For three years he studied with Vincent d'Indy and Albert Roussel. "At your age," Debussy said to him, "one can no longer change one's skin." "If I fail," Satie replied, "it means that I haven't got it in me to be a composer." After receiving a diploma duly signed by Roussel, Satie set out to compose a chorale and fugue in the tradition of his recent academic training. He then went on to write *En habit de cheval* (In Riding Clothes — 1911) starting off with two movements in academically formal style — a choral and a "liturgical" fugue; the "old" Satie took over before the work was completed and the third movement became the *Autre choral* (The Other Choral) and the finale a *Fugue de papier* (Paper Fugue).

The noted American composer and music critic Virgil Thomson has stated that Satie "had the firmest conviction that the only healthy thing music can do in our century is to stop being impressive." And this is what Satie did. He chose titles for his compositions that were ridiculous: "Desiccated Embryos" and "Truely Flabby Preludes for a Dog," or he gave directions to the performer that were absurd, "to be played dry as a cuckoo, light as an egg" or "Must sound like a nightingale with a toothache." He wrote music whose thematic line was direct, pointed, simple; the harmonization was always subservient to the melody. The orchestration was "without sauce" (as he called it), minimal.

"The new spirit," Satie said, "teaches us to aim at an emotional simplicity and a firmness of utterance that enable sonorities and rhythms to assert themselves clearly, unequivocal in design and accent, and conceived in a spirit of humility and renunciation."

Melody is the most important element in Satie's writing. The rhythm is usually most simple "in order to permit concentration on melody, and it is peculiar because the melody is peculiar, 'singing' as only the piano 'sings,' wandering over the twelve notes of the keyboard with blithe disregard of scales, yet often suggesting one or another diatonic mode. . . . Its articulation is clear and natural."

Satie's humor is generally to be found in words — the titles and performance directions — seldom in the urbane and charming music itself. He does, of course, invoke humor in his music when appropriate. One thinks of the busy, vapid fury of piano passages that are almost too fast to be articulated in *Celle qui parle trop* (She Who Talks Too Much), or the use of the reveille bugle call quoted in *La Réveil de la Mariée* (Awakening the Bride). Sometimes Satie employed unusual "effects" because of their appropriateness to the circumstances. In his ballet *Parade* (*"parade"* is the name given in France to the previews offered outside a side-show tent to lure people inside), he became, in 1917, one of the first to use extra-musical elements in the orchestra: sound splashes, lottery wheels, typewriters, fog horns and pistol shots.

But humor, effects, titles aside, Satie has written some truly beautiful music. To the uninitiated, one would recommend the *Gymnopédies* (literally "athletic exercises of Greek youths"), either in their original piano version or the orchestration of numbers one and three by Debussy. The music is serene, its beauty haunting. Another work worthy of study and enjoyment is "Sur un vaisseau" from *Descriptions automatiques* ("Of a Ship" from *Automatic*

Descriptions) which has a most lyrical quality. The harsh, dissonant chords and biting rhythms of "Sur un casque" (Of a Helmet) from the same piano suite forms an interesting contrast. The "Valse du 'Mystérieux baiser dans l'oeil" from *La Belle Excentrique* ("Waltz of the 'Mysterious Kiss in the Eye' " from *The Eccentric Beauty*) clearly illustrates the French style of piano writing later adopted and adapted by Darius Milhaud and others of the Group of Six in their works. Of Satie's ballet music (including *Les Aventures de Mercure* and *Relâche,* both of 1924), the already mentioned *Parade* is perhaps the most interesting with its lilting principal theme and amusing "cake-walk" section.

TROIS MORCEAUX EN FORME DE POIRE

2. Enlevé

The full title of this work printed on the music is: *Trois Morceaux en forme de Poire (à 4 mains) avec une Maniere de Commencement, une Prolongation du même & Un En Plus, suivi d'une Redite.* [Three Pieces in the Form of a Pear (for 4 hands) with a Kind of Commencement, a Prolongation of the same & One More, followed by a Repetition.] In other words, seven movements!

The story is well known that Debussy criticized some of Satie's early writings because he observed a lack of form in them. Supposedly Satie returned on his next visit from Arcueil with *Three Pieces in the Form of a Pear* to prove that he had "form" in his music. The humor goes further. *Poire* means not only "pear," but also, in slang, the dupe of a hoax, the butt of a joke. Was the music intended as a hoax? (Hardly likely.) Or, is Satie saying that he, himself is the butt of the hoax? Or Debussy?

It would seem that the broad humor is in the title, for the music itself — although at times "witty" — is not "funny." It is a suite of contrasting movements at once tuneful, rhythmically and harmonically interesting, and certainly not without an underlying form.

Of the "3 Pieces" which are the core of the suite, the second is in tripartite form: A–B–A. The first and last sections are marked *Enlevé* (carried away); the middle section, in contrast, is *De moitié* (half as fast).

   The first section is, itself, in ternary form. The first melody is stated immediately.

Example 1

PRIMA PIANO

   The second melody follows without pause and is repeated three times.

Example 2

PRIMA PIANO

Example 1 is heard once more.
   The middle section is in binary form. The first theme is a duet.

Example 3

PRIMA PIANO

The *prima* pianist starts the second theme; the *seconda* completes it.

Example 4

The repetition of the first section is exact.

III

ARNOLD SCHOENBERG (1874-1951) was a Viennese composer. He and Debussy stand in the greatest possible contrast to one another. The music of Debussy is widely performed today; the music of Schoenberg is performed much less frequently. Debussy formulated no theories about his style of composition; Schoenberg's theories concerning *atonalism* and *serial composition* have formed the basis for the most important school of composition in the 20th century. Debussy's "impressionistic" music is — according to the French poet Jean Cocteau — created by "a silken brush"; the "expressionistic" music of Schoenberg is hewn out "with an axe." Debussy's inspiration flowed from the heart; Schoenberg's works are the creation of a brilliant mind.

Arnold Schoenberg (his name had originally been spelled Schönberg) was born in Vienna, the only city that was a musical

Painting of Arnold Schoenberg done in the expressionistic style by the composer's friend, the Austrian artist and playwright, Oskar Kokoschka (1886-   ). Kokoschka is famous for portraits and dramatic landscapes done in the expressionistic style in which the representation of the face or scene is subordinated to the expression of emotion. In his plays, Kokoschka projected spiritual actualities, rather than naturalistic records of events.

rival of Paris, a capitol rich in the historical tradition of music. Reared in a home of great poverty, Schoenberg was not aware that he wished to become a musician until he was 16. He had, during his six years in school, played some with a chamber ensemble, received violin lessons and taught himself the cello. After he had finally made up his mind to follow a career in music, his father's death that year seemed to rule out any serious study of it for financial reasons.

Fortunately, when he was 20, some compositions of his aroused the interest of Alexander von Zemlinsky, a friend of Johannes Brahms. Zemlinsky took Schoenberg under his protective wing and for two years taught the young man composition, the only formal training that Schoenberg ever had. (Schoenberg was later to marry Zemlinsky's sister.) His first work to receive a public hearing was a string quartet which was received with favor. His songs, however, were more daring, less academic, and aroused violent objections.

Schoenberg's early works are direct descendents in style of the lush, chromatic harmonies of Wagner's operas *Parsifal* and *Tristan*, but the formal structure of Schoenberg's compositions is derived from J. S. Bach, his great idol. *Verklärte Nacht* (Transfigured Night) of 1899 for string orchestra and his massive *Gurrelieder* (Songs for Gurre) of 1901 for soloists, chorus and large orchestra are still, in spite of their great originality, within the Wagnerian orbit. His next works, extending up to 1907, show a steady but marked expansion of chromatic and contrapuntal devices that delay tonal resolutions over longer and longer periods. These works include the symphonic poem *Pelleas und Melisande* (written about the same time Debussy completed his opera on this text), the *String Quartet in D minor* and the *Kammersinfonie* (Chamber Symphony).

About this time Schoenberg became interested in the fine art of painting. He studied some himself, later painting quite a number of self-portraits. An exhibition of his paintings was held in Vienna. He also became friendly with several of the best artists in Vienna, Wassily Kandinsky, Oscar Kokoschka, Paul Klee and Franz Marc. Since, as Schoenberg said, "There is only one great goal toward which an artist strives, to express himself," it is perhaps logical that the style of these painters became know as *expressionism,* the German answer to French *impressionism.* There were also poets associated with this movement, among whom were Stefan George and Richard Dehmel. Perhaps one should even link the name of Sigmund Freud, the discoverer of psychoanalysis, with this movement, for it was his search into the subconscious that inspired the expressionistic school to try and represent on canvas, to *express,* the inner experience as the only reality, the shadowy terrain of the unconscious and subconscious. Many of the paintings were grotesque because the artist tried to express the unconscious, the hallucinated visions that differed from the traditional notion of beauty, the artist's powerful attempt to express his "inner self."

Schoenberg, in his musical compositions, sought similar goals. He felt the solution was to pull away from the 19th-century concepts of harmony and tonality. "Tonality is not an eternal law of music," he declared, "but simply a means toward the achievement of musical form." Tonality in western music had been based on the principle that seven of the twelve tones within an octave belong to a key, while five lie outside of it. The late 19th-century chromatic harmony — such as employed by Wagner — tended to lessen the distinction between the two groups. Schoenberg decided that the time had come to take the next step, make all twelve tones equal in importance and use, thus eliminating the sense of tonality or a tonal-center. Musicians labeled this principle *atonality.* Schoenberg disliked that term as much as Debussy did *impressionism.* "I regard the expression *atonal* as meaningless. *Atonal* can only signify something that does not correspond to the nature of tone. A piece of music will necessarily always be tonal in so far as a relation exists from tone to tone." Schoenberg suggested the use of the word *pantonal* in its place to signify "the syntheses of all tonalities." But, the word *atonal* stuck in the public's mind and is the term now in universal use.

One of Schoenberg's first works in the new *atonal* idiom was *Pierrot Lunaire* (Pierrot of the Moonlight), a setting of 21 poems for a vocal soloist and chamber ensemble.

Schoenberg next developed a method that formed the basis of most of his later compositions and which changed the western concept of composition for all time. "After many unsuccessful attempts during a period of approximately 12 years, I laid the foundations for a new procedure in musical construction which seem fitted to replace those structural differentiations provided formerly by tonal harmonies. I call this procedure *Method of*

Composing with Twelve Tones which are related only with one another."

Once again musicians and writers selected their own labels. Some called the music resulting from this method *12-tone* music, some called it *dodecaphonic* music, others *serial* music, (since in Schoenberg's "Method" the twelve tones are arbitrarily arranged in a "series" for each composition). The principles of this Method are summarized later.

During the years that Schoenberg was discovering and establishing his Method — the post-World War I decade — he conducted seminars on composition and also taught privately. Two of his students, Anton Webern and Alban Berg, went on to become outstanding composers and have almost surpassed their master as far as fame is concerned.

In 1925 . Schoenberg was appointed to the staff of the Prussian Academy of the Arts in Berlin, but resigned the post in 1933 when Hitler rose to power and started his pogroms against the Jews. Schoenberg moved first to Paris and later that year accepted a position with a conservatory in Boston. Because of a serious sinus condition, he moved to the more healthful climate of southern California the following year. There he taught harmony and composition at the University of California at Los Angeles, a position he occupied until his retirement in 1944 at the age of 70.

Few of Schoenberg's compositions in the twelve-tone idiom have become well-known or widely performed. A list of the more important works would include his opera *Moses und Aron* (1932-51), the *Concerto for Violin and Orchestra* (1936), the *Chamber Symphony No. 2* (1940) and the *Concerto for Piano and Orchestra* (1943). Although the musical world branded him and his Method as revolutionary, Schoenberg did not agree. "I personally hate to be called a revolutionary, which I am not. What I did was neither revolutionary nor anarchy."

PIERROT LUNAIRE

7. Der Kranke Mond

In 1912 Arnold Schoenberg's melodrama in the form of a song-cycle, *Pierrot Lunaire* (Pierrot of the Moonlight) shocked the musical public. Actual fist-fights broke out in the concert hall, and cat-calls and boos were the order of the day. The work is a setting of 21 poems arranged in three groups of seven. The poems were written by the minor Belgian symbolist poet Albert Giraud (1860-1929). Schoenberg used them in an unrhymed German translation by Otto Erich Hartleben (1860-1905). These lyrics make abrupt shifts from romantic to sordid imagery; in them there are self-conscious references to torment and ecstasy. There is no coherent narrative or argument in them, and no evident design in the sequence of the poems. There are only contrasts of mood. The 21 poems are united by references to the moon and the pantomime characters of Pierrot, Columbine and Cassander.

Schoenberg's setting of these lyrics was as novel as the poetry itself, as harsh and stark as the lines, as mystically shocking as the poems were revolting. He scored the work for soprano and five instrumentalists. The ensemble includes piano, flute interchangeable with piccolo, clarinet interchangeable with bass clarinet, violin interchangeable with viola, and cello. The vocal soloist, sometimes called the *reciter* in this work, does not sing the lyrics in the conventional sense of that word; rather she employs a form of song-speech known as *Sprechstimme.*

While *Sprechstimme* had been used in various ways before — even by Schoenberg himself, — in *Pierrot Lunaire* he used it exclusively.

Except for a few isolated notes in *Sprechstimme*, the vocalist must not sing, must not sustain a steady pitch, must not chant; nor can she simply speak. She must try to recreate the composer's speech-melody, observing the printed indications of rhythm, dynamics and gliding pitch inflections. She does not add any interpretation of her own. (Schoenberg was very specific in his dynamic markings.) To indicate in traditional staff notation the difference of *Sprechstimme* from normal song, X's are placed on the stems of the notes. (See the following examples.)

Each of the 21 pieces in *Pierrot* has its own tempo and instrumentation. Of the five players, one or more keeps silent in most of the songs. Because this is *expressionistic* music, the choice of instruments does not always follow the reality of the text. Thus, in *Serenade,* while Pierrot is described as playing on the viola, the cello, not the viola, accompanies the passage.

Although *Pierrot Lunaire* was not well received at its first performance (after more than 40 rehearsals) and was the object of much criticism and scorn, it has remained, over the years, one of Schoenberg's most frequently performed works. By 1965, six different performances of it had been recorded; four of them still remain active in the catalogue. Schoenberg thought *Pierrot* ought to be performed in English in English-speaking countries (a most logical idea), but only recordings of the work in German are available, hence the bilingual quotations below.

In *Pierrot*, Schoenberg employs motivic and intervalic constructions of every kind. They are incorporated into complex linear textures. It is these textures − fluid, flashing, chromatic − that provide for the listener the impact of this work, settings of extreme severity and profundity.

Der Kranke Mond (The Sick Moon), is the seventh and final song in Part I. It is a duet for flute and vocalist, cast in tight, two-voice counterpoint. The tempo is marked *Very Slow*; the flute enters before the voice. In Example 1, notice that every tone of the chromatic scale except D-sharp (or E-flat) has been used in the vocal line (from F-sharp to C in the first half and from C-sharp to F in the second half). The missing D-sharp (as E-flat) is prominent in the counterpoint of the flute.

Example 1

The duet continues:

dein Blick, so fiebernd Übergross,	*Your light, so fever swollen,*
bannt mich,	*Will pierce me,*
wie fremde Melodie.	*Like music from afar.*

A flute interlude precedes the opening of the second verse, Example 2.

Example 2

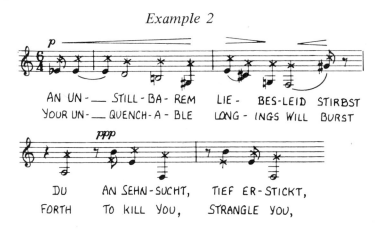

| du nächtig todeskranker mond, | *You twilight, deathly feeble moon,* |
| dort auf des Himmels schwarzem Pfühl. | *Floating on the sky's dark pool.* |

Another flute interlude precedes the third verse. Its text starts:

| Den Liebsten, der im Sinnenrausch, | *A lover, on his way in haste,* |

gedankenlos zur Liebsten geht,	*To meet his beloved one,*
belustigt deiner Strahlen Spiel,	*Is quite distracted by your beams,*

(The closing measures of this verse, Example 3, demand much of the vocalist.)

Example 3

PIANO SUITE (Opus 25)

5. Minuet

If Arnold Schoenberg had provoked the musical public with his "atonal" works such as *Pierrot Lunaire,* he shocked them even more in the 1920's as he worked out his "Method of Composing with Twelve Tones." "This Method," the composer wrote, "consists primarily of the constant and exclusive use of a set [or "row" or "series"] of twelve different tones." He then goes on to say that it "is no system, but only a method, which means a *modus* of applying regularly a preconceived formula."

Perhaps the most succinct example is his use of the row in his *Piano Suite,* Opus 25. Its basic row is:

Example 1

The rules of the method, the "preconceived formula," can be paraphrased as follows:

1.   Once a tone in the row is sounded, it is not repeated until the series has been completed. However, under certain conditions, tones can be repeated for reasons of sonority or rhythm, when used as a pedal point, in a trill or in tremolo figures.

2.   The row may be used in one of four basic forms: Original, Retrograde or backwards, Inverted or turned upside down, and Inverted Retrograde or backwards turned upside down.

3.   The series can be used both horizontally as melody tones, or vertically as accompanying chords, or in a combination of both.

4.   The series may be transposed to any of the other eleven pitches. (This means with four forms of the row and the possibility of 12 starting tones, there are 48 different varieties of the row possible.)

5.   Any tone of the row can be sounded in any octave.

6.   Sometimes the row is subdivided into subgroups, for example: two groups of six tones each, or three groups of four tones, etc.

In defense of the 12-tone Method, Schoenberg said: "I offer incontestable proof of the fact that in following the Method, a composer is neither less nor more bound, hindered nor made independent. He may be as cold-hearted and unmoved as an engineer, or, as laymen imagine, may conceive in sweet dreams — an inspiration."

He goes on to say that "what can be constructed with these twelve tones depends on one's inventive faculty. The basic tones will not invent for you. Expression is limited only by the composer's creativeness and his personality. He may be original or moving, with old or modern methods. Finally, success depends only on whether we are touched, excited, made happy, enthusiastic . . . or not."

In his *Piano Suite,* Opus 25, Schoenberg has used the row in Example 1 as the basis for each of the dances in this suite, but because of meter, rhythm, tempo, plus the alterations possible under the previously listed rules, it sounds new to the ear in each dance.

The form of the "Minuet" from the *Suite* is strictly classical. But, one must almost *see* it on the printed page to perceive this structure and *see* the rhythm of a minuet. It is difficult, except for the most skillfully trained ear, to hear either the formal structure or the rhythm of a minuet.

At the opening of the Minuet, numbers 5 through 12 of the row appear in the right hand, while – in counterpoint – numbers 1 through 4 appear in the left.

Example 2

The first section of the "Minuet" is 11 measures in length and is repeated.

The second part of this binary form is twice as long, 22 measures, and is not repeated. Three times in these 22 measures Schoenberg changed from the minuet meter of 3/4 to 2/4, but it is difficult, if not impossible, for the ear to hear this change.

The "Trio" opens with a canon. The left hand immediately presents the row (Example 1) in its original form. The right hand answers in contrary motion at the tritone (transposition of an augmented fourth or "three" whole "tones" hence *tritone).* This, as seen in Example 2, is an example of the *"modus* of applying a preconceived formula." The right hand part is a new form of the same row.

Example 3

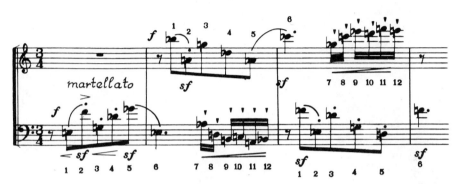

Next follows an inversion for the left hand while the right hand makes a simple transposition of the original row. This first section of the "Trio" is then repeated.

The second section of the "Trio" is also of four measures, repeated. It ends with a condensed form of the last part of Example 3 and the following two measures.

As in a classical minuet, the first part — the "Minuet" — is repeated without its internal repeats.

IV

BÉLA BARTÓK (1881-1945) was a quiet, shy and retiring man, a composer largely unheralded and ignored during his lifetime. No label such as "impressionism" or "expressionism" was affixed to his style by the critics; he did not develop a "method" or inspire a group of ardent student followers. Yet his contribution to 20th-

ARNOLD SCHOENBERG   BÉLA BARTÓK

century music was of epic proportion; few works of other composers are the equal of his best; none are better.

Bartók, although Hungarian by birth, first became familiar with music of the Germanic tradition, especially that of Brahms. Later he discovered the adventuresome, highly chromatic music of Richard Strauss; this opened new vistas for him in harmony, style and structure. Almost by accident, Bartók became acquainted with the folk music of Hungary, and later with that of Romania, Turkey, and the Arabs of North Africa. Bartók was affected by these influences, yet "the line of Bartók's creative development is more direct than that of most of his contemporaries," according to his principal biographer, Halsey Stevens. From the late 1920's on, "his tonalities are more sharply defined, his melodies more folklike and frequently of a highly organized motivic structure, his harmonics tending toward greater lucidity or even toward extreme simplicity, his rhythms vital and varied. Polyphonic manipulation is intensified, with stress on canon, fugato and free imitation. Thematic inversion is everywhere present." Stevens goes on to say that Bartók "seldom strayed far from the fundamental principles of classical structure." However, "as time went on, he found himself looking to earlier models than Haydn and Mozart: to Bach and the pre-Bach period for continuous or additive forms as opposed to the developmental and other closed forms of the Viennese composers."

The musical training of Béla Bartók, the lad with perfect pitch, began on his fifth birthday when his mother gave him his first piano lesson; less than a month later the two of them were able to play a duet for his father. The death of Béla's father two years later caused the family to make a number of moves to widely separated parts of Hungary. His mother gave piano lessons to help support the family; a private teacher was found for Béla and he acquired a solid foundation in the music of the Classical and Romantic eras. The works of Johannes Brahms made the strongest impression on him at this time. (His teacher allowed Béla to hear no work newer or more modern than Wagner's *Tannhäuser* which was then almost 50 years old.) In addition to his keyboard studies, Bartók composed some works of his own.

By the fall of 1899 Bartók was ready to enter the Academy of Music in Budapest. He took courses in piano, composition, score-reading and orchestration. Bouts with ill health − a bronchial condition among others − seemed for a time to preclude a career in music for him. A professor at the Academy advised his mother that the life of a professional musician was much too strenuous for a person of such frail stature and precarious health. Undaunted, Bartók resolutely continued with his studies at the Academy.

At the school he discovered the works of Franz Liszt (1811-1886) − a fellow Hungarian; later he was able to study the scores of Wagner's later operas. During the period Bartók devoted his attention to the piano, abandoning composition for two years. Then, in 1902, an event of great significance took place. "From this stagnation," Bartók wrote, "I was aroused as by a flash of lightning by the first Budapest performance of *Thus Spake Zarathustra* by Richard Strauss. "This work, received with shudders by musicians here, stimulated the greatest enthusiasm in me; at last I saw the way before me. Immediately I threw myself into a study of Strauss's scores, and again began to compose."

Another factor soon concerned the composer. A new nationalist current started to sweep across Hungary, an interest on the part of scholars to revivify the old Hungarian culture, to republish some of the early Hungarian writers and to resurrect the patriotic songs of the Rakoczy period, all suppressed since the catastrophic uprising of 1848-9. Through this renaissance of authentic Hungarian culture and history Bartók became interested in national music.

The discovery of Strauss's tone poems, coupled with the new national fervor, led Bartók to compose his first major work, *Kossuth,* a patriotic tone poem concerning a Hungarian "hero's life." The music was divided in ten tableaux which suggested various events in the 1848-9 war of independence led against Austria by Lajos Kossuth. The tone poem was successfully performed by the Philharmonic Society shortly after Bartók completed his studies at the Academy of Music.

The composer intended to continue his work in piano and planned to concertize. He made appearances in Berlin, Vienna and in England. He returned to Hungary, to an incidental experience that was to change the whole path of his career and affect every later composition. Sometime during that year (1904) Bartók heard an 18-year old girl in the little Hungarian village of Kibéd in the province of Maros-Torda sing a pleasant and intriguing little folk song. Bartók wrote it out in musical notation; for the first time he became aware that there was an indigenous Magyar* music of which he, like most of his colleagues, was unaware. Previously composers, including the Hungarian Franz Liszt and the German Johannes Brahms, had assumed that the gypsies had originated true Hungarian folk music.

Bartók now set out to locate, investigate, notate and classify this music. He discovered that he accomplished his purpose best if he went to the little rural villages and hamlets, and lived with the peasants, eating simple foods at their tables, living in their primitive homes. In this manner he gained their respect and friendship, finding them then willing to share music-making with him. For scientific purposes, he took with him a primitive spring-wound Edison cylinder phonograph (see photograph); sometime later he painstakingly would transcribe the melodies into standard musical notation.

The effect of these discoveries did not immediately affect Bartók's compositional style; the change evolved slowly over a long period of time. His first work based on his research was *Twenty Hungarian Folk Songs* for voice and piano; in this he collaborated

---

* Magyars form the predominant ethnic group in Hungary and are of Finno-Urgic stock.

in 1906 with his friend and fellow composer, Zoltán Kodály (1882-1967), each contributing ten songs. There followed numerous folk song settings — for piano, for voice, for chorus, for solo instruments. Beginning in 1908 Bartók started publishing a long series of monographs on his musico-ethnological investigations. Gradually the results of these studies influenced his original compositions "not by a simple borrowing of melodies or motives or a spicing of conventional patterns with evocative modal or rhythmic procedures," writes Halsey Stevens, "but by a detailed examination of the melodic and rhythmic characteristics of the peasant tunes, and by the derivation of harmonies for them, the discovery of the intrinsic nature of Magyar peasant music, and finally its amalgamation with the techniques of art music."

In 1907 Bartók was appointed to the staff of the Academy of Music in Budapest, a post he was to occupy for some 30 years. He did not, however, teach composition; this he always refused to do, fearing probably, that it would interfere and affect his own style and method of composition. He took brief leaves from the Academy from time to time, occasionally because of ill health, frequently to go on folksong collecting trips. He was joined a year after his appointment at the Academy by his friend Zoltán Kodály who became head of the composition department until his death in 1967. Together, Bartók and Kodály exercised the strongest possible influence on future generations of Hungarian composers.

While Kodály confined his research exclusively to the music of the Magyars, Bartók branched out. In 1915 a number of his compositions were based on tunes he discovered in Romania: a *Sonatina* for piano, the *Romanian Folk Dances from Hungary* (see following section), *Colinde* (Romanian Christmas songs) and others. Unfortunately World War I closed the borders of European countries for travel, thus restricting Bartók's research expeditions. The first performance of two major works, however, date from this period. His one-act ballet, *The Wooden Prince,* completed in 1916, was first performed at the Hungarian State Opera House on May 12, 1917. A little over a year later his one-act opera, *Duke Bluebeard's Castle,* was first performed in Budapest. He next turned to the completion of a one-act pantomime, *The Miraculous Mandarin,* completing it in May of 1919.

During the 1920's and early 30's, Bartók traveled widely, but his music "was so uncompromising, so unyielding, that the general public was left far behind." In 1934 he resigned from the Academy of Music and became a working member of the Hungarian Academy of Science so that, free from classroom duties, he could devote all his time to the systematization of the large collection of folk music that he had amassed. He traveled to Turkey to do further research, then on to North Africa.

Despite the clouds of World War II that hung over Hungary in 1936-7, Bartók completed two major compositions: *Music for Strings, Percussion and Celesta* and the *Sonata* (later *Concerto) for Two Pianos and Percussion.* He also completed in 1937 a series of 153 graded, short pieces for piano begun in 1926, *Mikrokosmos.* The death of his mother just before Christmas, 1939, severed Bartók's last strong tie to his beloved Hungary and he emigrated, along with his wife and son, to the United States. A position was found for him at Columbia University at a salary of $3000 a year doing folk song research. When that special fund was exhausted, a position was found for him at Harvard, but his health was already seriously undermined. He was also depressed by the war and the fate of his beloved homeland.

After a lengthy stay in the hospital during the spring of 1943, Bartók planned a summer vacation at Saranac Lake in upstate New York. Just before leaving, Serge Koussevitsky, conductor of the Boston Symphony Orchestra, paid him a visit in his hospital room. He offered the composer a commission of $1,000 to write an orchestral work. At first Bartók refused, afraid that his health might not permit him to complete such an arduous task. Koussevitsky left the room after giving Bartók a check for $500 and a promise that the other $500 would be paid at the time of the first performance. Bartók's finest and most popular orchestral work was the result of this commission, the *Concerto for Orchestra.* The last major work he finished was his third *Piano Concerto.* A *Concerto for Viola* was left incomplete at the time of his death.

ROMANIAN FOLK DANCES

1. Joc cu bâtă

In 1915 Béla Bartók took seven of the dance tunes that he had collected in his expeditions around the Romanian section of

Béla Bartók recording peasant songs on a hand-wound Edison phonograph in Hungary in 1908. Zoltan Kodaly took this picture as Bartók recorded a tune sung into the machine.

Romanian peasants perform the stick dance, *Joc cu bâtă,* in native costume.

Hungary and created a suite for piano from them. He took as his over-all model the structure of the Baroque dance suite, a series of dances in related keys. For the internal structure of the dances, Bartók relied heavily on the simple binary and ternary forms. The composer made few if any changes in the Romanian melodies or rhythms as he had notated them. Since the melodies were largely modal, he chose appropriate and simple harmonies with which to accompany them. He called his piano suite, *Romanian Folk Dances from Hungary.* The composer was later encouraged to score the suite for small orchestra.

During one of his expeditions into Romania, Bartók wandered into a village-tavern in the Maros-Torda district of Transylvania one evening. There he heard an old gypsy violinist play a beautiful tune, one used to accompany a dance-game played with sticks, *Joc cu bâtă* — literally "Dance with Sticks." The gaily syncopated melody was both merry and energetic. Bartók used this melody — *Joc cu bâtă* — for the first movement of his suite.

Repeated chords serve as an introduction to the dance, establishing its basic pulse in duple meter. In the fourth measure, the clarinet and violins play the gypsy melody, Example 1, while the rhythm of the dance is provided by the harmony of the second violins, violas, cellos and basses.

Example 1

Example 1, with its rhythm varied slightly, is repeated.
The violins play Example 2, a melody which ends *pizzicato.*

Example 2

With very slight changes, Example 2 is repeated. This brings the short dance movement in simple binary form to a close.

Note in these naive Romanian melodies the use of rhythmic motives, Figure A in Example 1, Figure B in Example 2. It was this type of rhythmic (or melodic) motive that later became a pervasive part of Bartók's idiom in original compositions.

CONCERTO FOR ORCHESTRA
4. Interrupted Intermezzo

Mention has already been made concerning a commission for an orchestral work given to Bartók by Serge Koussevitsky, the musical director of the Boston Symphony Orchestra at a time when Bartók was gravely ill. The commission worked wonders for Bartók; his health improved. The composer was not quite certain whether he was able to complete his *Concerto for Orchestra* because he felt better, or felt better because he was able to complete the work. At any rate he wrote to a friend, saying:

> At present I feel in the best of health, no fever, my strength has returned, I take fine walks in the woods and mountains – actually I climb the mountain (of course, only with due caution). In March my weight was 87 pounds; now it is 105. I grow fat. I bulge. I explode. You will not recognize me.[2]

In preparing the program notes for the first performance of his *Concerto for Orchestra,* Bartók wrote that "the title of this symphony-like orchestral work is explained by its tendency to treat the single orchestral instruments in a concertant or soloistic manner." It was, in a manner of speaking, an adaptation of the Baroque *concerto grosso* idea as employed by Bach and his contemporaries.

The fourth movement is subtitled *Interrupted Intermezzo.* "The form of the fourth movement," the composer wrote, "could be rendered by the letter symbols A B A — interruption — B A." His son later said that the ludicrous theme for the interruption occurred to his father after listening to a radio broadcast of one of Shostakovich's symphonies with bizarre and ribald themes.

The score is marked *Allegretto.* After a three measure introduction by the strings, the oboe announces the "A" theme, Example 1. Note the repeated use of both melodic and rhythmic motives.

Example 1 ("A" theme)

Example 1 is repeated in octaves by the flute and clarinet while the bassoon inverts it. Example 1 in inversion is then heard by itself, played by the flute. The French horn follows with a variant of the original form of Example 1. Next, the oboe repeats Example 1 in its original form.

The *Allegretto* changes to *Calmo;* the violas play the lyrical "B" theme, Example 2.

Example 2 ("B" theme)

The violins repeat Example 2, canonically imitated by the English horn two beats later.

The oboe repeats Example 1.

The "interruption" of the *Intermezzo* now occurs. As the tempo accelerates, the clarinet announces the saucy theme of the interruption, Example 3.

Example 3

After a humorous, mocking passage for the woodwinds as they descend the scale, a trombone *glissando* is heard twice. Bartók then employs the woodwinds in a rhythmic section suggestive of a

German band while the violins play a rhythmic variation of
Example 3. A loud crash on the Chinese gong announces the end
of the interruption.

The upper strings play the lyrical "B" theme, Example 2.

The English horn is heard with the "A" theme, Example 1.
Following a flute *cadenza*, the "A" theme in an inverted pattern
passes from oboe to bassoon to piccolo. The movement ends with
three *staccato* notes for the woodwinds.

V

IGOR STRAVINSKY (1882-   ) has said of himself:

> I was born out of time in the sense that by temperament and
> talent I would have been more suited for the life of a small Bach,
> living in anonymity and composing regularly for an established
> service and for God.[3]

But such was not to be his fate. His fame and popularity have
greatly overshadowed that of Schoenberg, and by the sheer number
of major compositions he has written, his name is well-known in
circles that have never heard of Béla Bartók. Through longevity —
more than four generations — he has lived from the days of Liszt,
Wagner, Tchaikovsky and Brahms, to the most *avant-garde* composers of the late 20th century.

Stravinsky was born in Oranienbaum, Russia, a summer resort
a short distance from St. Petersburg (now Leningrad). His father,
Feodor Stravinsky, was the leading bass at the St. Petersburg
Opera, and because of this, Igor grew up surrounded by the world
of French, Italian and Russian opera. By nine he could play the
piano and began reading through his father's library of opera
scores.

At first no thought was given either by Igor or his family to a

IGOR STRAVINSKY

Cover design by Picasso for Stravinsky's piano work, *Ragtime.*

Balanchine's production of *Le Sacre du printemps* produced for La Scala in Milan.

professional career in music. He hated the routine piano exercises he was assigned, and was bored by the lessons in traditional harmony. After becoming acquainted with Brahms' quartets and Wagner's operas, he studied the works of Gounod, Bizet, Delibes and Chabrier. He decided, however, on a career in law and entered the University of St. Petersburg to study jurisprudence. At this time Stravinsky became acquainted with the famous Russian composer Nicholas Rimsky-Korsakov and requested lessons in composition. From 1903 until Rimsky-Korsakov's death in 1908, the two of them worked closely together. Stravinsky's *Symphony, Opus 1*, composed "under Rimsky's control" is therefore a much more professional and polished early work than Schoenberg's first *Quartet* or Bartók's tone poem *Kossuth.*

The whole early phase of Stravinsky's career was shaped by the events that followed a performance of his youthful *Fantastic Scherzo* at a concert in Paris. The Russian ballet impresario, Serge Diaghilev, heard the performance and was so impressed that when he returned to Russia he requested Stravinsky to arrange and orchestrate Chopin's *Valse Brilliante* and a *Nocturne* for his proposed ballet, *Les Sylphides,* to be given in Paris the following season. Diaghilev was pleased with the results; he next commissioned Stravinsky to compose a ballet based on the Russian fairy tale of "The Firebird."

From this association of Diaghilev and Stravinsky in Paris came three of the greatest masterpieces of 20th-century music, three ballets: *The Firebird* in 1910, *Petrouchka* in 1911 and *The Rite of Spring* in 1913. All three reflect Stravinsky's Russian background but nevertheless established an idiom for the 28-year old composer that was unique and individual. He revolutionized the concept of rhythm with units of seven, eleven or thirteen beats in a measure, a continual shifting from one meter to another, and a dislocation of accents by means of intricate patterns of syncopation. This tended to give the music powerful but controlled thrust and tension. He avoided the lush chromaticisms of the late Romantics, instead changing tonalities frequently and at times employing more than one simultaneously (polytonality). However, his melodies and harmonies, no matter how complex in structure, always seemed to revert back to or center around a basic key or tonality. His orchestrations were superb, for he was a pupil of one of the greatest authorities on orchestration the world of music has known, Rimsky-Korsakov.

After the three ballets, Stravinsky returned to work on an opera, *The Nightingale,* which had been interrupted by Diaghilev's commission. Portions of it show the strong influence of Debussy at that time on the style of Stravinsky.

World War I disrupted all of Europe and its music-making. Stravinsky fled first to Switzerland, and then after the war settled in Paris for 15 years. This upheaval caused Stravinsky to make important changes in his next major composition, a cantata entitled *The Wedding,* a work based on the customs of Russian folk weddings. Originally he had planned to use an orchestra of about 150 to accompany the chorus and soloists. When it was finally readied for the stage after the war, the composer pared the accompaniment down to four pianos and percussion.

An economy of means is suggested in Stravinsky's next two works for the stage: *The Soldier's Tale* of 1918, to be "read, played and danced," and *The Fox* of 1922, a "burlesque tale."

American jazz exerted an influence on Stravinsky. "In 1918 Ernest Ansermet [the Swiss conductor] returning from an American tour, brought me a bundle of ragtime music in the form of piano reductions and instrumental parts, which I copied out in score. With these pieces before me, I composed the *Ragtime* in [The Soldier's Tale] and, after completing [it], the *Ragtime* for eleven instruments."

Some writers have called the following years of the composer's career his *neo-classical period* because he followed the principle of the Baroque concerto grosso, the pitting of one tone mass against another. Examples include the *Symphonies of Wind Instruments* of 1920, and the *Octet for Wind Instruments* of 1923. The "return to Bach" really crystallized in the *Piano Sonata,* the *Concerto for Piano and Wind Orchestra* and the *Serenade in A*, all of which date from 1924-25.

But, Stravinsky's music defies categorization. Parallel, first to his interest in jazz and later to his "neo-classical" works, are a series of works based on the melodies of other composers. First came *Pulcinella* (1919), a ballet score based on the tunes of Giovanni Pergolesi (1710-1736). The ballet *Le baiser de la fée* (The Fairy's Kiss), of 1922 was "inspired by the Muse of Tchaikovsky." His one-act opera of the same year, *Mavra,* is dedicated "to the memory of Pushkin, Glinka and Tchaikovsky." A brilliant concert piece of 1929, *Capriccio,* pays homage to Weber and Mendelssohn.

Stravinsky suggested to the French poet Jean Cocteau that they collaborate in the creation of an opera-oratorio in Latin which would present the ancient Oedipus story in terms at once monumental and modern. The resulting *Oedipus Rex* was epoch-making both as theater and as music. "My idea," the composer writes, "was that the actors should stand on pedestals . . .and become vocally, though not physically, galvanized statues. Oedipus himself should stand in full view throughout . . His self-violence is described, but not enacted: he should not move."

Another work in Latin followed, *The Symphony of Psalms,* commissioned by the Boston Symphony Orchestra to celebrate their 50th anniversary in 1930. Four years later he completed his ballet *Persephone* for Ida Rubinstein, the dancer-choreographer. This was followed by *Card Party,* a ballet in "three deals" for presentation at the Metropolitan Opera House under the composer's baton. In 1939 he was invited by Harvard University to deliver a series of lectures; he was there when World War II broke out, and decided to remain in the United States, moving to Beverly Hills, California. He became a U.S. citizen in 1945.

During the war, a strange series of works flowed from Stravinsky's pen. "These were all journeyman jobs," the composer states in defense of them, "commissions I was forced to accept because the war in Europe had so drastically reduced the income from my compositions." These "commissions" included a *Circus Polka* (1944) for the Ringling Brothers, Barnum and Bailey Circus; *Scenes de Ballet* (1944) for Billy Rose's "Seven Lively Arts"; *Ebony Concerto* (1946) for Woody Herman's band; and *Praeludium*, a work of 30-odd bars meant as a signature for a dance band.

The Symphony in Three Movements of 1945 is another of Stravinsky's monumental works, a comprehensive one embodying all of his compositional "techniques" to date. His *Mass in G* followed in 1948. It was meant not for concert performance but for liturgical use.

Stravinsky, now nearing 65, happened to see a series of engravings by the English artist William Hogarth (1697-1764) on a visit to the Chicago Art Institute. Satirical sketches of debauchery in the life of one "Tom Rakewell", the prints collectively were known as "A Rake's Progress." "They immediately suggested a series of operatic scenes to me," Stravinsky said. "I was, however, readily susceptible to such a suggestion, for I had wanted to compose an English-language opera ever since my arrival in the United States. I chose Auden [to write the text] on the recommendation of my good friend and neighbor Aldous Huxley." At the composer's invitation, Auden came to Hollywood and in ten days he and Stravinsky had crafted the libretto. The opera was first performed in Venice on September 11, 1951.

In the following ten years Stravinsky composed six more works with English texts: a *Cantata* (1952) on anonymous medieval poems, three settings of Shakespeare texts (1952), a poem of Dylan Thomas (*In Memoriam Dylan Thomas* – 1954), the *Sermon, Narrative and Prayer* of 1961, the dance-drama for television known as *The Flood* (1962), and "The Dove Descending" from T. S. Eliot's *Four Quartets* (1962).

Alongside the English works were two set to Latin texts. *Canticum sacrum* (Sacred Song) was composed to honor the name of St. Mark for a celebration at St. Mark's Cathedral, Venice, in 1956. *Threni* (Threnody) dates from 1958, and is the composer's first work to be conceived exclusively in the 12-tone technique. In it he not only adapts the "tone row" technique of Webern to serve his own purposes and style, he also relies heavily on the contrapuntal techniques of the old polyphonists, including the great Josquin des Prez (c. 1440-1521).

During the same decade, Stravinsky added one more ballet to his "catalogue." To honor his 75th birthday in 1957, a concert version of *Agon* (Dance Contest) was presented at the University of California in Los Angeles. It had a complex score with carefully worked out details of polyphony, harmony and over-all sonority. (The work was not entirely in the 12-tone system.)

The composer's 80th birthday, in 1962, was celebrated by his first return to Russia in 53 years. In addition to conducting concerts of his music in Moscow and Leningrad, he spent an afternoon visiting with Khrushchev. "He is like a composer playing you the composition he is working on," said Stravinsky as he rode away from the Kremlin, "a composition of which he is very proud."

The tragic assassination of President John F. Kennedy led Stravinsky to collaborate once again with the poet W. H. Auden. Stravinsky set some verses of *haiku* by Auden for mezzo-soprano and three clarinets. Entitled *Elegy for J. F. Kennedy,* the work was premiered in New York on December 6, 1964.

LE SACRE DU PRINTEMPS

1. Introduction
2. Danses des adolescentes

Igor Stravinsky's first efforts for the Russian ballet impresario Serge Diaghilev were concerned with the orchestration of two piano works of Chopin for the ballet *Les Sylphides.* The two artists then collaborated in three of the 20th century's most outstanding ballets: *L'Oiseau de feu* (The Firebird), *Petrouchka* and *Le Sacre du printemps* (The Rite of Spring).

In his autobiography, Stravinsky details the origin of the third and finest of the three ballets:

> One day while I was finishing the last pages of *The Firebird* in St. Petersburg, I had a fleeting vision that came to me as a complete surprise. I saw in my imagination a solemn pagan rite: Sage elders, seated in a circle, watching a young girl dance herself to death. They were sacrificing her to propitiate the god of spring. Such was the theme of *The Rite of Spring.* I must confess that this vision made a deep impression on me, and I at once described it to my friend, Nicholas Roerich, he being a painter who specialized in pagan subjects. He welcomed my inspiration with enthusiasm, and he became my collaborator in this creation. In Paris, I told Diaghilev about it, and he was at once carried away with the idea, though its realization was delayed by the production of Petroushka.[4]

The Rite of Spring, subtitled "Scenes of Pagan Russia," is primitive both in story and music. Harsh dissonances, barbaric polyrhythms and polytonality characterize the score, but the music never loses its "vibrating transparency," to use Erik Satie's phrase. The work is scored for a very large orchestra: two piccolos, two flutes, flute in G, four oboes, English horn, the shrill E-flat clarinet, three regular clarinets, a bass clarinet, three bassoons, a contrabassoon, eight French horns, a high D trumpet, three regular trumpets, a bass trumpet, three trombones, two tubas, four timpani, bass drum, tambourine, cymbals, antique cymbals, triangle, guiro and the usual complement of strings.

The ballet is divided into two parts: "The Adoration of the Earth" and "The Sacrifice." Each of these "acts" is further subdivided. "The Adoration" begins with an *Introduction* played before the curtain rises; it is intended to suggest "the mystery of the physical world in spring." It leads without pause into the *Dance of the Adolescents* — a ceremonial worship of the earth, danced in forceful steps to a system of curiously placed accents.

The scandal created at the theater during the first performance of *The Rite* is one of the well-known legends of the 20th century. Stravinsky himself had not expected anything unusual, as he later said, since "at the dress rehearsal to which we had, as usual, invited a number of actors, painters, musicians, writers and the most cultured representatives of society, everything had gone off peacefully and I was very far from expecting such an outburst."

Then came that fateful night of May 28, 1913 at the Théâtre des Champs-Elysées in Paris. Nijinsky had done the choreography, Pierre Monteux was to conduct.

> The first bars of the prelude [Stravinsky later said] evoked derisive laughter. I was disgusted. These demonstrations, at first isolated, soon became general, provoking counter-demonstrations and very quickly developing into a terrific uproar. During the whole performance I was at Nijinsky's side in the wings. He was on a chair screaming: 'Sixteen, seventeen, eighteen! ' — they had their own methods of counting to keep time. Naturally the poor dancers could hear nothing by reason of the row in the auditorium and the sound of their own dance steps. I had to hold Nijinsky by his clothes — he was furious and ready to dash on stage at any moment and create a scandal.[5]

Fortunately for the composer who escaped through a dressing room window with the conductor after that first performance, a concert performance of the music a year later was more peaceful. "It was a brilliant renascence of *The Rite,* after the Théâtre des Champs-Elysées scandal. The hall was crowded. The audience, with no scenery to distract them, listened with concentrated attention and applauded with an enthusiasm I had been far from expecting and which greatly moved me. Certain critics who had censured *The Rite.* the year before now openly admitted their mistake. This conquest of the public naturally gave me intense and lasting satisfaction."

The *Introduction* is scored almost exclusively for woodwinds (the French horns being equally a part of this family); only in a few places does Stravinsky employ the strings. The high D trumpet is used once, the other brasses and percussion not at all. It opens with a bassoon solo, scored very high in its register (Example 1). At first this melody is unaccompanied; a soft French horn enters contrapuntally in the second measure; in the fourth bar, the clarinets join in. The bassoon melody, Example 1, is an adaptation by Stravinsky of a Lithuanian folk song which he discovered in an anthology, one whose character he changed by adding a shortened chromatic phrase to the originally symmetrical tune.

Example 1

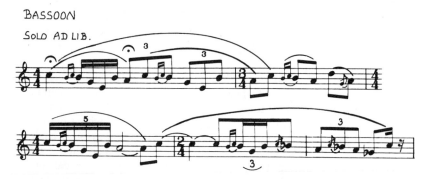

A measure later the solo bassoon repeats a truncated variant of the first three measures of Example 1. An English horn sounding almost like a shepherd's pipe, responds. The bassoon, in turn, answers with a one-measure excerpt from Example 1.

The tempo becomes a little faster; three bassoons and the English horn are heard in a highly chromatic and contrapuntal passage. Four quick pizzicato notes in the violas and cellos introduce the shrill soprano clarinet which plays a highly chromatic melody whose compass is only a fourth. A melody of widely spaced leaps for the flute follows; the English horn again becomes prominent and is soon joined contrapuntally by the bass clarinet.

A legato passage for three flutes and English horn is almost organ-like in its texture. It is interrupted by a persistent rhythm established by the bass clarinet and a single cello *pizzicato,* which stops only for a one-measure bassoon passage. Its resumption is short lived; the solo bassoon enters again. Soon the shrill voice of the soprano clarinet is heard above it, then the flute.

The oboe introduces a new melody, Example 2, which is folk-like in nature.

Example 2

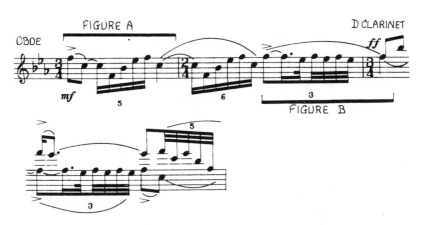

Clarinets become prominent against muted strings in harmonics; a cello *(pizzicato)* and two bassoons supply the rhythmic pulse of this passage. Flute and piccolo arpeggios are answered by "flutter tongued," descending, chromatic, parallel thirds in the oboes. A muted D trumpet is heard with Figure A from Example 2; this is followed by Figure B from the same Example. The texture then becomes very thick.

Suddenly the original tempo returns and the solo bassoon re-enters with a variant of Example 1. A clarinet trill against violins *pizzicato* interrupts it. A descending figure for solo clarinets leads to a string chord in harmonics. The pizzicato figure in the violins concludes the *Introduction,* leading without pause to the following dance.

The tempo doubles (*Tempo giusto* — "a moderate, strict tempo") at the opening of the *Dance of the Adolescents.* A syncopated rhythm, Example 3, is established immediately by the strings; horns punctuate the accented beats. The harmony in this passage is polytonal, an E-flat seventh chord superimposed on an F-flat chord. Stravinsky claimed this polytonal chord, with its double "axis" (E-flat and F-flat) was the fundamental musical idea of the entire score.

Example 3

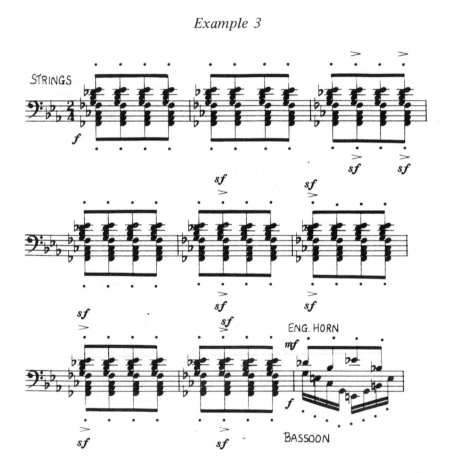

Soon a descending, chromatic figure, Example 4, moves back and forth between the muted trumpet, oboes and violins *pizzicato*.

Example 4

As the texture becomes thicker, brief figures for the piccolo can be heard.

A return is made to the opening rhythmical passage, Example 3. This *ostinato* becomes soft as a theme emerges from it in the bassoons:

Example 5

Over a continuation of the *ostinato,* pert figures are heard in the oboe answered by the flute. The music then halts suddenly, the pounding of the timpani echoing in the listener's ear.

A descending *arpeggio* in the woodwinds leads to a solo violin trill. A solo trumpet, *staccato,* takes up an insistent two-note figure. A bassoon and violin trill interrupts, leading to a new theme, Example 6, the principal theme of the dance (again in folk-song style) played by the French horns.

Example 6

A countermelody for solo flute appears over the sustained tones of the French horn melody. Soon a figure in repeated tones is heard in the oboes; twice the trumpet answers this with Figure C from Example 4.

The alto flute plays the principal theme, Example 6. Figures from it are then repeated.

Pairs of trumpets introduce a new, polytonal melody, one based around the centers of D-flat and G-flat.

Example 7

Figures from Example 7 are extended over the following ten measures.

The dynamic level subsides; only the strings are heard. After the woodwinds start to punctuate the string passage, a piccolo enters with a variant of the principal theme, Example 6.

From this point on, the texture thickens, the dynamic level increases, the pulse becomes stronger. Cellos are heard undergirding the rhythm; trumpets enter with insistent figures. The music builds, moving inexorably to its bold conclusion.

SYMPHONY OF PSALMS

3. Psalm CL

The *Symphony of Psalms* is one of the greatest masterpieces, if not *the* greatest masterpiece of 20th-century choral music. The work was commissioned by the Boston Symphony Orchestra in honor of its 50th anniversary in 1930.

Stravinsky chose an unusual orchestral combination; he eliminated the violins and clarinets as well as the violas since their timbre was perhaps too sensuous for a religious work. An all-male chorus is specified in the score, boy sopranos and altos along with the usual complement of tenors and basses. For a text, he selected Psalms 38, 39 and 150 of the Vulgate Bible, setting the verses in Latin. (Psalms 39, 40 and 150 are the equivalent in the King James version of the Bible.)

His first inspiration for the Symphony was a rhythmic figure to be embodied in the Psalm 150 section, but Stravinsky felt that he could not compose that Psalm setting until he had completed the second section, Psalm 40, "which is a prayer that a new canticle may be put into our mouths. The Allelujah is that canticle." The composer goes on to say of Psalm 150, "The *allegro* . . . was inspired by a vision of Elijah's chariot climbing the Heavens; never before had I written anything quite so literal as the triplets for horns and piano to suggest the horses and chariot. The final hymn of praise must be thought of as issuing from the skies, and agitation is followed by 'the calm of praise.' "

Psalm 150 opens with a slow introduction — an ethereal Alleluia (the "new canticle") followed by the Laudate Dominum, "a prayer to the . . . infant Christ." It is set harmonically against a C-major pedal in the orchestra.

Example 1

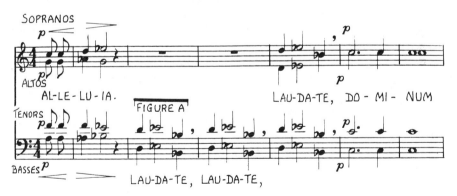

The slow introduction continues; Figure A is prominent throughout.

Psalmus CL (Vulgate)	*Psalm CL (King James Version)*
Alleluia.	*Praise ye the Lord.*

Laudate   Dominum   in   sanctis   *Praise God in His sanctuary:*
      Ejus:.
Laudate Eum in firmamento vir-   *Praise Him in the firmament of*
      tutis Ejus.   *His power.*
Laudate Dominum.   *Praise ye the Lord.*

The *Allegro* proper opens with the rhythm that was Stravinsky's first inspiration concerning the Symphony, one he jotted
down in his note book as ♪ ♫♫♩. . A C-major chord for bassoons
and French horns is repeated in this rhythm, off-set by a driving,
rhythmic *ostinato* in the bass viols, played *pizzicato* the first few
times.

Example 2

BASSOONS, FRENCH HORNS

The upper winds make staccato interjections during repetitions of the figures of Example 2. Syncopation is achieved, as
Stravinsky frequently does, by the shifting of the *ostinato* pattern
to various beats of the measure.

The dynamic level builds, as triplet figures — frequently in
descending chromatic motives — become prominent.

The sopranos enter on the *Laudate* with a two-note motive
(from the opening movement); the altos soon join them contrapuntally:

Example 3

Laudate Eum in virtutibus Ejus.   *Praise Him for his mighty acts.*

The dynamic level drops; the sound of the piano becomes prominent in the accompaniment. Altos and tenors, at the octave, declaim the text in a highly rhythmic passage:

Example 4

ALTOS, TENORS (OCTAVE LOWER)

LAUDA-TE DO-MI-NUM   IN   VIR - TU-TI-BUS   E -

JUS,   LAUDATE DOMINUM   IN SANCTIS   E - JUS.

Laudate Dominum in virtutibus   *Praise Him for his mighty acts:*
    Ejus,
Laudate Dominum in sanctis   *Praise God in his sanctuary:*
    Ejus.

The rhythmic Figure B continues in trumpets and horns; the ascending and descending chromatic figures in the wood winds are heard again. The basses start out, soon imitated contrapuntally by altos and tenors, then by sopranos.

Laudate Eum secundum multi-   *Praise Him according to his ex-*
    tudinem magnitudinis Ejus.   *cellent greatness.*
Laudate Eum in sono tubae;   *Praise Him with the sound of*
                                  the trumpet.

There is a sudden return to the slow tempo of the intro-duction; the "Alleluia" (Example 1) is heard again.

The tempo returns to *Allegro.* In an extended passage the rhythm of Figure B (Example 2) is prominent; the men — soon joined by the boy sopranos and altos — boldly proclaim the text. Orchestral interludes separate the restatements of the text.

Laudate Dominum　　　　　　　Praise God
Laudate Eum.　　　　　　　　　Praise Him.

Suddenly the dynamic level drops; the tempo slows to that of the Introduction. In a contrapuntal section of rare beauty, the chorus becomes prominent. The sopranos lead off, imitated one measure later by the basses; the inner voices — altos and tenors in unison — enter later.

Example 5

Laudate Eum in timpano et choro,　　　*Praise Him with the timbrel and dance:*
Laudate Eum in cordis et organo　　　*Praise Him with stringed instruments and organs.*

The music suddenly becomes "very soft and very singing." This serene Coda, which takes up about one-third of the movement, is in a slow, stately tempo marked "rigorous" by the composer. Its melodic development unfolds over a four-note *ostinato* bass (Figure C) which, because of the 3/4 meter signature, constantly shifts its point of accent. The tonality now centers around E-flat major.

Example 6

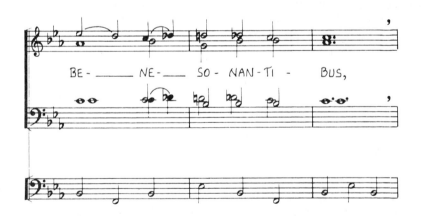

Laudate Eum in cymbalis, bene sonantibus,	*Praise Him upon the loud cymbals;*
Laudate Eum in cymbalis jubilationibus.	*Praise Him upon the high sounding cymbals.*
Laudate Dominum	*Praise God*

| Laudate Eum omnis spiritus lau-
  det Dominum
Laudet Eum | *Let everything that hath breath*
praise the Lord.
Praise ye the Lord. |

  The *Psalm 150* ends as ethereally as it began; the opening "Alleluia" (Example 1) is repeated, closing once again on a C-major chord.

VI

ANTON VON WEBERN (1883-1945) is one of the original triumvirate of twelve-tone or "serialist" composers: Webern himself, his teacher Arnold Schoenberg (nine years his senior) and fellow pupil Alban Berg (two years his junior). Webern's position within this group, however, is unique. "There is no other composer of similar significance in the whole history of music," states Ernst Krenek (a friend of both Webern and Schoenberg) "whose entire life's work (as left by himself to posterity) takes not more than about three hours of performance time." He goes on to say:

> Of Webern's 31 officially numbered works only his last, a cantata, is a little longer than ten minutes. The shortest lasts less than two minutes. But the small size of Webern's compositions is not the only unusual aspect of the composer's personality and work. While alive, he was highly respected by a few colleagues and experts, but his music was very little known at large, and the majority of those who came into contact with it turned away in anger or derision, despising its originator as the most insane among a group of mentally disturbed modern composers, and his work as even worse than the most exasperating excesses of Arnold Schoenberg, among whose original disciples Webern belonged.
> And yet, immediately after Webern's untimely death in 1945 his influence upon a younger generation of musicians spread with incredible intensity and speed, until even such a master as Igor Stravinsky in his advanced years adopted many of Webern's ideas and adapted them to his own creative purposes. [6]

ANTON WEBERN

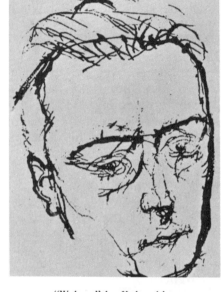

"Webern" by Kokoschka

"Berg" by Schoenberg

ALBAN BERG

Anton von Webern (he himself dropped the royal *von* from his name after the 1918 revolution in Austria) was born in Vienna on December 2nd, 1883. He was the son of a mining engineer whose duties led the family to move first to Graz, then to Klagenfurt, both cities in southern Austria. In the latter city Anton, at ten, was enrolled in the public school and took private lessons in piano, cello and music theory. When Anton completed his public schooling at 18, his family gave him a trip to the Wagner festival at Bayreuth as a graduation present. This inspired the youth to compose his first large-scale work, a ballad, *Young Siegfried* for soprano and orchestra.

That fall Webern enrolled at the University of Vienna to study musicology, also taking lessons in harmony and counterpoint. It was during his university days, actually in the autumn of 1904, that Webern first met Arnold Schoenberg and his pupil, Alban Berg. Formal lessons with Schoenberg lasted either until 1908 or 1910. The teacher-pupil relationship soon developed into a deep, lifelong friendship which benefited Schoenberg as much as it did Webern.

Webern's professional career began in 1908, one spent largely as a conductor. He started as the second conductor of the Spa orchestra and summer theater at Bad Ischl. Then for 12 years, with short interruptions for a stay in Berlin in 1911 and for military service during World War I (1915-1916), Webern conducted orchestras in Vienna, Teplitz, Danzig, Stettin and Prague. In 1920 he gave up orchestral conducting to settle in Mödling, near Vienna, conducting choruses and accepting a few pupils for private study. Two years later he came into contact with the Vienna Education Center of the Social Democratic Party, and took up duties as conductor of the Vienna Workers' Symphony Concerts. He then founded the Vienna Workers' Chorus.

Webern's earliest works were in the harmonic vein of their day, a *Passacaglia for Orchestra* (1908), songs and choruses (dating from 1908 to 1926), music for string quartet (1909 and 1913), *Six Pieces for Large Orchestra* (1910) and *Five Pieces for Orchestra* (1911-13). Toward the last of these compositions, the use of twelve tones may be found to occupy a more important function. His adoption of the *Method* of Schoenberg was gradual. "You musn't imagine that it was a sudden moment," he said. "The links with the past were most intense."

Webern felt that the 12-tone Method would enable a composer to have that "greatest possible unity," one of the fundamental concepts of music in his mind. "Unity is surely the indispensable thing if meaning is to exist. Unity, to be very general, is the establishment of the utmost relatedness between all the component parts."

Webern, in a series of lectures given in 1932, describes how he first encountered the principle of 12-tones:

> I went to see [Schoenberg] one fine morning, to tell him I had read in some newspaper where a few groceries were to be had. In fact I disturbed him with this, and he explained to me that he was 'on the way to something quite new.' He didn't tell me more at the time, and I racked my brains — 'For goodness' sake, whatever can it be? '. . .

> One day Schoenberg intuitively discovered the law that underlies twelve-note composition. An inevitable development of this law was that one gave the succession of notes a *particular order* the 'row' or 'series'.

> . . .Today we've arrived at the end of this path, i.e., at the goal; the twelve notes have come to power and the practical need for this law is completely clear to us today. [7]

Unlike his mentor, Schoenberg, who later occasionally reverted to the use of tonality, Webern, starting with the *String Trio* of 1927, employed the 12-tone Method exclusively thereafter.

Webern had a great love of nature; walks in the woods were journeys to discover the most minute forms of plant life: lichens, fungi and mosses. A neighbor of the composer remarked that "Webern's very touching joy in the little wonders of nature, especially in the world of vegetation, was known to all who came close to him. . . When he observed a fern or a mountain flower, it was preferably in its habitat." Webern felt strongly that the same law of nature which governed the plant and animal kingdoms also affected music. He said in a lecture:

> Man is only the vessel into which is poured what 'nature in general' wants to express. . . . Just as a researcher in nature strives to discover the rules of order that are the basis of nature, we must strive to discover the laws according to which nature, in its particular form 'man' is productive. And this leads us to the view that the things treated by art in general, with which art has to do,

are not 'aesthetic,' but that it is a matter of natural laws, that all discussion of music can only take place along these lines. . . .

Music is natural law as related to the sense of hearing. [8]

In 1927 Webern was appointed conductor of and later adviser for modern music for Radio Austria. He also made appearances throughout Europe as a conductor. But in 1934, the Social Democratic Party was dissolved, and with it Webern's official appointments disappeared. Then came Hitler's *Anschluss* of 1938. Webern lost his position at Radio Austria. "This job has been liquidated," he wrote to a friend. His publisher, Universal Editions, came to a partial rescue. The firm hired Webern as a proof reader and asked him to make piano reductions of orchestral scores. "Just think," the composer complained, "now I have to work for U.E., to make a huge, fat piano score. So I have to postpone work on my *Cantata* for a bit, otherwise it would be finished by now."

As World War II progressed, Webern's finances dropped to a new low; his only income came from lessons given a few private pupils. As the army fled the advance of the invading Russian troops, Webern moved his family to Mittersill, not far from Salzburg, where he resumed work on his *Concerto in Three Movements*. His work was interrupted by the tragic news that his son had been killed at the front and his house near Vienna destroyed by a bombing attack.

As the final days of the war approached, Webern's future suddenly looked brighter. He had received official letters from Vienna asking him to play a large part in the reconstruction of Austrian cultural life after the war. At the time he was living at the home of his son-in-law in Mittersill. The officers of the U.S. Army of occupation suspected this son-in-law of carrying on black market activities and sent a guard to search the house one evening. Unsuspectingly Webern stepped outside to smoke a cigarette, not knowing that the house was surrounded. He was shot and killed by an American soldier who, full of wartime hysteria and obeying orders too rashly, wasn't aware of what Webern was doing in leaving the house under search.

Perhaps the best epitaph for Webern and his work was voiced by Igor Stravinsky who said:

We must hail not only this great composer but a real hero. Doomed to a total failure in a deaf world of ignorance and indifference, he inexorably kept on cutting out his diamonds, his dazzling diamonds, the mines of which he had such a perfect knowledge. [9]

FIVE PIECES FOR ORCHESTRA (Opus 10)

1. Sehr ruhig und zart
2. Lebhaft und zart bewegt

The *Five Pieces for Orchestra* of Anton Webern is one of the most unusual compositions in all orchestral literature. The entire work of five movements lasts a bare six minutes in performance time (the fourth movement is only 6 1/3 measures in length!) and the "orchestra" consists of only 17 soloists who never all play at any one time!

In *Five Pieces for Orchestra* Webern had not yet discovered or adopted the 12-tone Method of Schoenberg in his writing, but the atonal, expressionistic influence can be heard immediately. The

Webern poses at his home in Mödling around 1920.

"atonalism" is achieved by the consistent use of all 12 tones of the chromatic scale, although they are not yet established in a "row" or "series." Dissonances occur when these chromatic tones form an unusual vertical interval such as a minor second or seventh. Probably the chief characteristic of Webern's writing in this work is the "breaking up" of the melodic line or melodic motives into single tones, each of which is assigned to a different instrument, resulting in a multi-timbred melodic motive. It is this characteristic of Webern's later works that has been much imitated by his "disciples" in the late 1950's and 60's

Each movement is compact, concise. Each tone has its place and function. The composer is most explicit as to the performance of each tone: its dynamic intensity, its duration, its quality or timbre (i.e. flutter tongue, muted or "sweet").

The first movement in 2/4 meter, is marked *Sehr ruhig und zart* (very calmly and softly) and is scored for flute, B-flat clarinet, muted trumpet and trombone, celesta, harp, glockenspiel, and muted strings: violin, viola and cello. It is a little over 12 measures in length.

The piece opens with single tones on muted trumpet and harp followed by a chord for viola, harp and celesta, and a single note flutter-tongued by the flute (Example 1). In the first six measures (one-half of the movement) all tones of the chromatic scale except E-natural are employed.

From the climax in measure 6 of Example 1, the texture thins out again; the dynamic level drops back to *ppp*. Single tones (in turn) for the harp, flute, muted trumpet and celesta conclude the brief movement.

The second *piece* is in 3/4 meter (except for two brief measures in 2/4) and is marked *Lebhaft und zart bewegt* (Lively, moving softly). It is the only fast or "lively" piece in this set of five. Fourteen measures in length, it is scored for piccolo, oboe, two clarinets, muted horn, trumpet and trombone, harmonium, celesta, harp, glockenspiel, cymbals, triangle, and muted solo strings.

Within the first measure and two-thirds the composer has employed all 12 tones of the chromatic scale. In contrast to the first piece, thematic motives are more in evidence. At the opening (see Example 2) the clarinet states its motive in counterpoint to that of the violin. The oboe soon joins in.

Example 1

Example 2

In the next five measures, single tones for different instruments form the motivic outline, either *pp* or *ppp*. A sense of urgency occurs in an *accelerando* that builds to the final measures for winds, triangle and glockenspiel *fortississimo (fff)*.

VII

ALBAN BERG (1885-1935) was a disciple and pupil of Arnold Schoenberg and a close friend of Anton Webern. Although he was the youngest of this triumvirate, his music has been more frequently performed over the years than that of the other two combined. His two operas, *Wozzeck* and *Lulu* have almost become repertory works at several opera houses. His *Concerto for Violin and Orchestra* is one of the masterpieces of 20th-century literature.

Alban was one of four children reared in a Roman Catholic home. His father owned a shop near St. Stephen's Cathedral in Vienna which dealt in the sale of saints' pictures and Catholic church furnishings.

In a letter written later in life, Berg recalled that as a youth "I wanted to become a poet. . . and, further back still, as a child I used to paint and draw, prompted by a certain manual skill which I mistook for talent."

The youth first turned to composition when he was 14, but the death of his father a year later destroyed the boy's hopes of successfully developing those talents in financial security. In the same year as his father's passing, Alban had his first attack of asthma. It was his poor health, along with a concentrated effort to compose about 70 songs and duets — studying Ibsen's plays during his "free" moments — that caused him to neglect his school work. When he failed to pass his final examination at the end of the 1903 school year he contemplated suicide. His frame of mind was not helped by a youthful romance that was thwarted at the same time.

The following year he successfully passed the examination and graduated. He then accepted a position as an unpaid probationer-accountant with the government. He decided to continue in music in his spare time. One day he gathered up a sheaf of songs and called on a teacher of composition whose advertisement he had seen in the paper, Arnold Schoenberg. Berg at this point was a fair amateur pianist and a good choral singer; he was ignorant of the music of Richard Strauss or Gustav Mahler. Schoenberg looked at these early songs and described them as "between Hugo Wolf and Johannes Brahms." Berg studied for two years on a part-time basis with Schoenberg, then, as the result of inheriting some money, he was able to study full-time for five more years, stopping only when Schoenberg moved to Berlin in 1911.

The early compositions of Berg show a graudal evolution. Opus 1, a *Piano Sonata* of 1909 is Wagnerian in its reliance on chromatic harmony; his Opus 2, four songs completed later in 1909, show influences of Mahler with whose music he had become acquainted. In the last of the four songs, Berg abandons the use of a key signature. The *String Quartet* that followed (1910) was cast in two movements, almost an "exposition" movement and a "development" movement, as the two are thematically related; the tonality throughout is ambiguous. This was the last "free" composition written by Berg while he was studying with Schoenberg.

By Opus 4, *Five Songs* for voice and orchestra completed in 1910, Berg was already experimenting with a "tone row" in the last of the group, a passacaglia. Opus 5, *Four Pieces for Clarinet and Piano,* was dedicated to his teacher the year after lessons had stopped. These pieces are miniatures, composed purposely to contrast with the gargantuan works of Mahler, Scriabin and Strauss. Many of the expressionist "tricks" may be found in these Berg pieces: *glissandi,* trills, flutter-tonguing, tremolos, and irregular note-repetitions. The work actually forshadows the intensity and drama of his later opera *Wozzeck.*

The *Three Orchestral Pieces* of 1914, probably Berg's most frequently performed orchestral work, follows the pattern established by Schoenberg in his *Five Orchestral Pieces* and Webern's *Five Pieces* for orchestra. In these, the composers sought to escape from the traditional cyclic symphonic forms in favor of several short, self-contained movements.

Berg now became divided in his allegiance and inspiration.

The large symphonic style of Mahler attracted him once again, especially those symphonies of Mahler that made use of voices. In the summer of 1912 Berg wrote to his friend Anton Webern and announced his new project: "This winter I intend to compose a big symphonic movement and I plan to let it end with a boy's voice singing (from the gallery) words from 'Seraphita' a mystical novel by Balzac! " But, the idea came to nothing. Instead, Berg returned to the fold and completed *Three Orchestral Pieces* in honor of Schoenberg's 40th birthday.

Alban Berg was conscripted into military service in 1915 and trained for active duty. A medical examination proved him unfit for combat; he was then assigned to duty in one of the war offices in Vienna. On a military leave spent at the mountain estate of his wife's family, the composer's thoughts turned to music, for "there begins to stir in me the urge to work again, as in previous summer holidays. The musical setting, planned more than three years ago, of Büchner's play *Wozzeck* occupies me again." But the need to return to the war office within the week prevented any actual work. His health was seriously weakening; he wrote that he had "attacks of asthma of such virulence that I believed, literally, that I could not last the night."

The final collapse of Austria in 1918 released Berg from military service, but it threw him into the maelstrom of Viennese who had to struggle financially for a living because of inflation. At first the composer managed his family's estate, but that had to be sold later the same year. "I must concentrate on earning a living," appeared over and over again in his letters. He turned to teaching composition, and became quite successful at it.

His great masterpiece, the opera *Wozzeck,* was completed in 1921 and the vocal score was published with the financial assistance of Mahler's widow to whom the work was dedicated. About a year later the opera was taken over by Universal Editions of Vienna, a publishing house that extended a contract for all future creations of Berg, thereby guaranteeing him some financial security.

Berg now became absorbed in the "serial" technique, the twelve-tone method of Schoenberg. The *Chamber Concerto* of 1925 also shows the composer's interest in allusive quotations and musical anagrams. The principal theme of the *Concerto* includes the names of Arnold Schoenberg, Anton Webern and Alban Berg in so far as there are note equivalents for the letters (in German B-flat is known as G and E-flat as S.) The *Concerto* was followed by the *Lyric Suite* (1926), a work for string quartet in strict serial form.

Throughout his serial compositions, Berg was able to preserve bits and pieces of diatonic melody, dance-like rhythms, triads and seventh chords and even, occasionally, strong progressions of chords, all amid a rich use of chromatic, syncopated, dissonant counterpoint. His wide range of style allowed him to quote from Wagner in the *Lyric Suite,* from Bach and folksong in his *Violin Concerto* (see the following section), and to make use of jazz elements in a concert aria *Der Wein* completed in 1929. He developed a style and idiom quite independent of either Schoenberg or Webern, one which showed his gift for lyrical melodies and dramatic forms. He expressed a unique pathos in his writing quite in contrast to Schoenberg's theosophy and Webern's nature-religion.

Among the few official honors bestowed on Berg during his lifetime was his nomination, largely as the result of the success of *Wozzeck,* to become a member of the Prussian Academy of Arts on January 30, 1930 — exactly three years before Hitler's appointment as Reichs-Chancellor automatically erased Berg's name and banished his music from the German musical world.

Always in poor health, Berg reported in a letter from his little mountain cottage on August 27th, 1935, that he had been stung by a bee. This led to a carbuncle followed by blood-poisoning. The sting must have occurred about the same day that his *Violin Concerto* was completed. The composer then turned back to the orchestration of the third act of his opera *Lulu* — work that had been interrupted by the creation of the *Concerto.* Berg moved back to Vienna exhausted and ailing, the orchestration of *Lulu* incomplete. Although gravely ill, he attended a performance of his *Lulu Symphony* derived from the opera. This was his last public appearance; he passed away at one in the morning on December 24, 1935, of pernicious blood poisoning.

VIOLIN CONCERTO

2. Allegro

A double tragedy surrounds Berg's *Violin Concerto*, a work

commissioned by the American violinist Louis Krasner. During the composition of the *Concerto,* Berg's thoughts turned frequently to the then recent, tragic death from polyiomyelitis of the beautiful 18-year old daughter of Alma Mahler Gropius, Gustav Mahler's widow. The title-page of the *Concerto* bears the inscription: "To the Memory of an Angel." It served as a "requiem" for the young and talented girl for whom Berg had such a fatherly affection. In the last section of the *Concerto* he used the choral tune of Johann Rudolph Ahle (1626-1673) that Bach himself employed in his Cantata No. 60, "O Eternity, Thou Thundrous Word." In the conductor's score of the *Concerto* Berg quotes the text of the choral underneath the solo violin staff: "It is enough, Lord, when it is Your pleasure." The other tragedy associated with the *Concerto* is, of course, Berg's own tragically early death at 50.

For the first performance of the *Concerto* in Barcelona four months after the composer's death, his close personal friend and biographer, Willi Reich, wrote the following program notes for the second (and final) movement:

> A turbulent passage introduces the Second Part, which is con-ceived as a free, restless and stormy cadenza for the violin. The music drives its demonic and irresistible course, relieved only by a short and peaceful intermezzo, to the catastrophe. Heavy laments and sharp outcries are heard in the orchestra; then, over a long pedal-point, a gradual fading away. At this poignant moment, there suddenly is introduced by the solo violin the grave choral of J.S. Bach, derived from J.R. Ahle: 'It is enough.' The woodwinds, in an organ-like choir, answer each strophe with the original harmony of the classical prototype. Then there begin artful variations in which the original choral melody always lingers, the 'misterioso' rising from the bass, while the solo violin adds a moving elegy. The death-song grows more distinct, the soloist visibly takes the lead of the whole body of violins and violas, drawing them intensely into unison with its voice, then gradually detaching itself. A fleeting recollection of the lovely girl's image, and the choral, in bitter harmonization, and mingled with a tender melody of the solo violin, brings the tragic work in coda-fashion to its close.[10]

The *Concerto* is written in the 12-tone Method. It is in two parts, each containing two movements. The Second Part opens with a tripartite *Allegro:* a turbulent cadenza section, a more calm and tranquil middle section, and a pseudo-recapitulation of the cadenza section. The second movement in Part II is an *Adagio:* a choral, two variations on the choral and a Coda.

The "row" or "series" on which the Second Part is based is a retrograde (or backward) form of the row of the First Part. The opening measures announce the 12 notes of the series, telescoped into a harsh chord whose notes rise from a low C on the double bass to a high C-flat for the flute. The timpani responds with a G-minor chord, first struck, then continued in a roll:

Example 1

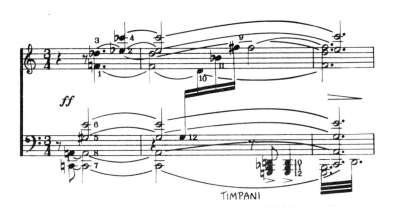

The score is marked *Allegro, but always rubato, free like a cadenza.* The solo violin immediately launches into a series of turbulent passages, many in double stops, cadenza-like in nature and derived from the basic row and its variants.

Following a three-octave descent in measure twenty-two by the solo violin, the dominating rhythmic figure of the *Allegro* is heard in the French horns and woodwinds:

Example 2

FRENCH HORNS

BASSOONS

This rhythmic figure is repeated numerous times by the horns and woodwinds while the solo violin continues its "free flowing" cadenza. Ten measures later all but the low woodwinds drop out and the solo violin takes up the rhythmic motive of Example 2.

Berg marks the middle section of this tripartite *Allegro* "always free, the same tempo, but less rhythmical; tranquil but not dragging." The solo violin plays a descending passage (the first four notes of the row) leading to double stops (the lower tone *pizzicato)* and eventually broken chords. The woodwinds have a soft, sustained accompaniment while the solo violin passage derives its rhythm from Example 2.

Throughout much of this middle section, the solo violin is accompanied only by the violas and cellos. Eventually, two clarinets enter "scherzo-like"; the solo violin plays a descending figure in double stops.

The tempo returns to *Allegro rubato.* Reminiscences of the first section are heard. The movement reaches its climax when the full orchestra, *fff* (and marked in the score, "high point of the *Allegro")* intones the rhythmic motive of Example 2. The music subsides to *ppp* ten measures later, leading without pause to the next movement.

The second movement, an *Adagio,* is also in tripartite form: the choral tune, two variations on the choral tune and a reminiscence of the First Part, and a closing Coda. The *Adagio* immediately introduces the choral tune, the clarinets repeating, in Bach's harmony, each statement of the solo violin. The whole-tone notes at the beginning of the row form the opening pitches of Bach's choral tune.

Example 3

In Variation I the cellos play the choral tune accompanied by sustained horns; the harp canonically repeats the choral tune a sixth higher in pitch. The tune then becomes hard to discern as the solo violin plays a rhythmical and melodic variant of it. Soon all the violins and, eventually, the violas join in unison with the solo violin which "acts as a leader of the string section."

In Variation II horns in unison play the choral tune in inversion; the first violins continue in unison with the solo violin as it plays arabesques that grow faster and faster, leading to "the highpoint of the *Adagio.*" As the dynamic level subsides, fragments of the choral melody appear first in the trombones and tuba, then in the cellos. The upper woodwinds and strings drop out except for the solo violin. Suggestions of a Corinthian folk-tune used in Part I of the *Concerto* are heard.

The Coda opens with a statement by the woodwinds (without clarinets) of the choral melody, Example 3; the solo violin plays a countermelody derived from the tone-row. The string section joins the woodwinds in the choral, answered by the solo violin with fragments of the melody. The French horns complete the choral melody as an ascending passage derived ·from the tone row is started by one viola, continued by one violin and completed by the solo violin. Soft chords by the woodwinds lead to the closing measures in which the violins and double basses play an *arpeggio* derived from the tone row.

Heitor Villa-Lobos at work on one of his more than 3,000 compositions.

VIII

HEITOR VILLA-LOBOS **(1887-1959)** was a composer of most unusual and eccentric nature, a study in contrasts. He could write some of the New World's finest music, yet he also composed a large quantity of trivia. Largely self-taught both in music and academic subjects because he hated school, he later in life became the Superintendent of Musical Education for Brazil. His tastes ran the gamut, from café music to symphonic literature. He was a great story teller, which makes it difficult for the historian or biographer to determine which anecdotes are true, and which are simply stories.

Even the date of Villa-Lobos birth and the details of his childhood are shrouded in mystery and conflict. He was born in Rio de Janeiro, but the year of his birth is listed by different authorities as 1881, 1887, 1890 or 1892. His father was a writer, amateur cellist and pianist, and/or a "man of the people," as the case may be. At an early age — some say six — Heitor learned to play the viola, the cello, or the guitar (and/or any number of wind instruments). He once claimed that he taught himself the violin, learning to play it by holding the instrument in a vertical position such as one does the cello!

He disliked school and teachers. A friend said: "Villa was a rebellious youth who took not at all to formal education. He apparently did run away (or was expelled) from school, and his studies at the Instituto Naccional de Musica began and ended almost simultaneously. He really studied with nobody on a master-and-pupil basis but learned everything he knew (which was considerable) from intelligent listening and score reading."

His father died when Villa-Lobos was still young. The boy then turned to playing popular music in theater and restaurant orchestras. Every free moment he spent in various haunts which specialized in the popular songs and dances of Brazil. He composed a number of popular songs himself. His first symphonic composition, *Canticos Sertanejos* (A Forest Hymn), a suite for orchestra based on Brazilian country airs, was completed in 1909, when Villa-Lobos was about 22.

The next year he decided to come to the United States. Along the way — for he was traveling on a shoestring budget — he was marooned in Barbados. He became fascinated by the music he heard there, largely chants of the native Africans and their descendents who lived on the island. His *Three African Dances,* based on melodies and rhythms heard in Barbados, also included the use of folk instruments.

Villa-Lobos never completed *that* journey to the United States. Instead, in 1912, he made the first of many trips to the interior of Brazil to discover more about the music, rites and ceremonies of the natives who lived there, representatives of the cultures of the Brazilian Indians, the Africans, the Afro-Indians, and the Afro-Indian-Portuguese. He wandered, according to his own account, not only through the Amazons, but over the entire face of this huge country, from Pernambuco to Rio Grande do Sul.

He claimed that he never used any of this Brazilian folk music as such in his own work. "I compose in the folk style," he once told a music critic. "I utilize thematic idioms in my own way. An artist . . . must select and transmit the material given him by his people. To make a potpourri of folk melody and think that in this way music has been created, is hopeless."

In 1915 a concert devoted exclusively to the compositions of Villa-Lobos was given in Rio de Janeiro. Unfortunately the public was not ready for his idiom. For the average symphony patron — oriented in the European tradition — the music of Villa-Lobos smacked of Brazilian popular music and folk rhythms; for the man in the street who enjoyed popular music, his compositions were too formal!

Two internationally famous musicians affected to a slight degree Villa-Lobos' career as a composer. Darius Milhaud, the noted Parisian composer, was assigned as secretary to the French Ambassador in Rio de Janeiro during World War I. Milhaud was the first "great" composer that Villa-Lobos had ever seen. He met the Frenchman, heard concerts of his music and through him, became acquainted with the works of other French musicians. These influences may be found in such works as the *Suite floral* (Flower Suite) of 1917 which is impressionistic in nature, and *Epigramas irônicos a sentimentais* (Ironical and Sentimental Epigrams) of 1921 which hints, even in its title, of the works of Erik Satie, the French "rebel."

In 1919, the world-renowned Polish-American pianist Artur Rubinstein appeared in Rio de Janeiro. While there, he heard some of the music of Villa-Lobos. Impressed, Rubinstein asked the Brazilian composer to write some works that he could play on his concert tours. This was the start of Villa-Lobos's fame outside of Brazil.

A grant from the Brazilian government enabled Villa-Lobos to go to Paris where he lived off and on from 1923 to 1930. While in Paris, he claimed, "I listened attentively, but never allowed myself to be influenced by any of the novelties I heard. I claim to be all myself, and I conceive my music in complete independence and isolation."

From Paris Villa-Lobos returned to Brazil and became its Director of Musical Education. His approach to this challenge was very different. He had the children taught to sing in large choruses, not from printed notes, but by the position of the fingers, indicating the degrees of the scale. The children sang everything, all the way from the works of Bach to popular songs. They performed these with stamping, hissing, whistling, shouting, clapping and swaying when appropriate to the music. Villa-Lobos himself organized a series of open-air concerts which involved a chorus of 30,000 school children and an orchestra of 1,000 players. For these concerts he invented a system whereby he conducted with signal flags from a high tower in the middle of the huge stadium. One of his principal contributions to the world of music was his *Guia prático* (Practical Guide), a series of music texts for the public schools of Brazil.

In the field of orchestral literature, Villa-Lobos devised two categories of compositions. He called them *Chôros* and *Bachianas Brasileiras.* The Chôros, (literally "Choruses") of which he wrote 14, were "street serenades" which emphasized the rhythm and melodies of Brazilian, Indian and popular music. The *Bachianas Brasileiras* are a combination of contrapuntal writing, based on the earlier style of J. S. Bach, and native elements of Brazilian music. He composed nine of these latter suites. Several of his dozen symphonic poems evoke the atmosphere of the jungle, Afro-Brazilian rhythms and tribal rites. The best known is *Amazonas* (1917), which depicts the adventures of an Indian maid alone in the tropical jungle. Among his 18 ballets are *Uirapuru* (1935), the story of the legendary Indian chieftain whose flute playing puts young girls under his spell, and *Dança da terra* (Dance of the Earth—1943), a primitive ritual of earth-worship.

Villa-Lobos was at his best in the lyrical, improvisational forms. Although he composed 12 symphonies, their rigid and formal structure did not show off his originality and talent to the best. Essentially he was a tonal composer, although his works frequently wander through many keys and some are polytonal in nature. *Ostinato* rhythms and a rich exploitation of percussive effects mark a chief characteristic of his personal idiom. Any "French influence" disappeared after his early works. The "Brazilian influence" is achieved, as has been said before, by the use of typically Brazilian melodies, harmonies and rhythmic traits; actually it is more a question of atmosphere and feeling, a kind of "Brazilian accent."

Altogether Villa-Lobos composed close to 3,000 works. They

represent the outpouring of a gifted musician who worked chiefly by intuition.

In 1944 he visited the United States for the first time, a trip arranged through the combined efforts of the Janssen Symphony Orchestra of Los Angeles and the U.S. State Department. The success of his concerts in Los Angeles, Boston and New York was such that he returned a number of times to New York.

His last years were marked by a series of miseries, ailments and illnesses to which any ordinary human being would have knuckled under years earlier. "It was Villa's tremendous will power," a friend said, "and his affirmation of life that kept him going long after the medical profession had declared his case hopeless."

BACHIANAS BRASILERIRAS NO. 5

1. Aria

Each of the Bachianas Brasileiras suites is scored for a different instrumental combination, much the same way Bach utilized various instrumental groupings in his Suites. The *Bachianas Brasileiras No. 5* is scored for eight solo cellos and a soprano soloist. There are two movements in the suite. The first is titled "Aria" and was completed in 1938. The second movement, "Dansa" (Dance) was added in 1945.

In the "Aria," two of the cellos double the soprano vocal line; the others provide an accompaniment which is predominantly *pizzicato,* suggesting the native guitars of Brazil. The "Aria" is cast in ternary form. The first and last sections are without text, the soprano singing either on the neutral syllable "ah" or humming. The middle section is a setting of a poem in Portuguese by Ruth V. Corrêa.

The "Aria" opens with a two-measure instrumental introduction. In the contrapuntal style of Bach, the outside (highest and lowest) cello voices move in contrary motion.

The soprano enters on the neutral syllable *ah.* The melody, the beginning of which is quoted in Example 1, is long phrased, lyric, and employs melodic turns characteristic of native Brazilian music. Although the meter changes frequently, the beats or pulsations are steady and equal; the onward "push" of this rhythm is a Brazilian characteristic.

Example 1

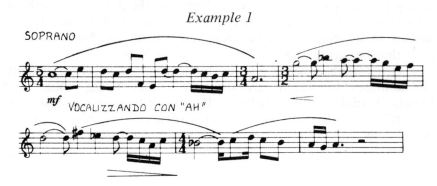

A three measure interlude follows the soprano melody, the start of which is quoted in Example 1. That melody is then repeated by a solo cello; the soprano soloist is silent during this repetition.

The middle section resembles a Brazilian popular song. It is full of syncopation and *rubatos.* The soloist sounds almost as though she were improvising or creating the melody as she sings along. The harmony is particularly interesting. It begins:

Tarde, uma nuvem rósea	*Lo, at midnight, clouds are slowly*
Lenta e transparente,	*Passing, rosy and lustrous,*
Sobre o espaço sonhadora e bela!	*O'er the spacious heaven with loveliness laden!*
Surge no infinito a lua docemente,	*From the boundless deep the moon arises wondrous,*
Enfeitando a tarde, qual meiga donzela	*Glorifying the evening like a beauteous maiden,*
Que se apresta e alinda sonhadoramente,	*Now she adorns herself in half unconscious duty,*
Em anseios d'alma para ficar bela,	*Eager, anxious that we recognize her beauty,*
Grita ao céo e a terra,	*While sky and earth, yea all nature*
Toda a Natureza!	*With applause salute her.*

Example 2

* * * *

| Cala a passarada aos seus tristes queixumes, | *All the birds have ceased their sad and mournful complaining,* |
| E reflete o mar toda a sua riqueza | *Now appears on the sea in a silver reflection* |

Suave a luz de lua desperta agora,	*Moonlight softly waking the soul and constraining*
A cruel saudade que ri a chora!	*Hearts to cruel tears and bitter dejection.*
Tarde, uma nuvem rósea lenta e transparente,	*Lo at midnight clouds are slowly passing rosy and lustrous*
Sobre o espaço sonhadora e bela!	*O'er the spacious heavens dreamily wondrous.*

The soprano theme from the opening section is repeated; this time the solosit hums it. As she finishes this haunting melody, the "Aria." comes to an end.

IX

SERGE PROKOFIEV (1891-1953) was most precocious as a child. Having heard his mother play Beethoven sonatas and Chopin waltzes, he demanded to play the piano too. So, as soon as he could balance himself on a piano stool, his mother started giving him lessons. At five and a half, Serge composed his first piano piece, picking out the notes to form a tune and playing them over and over again until his mother was able to write them down. Serge called the piece *Indian Galop*, a high-spirited tune inspired by the family discussions of India that he had overheard. Six months later (at age 6!) he composed and wrote down a waltz, march and rondo. The following year he completed a duet which he and his mother could play.

Serge's father was the Agricultural Manager for the great Sontsov estates in the Ukraine. While he was pleased that his son liked music, he saw to it that Serge also received lessons in riding as soon as he could sit in a saddle. Every morning began with a

"Prokofiev" in 1921 by Matisse.   Prokofiev in 1940.

swim for the boy in the river bordering the estate. His garden was not just a pleasant "child's past-time," but was developed according to lessons learned from his father, the agriculturist. Serge learned chess at a very early age, becoming an expert far beyond his years. Later, as an adult, he won many distinctions in national and international chess tournaments.

The interest of her child in music led Serge's mother to take him on a second visit to Moscow in 1902 to try and learn from experts whether her son's talent in music should be developed. The 11-year old lad took with him the partially completed score of his second opera, *Desert Islands*. In Moscow, mother and son met Serge Taneyev, the great Russian authority on counterpoint. He was so impressed by the boy's ability, he suggested to Mme. Prokofiev that she stay in Moscow until the end of the school year so that Serge could take lessons from him. As summer approached, Taneyev then counseled Mme. Prokofiev to hire an instructor in harmony and composition who could accompany them back to the Ukraine and give the boy lessons at home. The young Reinhold Glière was suggested by Taneyev and hired by the Prokofiev's.

By fall Serge was ready to return to Taneyev in Moscow. Glière said of the summer's work: "The boy showed an understanding of harmony and musical form quite remarkable for a boy of his age; . . . he was a good sight reader, had perfect pitch, an excellent memory, a rich creative imagination and an extraordinary feeling for harmony."

At his first lesson Serge gave Taneyev his *Symphony No. 1* which he had completed that summer under Glière's tutoring. The master praised the counterpoint, but said he found the harmony crude. "Mainly the tonic, dominant and subdominant chords," he said with a laugh. The laugh was not only biting but historic; Prokofiev never forgot it. "I was deeply hurt." The fact that the harmony was crude was worse. "The thought rankled. The seed had been sown and a long period of germination began." Never again was Prokofiev to be accused of crude harmony! The 12 year-old boy went on to give the world a new concept of harmony as a mature composer.

The following fall Serge was enrolled as a full-time student in the Conservatory of St. Petersburg. This was chosen over the one in Moscow because it offered training in general subjects in addition to its courses in music. Nicholas Rimsky-Korsakov was on the board of entrance examiners. When he looked at the fat folder Serge was carrying — containing four operas, two sonatas, a symphony and a number of piano pieces — he exclaimed: "What, are all these your own compositions? " When Serge admitted that they were, Rimsky-Korsakov told his colleagues, "Here is a pupil after my own heart."

At 17 Prokofiev made his first public appearance as a pianist. A series called "Evenings of Modern Music" had begun in St. Petersburg in 1901, and, as a student, Prokofiev had heard many new works at these concerts, compositions by Claude Debussy, Maurice Ravel, Max Reger, Paul Dukas, Vincent d'Indy and Richard Strauss. Now he performed his own Opus 4, *Diabolic Suggestions*, a work still in the active piano repertory today. It was bold, new, different. "Of course he loved to shock," a writer has said referring to this new work, "for he was a spirited young composer. But that, like his wish to be up-to-date, was an irrelevance. His music expressed himself."

The year 1911, Prokofiev's 20th, was a milestone in his career. In addition to completing his *Piano Concerto No. 1*, he was published for the first time (the *Sonata No. 1* as well as 12 short piano works) and heard the first professional performance of any of his compositions (*Dreams* and *Autumn Sketches*, both orchestral works).

After nine years of work, Prokofiev graduated from the Conservatory, appearing at the exercises as piano soloist in his own *Piano Concerto No. 2*. As a present to honor the occasion, his mother provided him with a trip to London. There Prokofiev met Serge Diaghilev, the ballet impresario whose Russian Ballet was appearing in the English capitol. Many talks were held concerning the possibility of a new ballet score. Diaghilev thought he could "tame" this lad, who, at this point, was an *enfant terrible* very much on the fringe of the musical world. Prokofiev thought the impresario could vault him to eminence and public recognition in much the same manner as he had earlier done for Stravinsky. Although the heavy clouds of World War I began to appear on the horizon, Prokofiev set out to work on the music; he was exempt from Russian military service as he was the only son of a widow. (His father had died when Serge was 19.)

Prokofiev chose for a ballet subject "a few Scythian characters, but could think of no plot." The exigencies of the war made it impossible for the ballet, as such, to come to life. The composer therefore took excerpts from his full score and called it the *Scythian Suite*. It was first performed in 1916 at Petrograd (formerly St. Petersburg, now Leningrad).

Prokofiev was back in Moscow early in 1917 to play his first all-Prokofiev recital. He returned to Petrograd just in time to see the outbreak of the revolution which led to Kerensky's government. Politics was outside his sphere. His reaction at first was to go on working as usual. He went off to the country and started to work on two compositions simultaneously, as he did frequently, a violin concerto and a symphony. He decided to write the latter (with tongue-in-cheek) in the spirit of Haydn had the old master lived in the 20th century. The result was the *Classical Symphony*, one of Prokofiev's most frequently performed works.

Word reached him in the country that all was not well in Moscow and Petrograd. The leaders of the February Revolution were calling for the closing of theaters, the shutting of art galleries, and the bolting of doors at concert halls. The following winter was so depressing for Prokofiev in Russia that he decided to visit the New World; his mother had visions of her son becoming fabulously wealthy in those far-off lands. On May 7, 1918, Prokofiev left Moscow for the 18-day train ride to Vladivostok. He then sailed for Tokyo where he gave two concerts, then on to Yokohama for one concert appearance. He next sailed for San Francisco via Honolulu. By September he was in New York.

His first recital in that city drew mixed reactions. The public admired his pianistic ability; they disliked his compositions. The music critics wrote that it was "a carnival of cacophony," "Russian chaos in music," "Bolshevism in art." Fortunately for Prokofiev, Chicago was more receptive. When performed by the Chicago Symphony, his *Scythian Suite* was so well liked that the director of the Chicago Opera decided to produce his new opera, *The Love for Three Oranges*, as soon as it could be completed. Prokofiev gave up the concert tour to concentrate for a year on finishing the opera. The director's death just before work was completed on it led to an indefinite postponement. He tried to resume his concert tour, but the audiences did not want to hear his music.

In desperation, Prokofiev left the United States and headed for Paris. There Diaghilev produced his ballet *Chout* (The Buffoon) with great success. In the meantime, Mary Garden had assumed the directorship of the Chicago Opera and decided to produce *The Love for Three Oranges*. Prokofiev traveled to Chicago to conduct the first performance of it on December 30, 1921; the opera was well received. This was not the case in New York, where its later production led one critic to write: "The production cost $130,000, which is about $43,000 per orange too much! "

For the next ten years Prokofiev made Paris his home, although he made frequent concert tours in Europe and the United States to perform his music. As time went on, however, he became homesick. "I've got to live back in the land of my native soil," he confided to a friend. "I've got to see real winters again, and spring that bursts into being from one moment to the next. I've got to hear the Russian language echoing in my ears. I've got to talk to people who are my own flesh and blood, so that they can give me back something I lack here — their songs, my songs. . . . Yes, my friend, I'm going back."

The 16 years of wandering (1918-1934) were followed by 19 years spent largely in his native Russia. His first major project on his return was to write the film score for the Russian motion picture *Lieutenant Kijé;* he applied the techniques of scoring for a film that he had learned on his visits to the studios in Hollywood. A few years later he delighted children (young *and* old) all over the world by writing the story and music known as *Peter and the Wolf* (1936). He also tried his hand at ballet once more, creating *Romeo and Juliet* (1936) first, then *Cinderella* ten years later.

Most of Prokofiev's works are marked by bold melodies with wide leaps and unexpected turns of phrase; his rhythms are likewise bold, strong, forceful, frequently march-like. His orchestrations show that he learned his lessons well from his teacher, Rimsky-Korsakov, one of the greatest authorities on orchestration the world has ever known. Prokofiev's harmony, while often dissonant, is always diatonic; sudden changes in key frequently add excitement to his music. Although there are atonal passages in his works, these are used (according to Prokofiev) "mainly for the sake of contrast, in order to bring the tonal passage to the fore." Prokofiev liked the classical forms, for he was a spiritual descendant of Scarlatti, Haydn and Mozart. "I want nothing better, nothing more flexible or more complete than the sonata form, which contains everything necessary to my structural purposes." This affinity shows in the catalogue of his works: seven symphonies (1916-1952); five piano concertos (1911-1932); two violin and one cello concerto (1916-1938); and nine sonatas for the piano (1907-1947).

As an artist who voluntarily returned to the U.S.S.R. when he could have enjoyed a professional career in western Europe and the United States, he was amply rewarded with prizes and money. In 1943 he received the Stalin Prize for his *Piano Sonata No. 7,* and a year later was decorated with the Order of the Red Banner of Labor for outstanding services rendered in the development of Soviet music. But Russian policy did an "about face." In 1948 Prokofiev, along with Shostakovich, Khatchaturian and Miaskovsky, was denounced by the Central Committee of the Communist Party because of the "bourgeois formalism" in their writing. The performance of their music was forbidden in Russia. The ban did not last long, however, since this group was the "Big Four" of contemporary Russian music. First Prokofiev's ballets, then his symphonies were performed. The composer now tried to meet the requirements of socialist-realist art and completed a sixth symphony and an opera based on Soviet life, *A Tale of a Real Man.*

Both were attacked in the press as being "formalistic"; *Pravda* said Prokofiev's music was penetrated to the core by "Western formalist decay."

Hurt, Prokofiev tried once again, crafting one of his finest works, his *Symphony No. 7* which received its successful premiere in Moscow in October, 1952. He died five months later, the day after Josef Stalin passed away. The Soviet government withheld the news for 48 hours so that, presumably, Prokofiev's death would not overshadow that of Josef Stalin.

CONCERTO NO. 3 FOR PIANO AND ORCHESTA

2. Andantino

The actual composition of Prokofiev's third piano concerto occurred after his first unsuccessful visit to the United States in 1918, although some of the themes had been conceived previous to the visit and some during the tour. Having successfully watched Diaghilev's production of his ballet *Chout* during the Paris season of 1921, Prokofiev went off to the Brittany coast for the summer, and started to work on some songs and his new piano concerto. The composer's account of how he "built" the Concerto is both mysterious and fascinating, an insight into the creative processes of his mind. In Brittany he only gave "form" to themes and ideas that he had been collecting over a period of years.

Ten years earlier he had decided to write a large, *virtuoso* concerto; only a passage of ascending parallel triads used in the Coda of the first movement survived from that idea of 1911. In 1916, before going off to Kiev to spend the summer with his old teacher Glière, Prokofiev sketched out two themes for the first movement and the theme and two variations for the second movement. Then there was another long break of 18 months. Just before leaving Russia for the United States, he began to write "a *white* quartet, that is, an entirely diatonic string quartet to be played on the white keys only of the piano. Some of these themes were composed in Petrograd, some on the Pacific and some in America. Then I began to think that a quartet of this kind would sound monotonous, so I decided to split up the material; I used the first and second themes of the *finale* for the *finale* of the concerto."

"So," he goes on to say, "when I began working on my *Concerto* in Brittany, I already had all the thematic material I needed except for the third theme of the *finale* and the subordinate theme of the first movement."

The first performance, with the composer as soloist, was given by the Chicago Symphony on December 16, 1921, just before the Chicago Opera unveiled its production of his opera, *The Love for Three Oranges*. Although the *Concerto* was not too well received by the public at its initial performance, it has since become the public's favorite of his piano concertos. The *Concerto No. 3* is characterized by the sharp, biting, sometimes satirical wit that is typical of Prokofiev's music. It is crisp, brilliant and full of sharp contrasts. The themes seem to propel their own energies.

The second movement, *Andantino*, consists of a theme with five variations. The tripartite theme is announced by the orchestra alone. It begins:

Example 1

The theme ends with a phrase derived from its opening phrase.

Variation 1

"In the first variation," the composer explained, "the piano treats the opening of the theme in quasi-sentimental fashion, and resolves into a chain of trills as the orchestra repeats the closing phrase."

Variation 2

"The tempo changes to *Allegro* for the second and third variations, and the piano has brilliant figures, while bits of the theme are introduced here and there in the orchestra."

The effect is tempestuous. Against rapidly moving figurations for the piano, a solo trumpet plays the opening measures of the theme. The strings repeat them with the eighth-notes inverted. The descending scale passage derived from Figure B is hidden in rapidly moving figurations, but it can be heard. The trumpet, now muted, returns with the closing measures of the theme.

Variation 3

Both Figure B and descending passages for the piano are prominent in this variation. After six measures the orchestra plays Figure B; then the woodwinds play a variant of the first phrase of the theme. The orchestra returns to Figure B; the piano recapitulates the opening phrase of this variation to bring it to a close.

Variation 4

"In Variation Four, the tempo is once again *Andante*, and the piano and orchestra discourse on the theme in a quiet and meditative fashion."

The rhythmic content of most of this variation is derived from the first four measures of the theme. The piano begins with it, although the eighth-notes move upward rather than downward. Later, the orchestra takes up Figure B. The piano returns with the concluding phrase, answered by the French horn with an octave leap upward on B-flat, a leap that has characterized this variation.

Variation 5

"Variation Five is energetic," the composer says in an understatement. After brilliant passage work for the piano, the next 24 measures are devoted almost exclusively to a rhythmic pattern derived from the first two measures of the theme; the piano, simultaneously, plays sparkling figures, chiefly in octaves. "Variation Five . . . leads without pause into a restatement of the theme."

Restatement

The theme returns in augmentation, the time value of each note doubled, but it sounds the same since the tempo has doubled. Against the theme in the orchestra, there is a "delicate chordal embroidery in the piano." The "embroidery" in staccato eighth-notes is colored by a spectral chromaticism that embodies the composer's love of the fantastic.

X

DARIUS MILHAUD (1892-   ) states his background very clearly in the opening sentence of his autobiography, *Notes Without Music*: "I am a Frenchman from Provence, and, by religion, a Jew." Those are the two principal sources of inspiration for him: his love of Provence and his Judaic background. Later, Brazil, jazz and Stravinsky became additional fountainheads of inspiration.

Of his childhood, Milhaud writes:

My parents settled at Bras d'Or in Aix-en-Provence. It was in this old house that my childhood was spent. . . We occupied the whole [second] floor of the Bras d'Or. My father who was the director of a firm exporting almonds (founded by my grandfather in 1806) had his offices on the ground floor . . .

Every summer my parents left their house and went to stay with my grandmother Précile on the outskirts of the town on an estate which had belonged to my greatgrandfather. . . At the beginning of

DARIUS MILHAUD

CARL ORFF

PAUL HINDEMITH

CARLOS CHÁVEZ

summer, all the inhabitants of the villages in the district sent their sheep to the mountains. In a noisy mass, the flocks pushed along the road to the Alps, and the familiar sounds of [our house] were submerged in a flood of continuous baa-ing. At night the long modulated notes of the nightingales thrilled me· with anguish, until they were resolved in a short, deliciously careless trill. A little later, a regular, full-throated chorus of frogs would strike up. . . . Even as I lay in bed I could see a tiny, gray owl in one of the tall cedars, and hear its plaintive hoot. Dawn was an explosion of cockcrows that mingled with the shrilling of the cicadas and the sound of bells, for we were surrounded on all sides by convents.

I could hear the Angelus from the convent of St. Thomas chiming out in triple time a major sixth, which hung in the air nearly as long as the note whose harmonic it was. Far off, like an echo, the bells of the Cathedral church of St. Saviour and of St. Mary Magdalen faintly answered. [11]

Was it any wonder that such a child with perceptive ears, with an interest in *sounds* would become intensely interested in music? He was not yet four when he first manifested signs of his "musical vocation" by groping at the piano after the notes of a tune he had heard some Italians singing under his window a few weeks earlier.

At seven he started with lessons on the violin; until he was ten, private tutors were provided in the academic subjects. He was then enrolled at the local public school and proved to be an excellent student. He continued his violin lessons and even arranged for some of his classmates to join him in playing string quartets. They played works by César Franck at a time when the public "found that composer's work too noisy." Also, in 1905, they studied Debussy's *Quartet*. Milhaud said that it was "such a revelation for me that I hastened to buy the score of *Pelléas.*" Opportunities for hearing symphony concerts were few and far between; what orchestral music he heard was the result of trips to Dieppe. He liked the symphony concerts, but disliked the Casino orchestra.

The family decided that the 17-year old boy should go to Paris and study at the Conservatory. "They thought I might become a virtuoso, and though they would assuredly have preferred me to go into my father's business, they put no obstacles in the way of my aspirations; throughout my childhood and thereafter, they gave me support, both material and moral."

Milhaud's knowledge of the literature of music enlarged as he attended concerts and operas in Paris. He was fascinated with Mussorgsky's opera *Boris Godunov*; he hated the Wagnerian music dramas. (He wrote about them: "bored to tears," "sickened . . . by their pretentious vulgarity," "leitmotiv − a childish device.") After seeing Diaghilev's production of Stravinsky's ballets, he praised Stravinsky as "the greatest musician of the century."

During the summer of 1911 Milhaud composed a *Sonata for Violin and Piano*, his earliest work which he thought worthy of preserving. After a performance of it at the Salle Pleyel in Paris a gentleman with a white moustache and goatee approached Milhaud backstage as he was putting his instrument away. The stranger announced, "I am Jacques Durand, I would like to publish your quartet. Come and see me tomorrow." And so Milhaud signed his first contract with the most distinguished publishing house in France. By the end of the following year he decided to abandon his career as a violinist in order to devote himself to composition.

All of Milhaud's youthful compositions were based upon or inspired by literary works, "not having experience yet to elaborate purely musical works." It was only logical, then, that Milhaud should turn to the theater after he had had "experience". He wrote a three-act opera on Francis Jammes' *La Brebis egarée* (The Lost Sheep). Shortly after that he met the poet Paul Claudel, who wrote the texts for many of his operas, theater pieces, choral works and songs.

World War I put an end to Milhaud's carefree days in Paris, although he was rejected for military service for medical reasons. In 1916 Claudel, who was a diplomat as well as a poet, was appointed as the French Ambassador to Brazil and asked his young friend Milhaud to accompany him as his diplomatic secretary. From February 1st of 1917 until after the Armistice was signed on November 11th, 1919, Milhaud lived in Rio de Janeiro, enjoying its sights and sounds, greatly impressed by native rhythms and dances. Many "Brazilian influences" are to be found in his music dating from this period and later.

After the war Milhaud returned to Paris and became active in that capital's artistic life. His circle of friends included the painters Picasso, Braque and Dufy, as well as the writers Jean Cocteau and Lucien Daudet, and composers such as Auric, Honegger and Poulenc.

After a concert one evening a Parisian music critic published a story entitled "Five Russians and Six Frenchmen." Thus was born the name, "Les Six" or "Group des Six," used widely by writers on subjects musical. "Quite arbitrarily he had chosen six names: Auric, Durey, Honegger, Poulenc, Tailleferre and my own, merely because we knew one another, were good friends, and had figured on the same programs; quite irrespective of our different temperaments. . . .I fundamentally disapproved, . . .but it was useless to protest. . . . This being so, we decided to give some 'Concerts des Six'."

The next 15 years Milhaud spent mostly in Paris, with frequent trips to all the musical centers of Europe to conduct. During the summer he and his wife usually visited his ancestral home in Provence. Attacks of rheumatism began to plague him, frequently confining him to a wheelchair, but this did not slow down Milhaud's agile pen, copious works still were turned out. His wife, Madeleine, was a constant help to him. She was, besides being a devoted wife and helpmate, a sensitive poet and actress who worked with Milhaud in a number of dramatic productions.

When France was overrun by Hitler's army during World War II, Milhaud, his wife and young son fled to the United States where they found a pleasant home in Oakland, California, and he located a teaching position at Mills College.

Since 1947 Milhaud has divided his time between his apartment in Paris (he is the Professor of Composition at the Conservatoire) and the United States. During the visits to the United States he has taught summer sessions at Mills College, the Berkshire Music Center at Tanglewood, the Music Academy of the West in Santa Barbara, and the summer school at Aspen, Colorado.

Over the years Milhaud has written so many works that they are too numerous to catalogue. By 1950 he had reached Opus 320, and in the last ten years he has composed at least 10 symphonies. An evaluation of Milhaud's "style" is best summarized by the gifted American composer Aaron Copland who says:

Milhaud's musical style is by nature essentially lyric. His music always sings. Whether he composes a five-act opera or a two-page song, this singing quality is paramount. The music flows so naturally that it seems to be improvised rather than composed. [12]

SCARAMOUCHE

3. Brazileira

Darius Milhaud's duet for two pianos, *Scaramouche*, is one of his most popular works and, at the same time, one of his most representative pieces — elegant, witty, urbane, sophisticated, civilized. The three movement suite is thematically derived from two earlier stage works. The third movement, "Brazileira," was based on some incidental music Milhaud wrote for a children's play, *The Flying Doctor*, produced at the Théâtre Scaramouche in 1937.

The music is characterized by a continual interchange of material between the players which constitutes the delight of two piano music. It suggests salon music, or, perhaps better, the spirit of the Parisian cafés and boulevards.

The *finale* of the suite, "Brazileira," is a *samba* that recalls Milhaud's youthful days spent in Rio de Janeiro. A saucy tune is immediately unveiled over a rhythmic accompaniment. It begins:

Example 1

PIANO I

After a repetition of that portion of the tune quoted in Example 1, the second piano counters with a little tune of its own.

Groups of three lush, ascending chords are heard four times; a persistent and rhythmic repetition of octaves follows.

A secondary theme, less brash and more like a dance-hall tune is introduced:

Example 2

The rising chords followed by the rhythmic repetitions of octaves is heard twice more, this time more forcefully than in its first appearance.

Example 1 returns three times: first in its original form, then in a modulating variant, and finally in its original form again. The two chords with which the tune ends also ends the "Brazileira" — as boldly and as surprisingly as imaginable.

XI

CARL ORFF (1895-   ) is an amazingly radical composer. His drastic, primitive style is such that he has received world-wide praise from conservative audiences and critics, but the *avant-garde* has scorned his work. Traces may be found in his music of folk songs, popular songs, and elements of Baroque, Renaissance and Medieval music. The simplicity of his writing is the opposite of the complex scoring of his German colleagues Wagner, Richard Strauss, Reger, Schoenberg and his own exact contemporary, Hindemith. Orff's "style" actually is a synthesis of many different experiences and influences during his long career.

Carl Orff was born in Munich, Germany, on July 10, 1895. He attended the local public school where he was said to be "an imaginative" pupil. His favorite subjects were German essay, literature, Latin, Greek, botany and natural science. His hobbies include insect collecting and gardening.

Although his love of music manifested itself at an early age, he hated practising the piano. A friend of his has said that "he has never enjoyed piano practise. His piano technique today is unremarkable, though his interpretations are invariably of great interest. It is not surprising, therefore, that he was more eager as a boy to play his own improvisations than to practise the Czerny studies. Improvising in both words and music is, indeed, his great passion."

His work with "words" dates from age ten when his first story was published in a children's magazine. At the time he was also working on a romantic nature book! Soon afterwards, he started composing music, writing out pieces to accompany the puppet-plays he had written. This "incidental music" was scored for piano, violin, zither and bells. The kitchen stove was used to produce the effect of thunder.

There was always much music in the Orff home: string quartets and piano quintets were played, Carl sang duets with his mother, and together they played four-hand piano transcriptions of both symphonic and operatic literature. From his tenth year on, Carl frequently attended concerts and plays. His first serious compositions were song-settings of poems that he had written himself. His first five songs were published when he was 16. Within the following year he composed 50 more songs! He then completed his first full-scale choral work, *Thus Spake Zarathustra* after Nietzsche's poem. (It followed by 15 years Strauss' tone poem of the same title. Since they were both residents of Munich, it seems likely that Orff knew of the Strauss tone poem.)

In July of 1913, Orff, then 18, completed his first opera, *Gisei, das Opfer* (Geisha, An Offering), a romantic interpretation of a traditional Japanese play. The music shows the composer was strongly influenced at this time by Debussy's music. That fall Orff enrolled at the musical academy, the Akademie der Tonkunst. In addition to private instruction in piano, organ and cello, he studied form and composition, but felt that his teachers were not sympathetic to his approach to music. Actually, Orff should be considered self-taught, for his basic knowledge was acquired by studying the compositions of the old masters, and his first songs were published before he had his first lesson in harmony.

A large orchestral work based on the writings of Maeterlinck was planned for 1914, but Orff never completed it. This was the end of his "Debussy" period. He now turned to the study of Schoenberg's music and transcribed the Viennese master's *Chamber Symphony* for piano duet. He next became fascinated with the tone poems of Richard Strauss. Orff started to work on a tone poem in the style of Strauss; it was to be based on Maeterlinck's *Monna Vanna*. Orff destroyed the fragments of it long before it was completed. Although some works remain from this period — two string quartets, choral music and songs — he was still searching for his personal idiom.

From 1915 to 1917 Orff was the conductor at a playhouse, the Munich Kammerspiele. During these years he was much more interested in plays than in opera. By conducting incidental music for them, he became acquainted with the stage works of Strindberg, Wedekind and Brecht among others. This association with the theater was abruptly cut short by World War I. Orff joined the Army.

After Germany's defeat, Orff returned to the theater briefly, then retired to devote himself exclusively to composition. He studied the works of the old masters: Lassus, Palestrina, Gabrieli and Monteverdi. Apart from their compositions, the only other music that fascinated him at this time were some dance accompaniments he heard played on African rattles. This led him, in 1924, to co-found the Günther School with Dorothea Günther, a dance specialist. She explained the guiding principle of their school: "a natural unity of music and movement — music and dance . . . (an) awakening in everyone of the sense of rhythmic movement, and of stimulating a love of dancing and music making." The dancers themselves played the musical instruments. The "school" traveled widely and was most active until it was disbanded after its studio was leveled by the wartime bombing of 1943.

Orff's experience with the Günther School led him to develop, between 1930 and 1935, the "Orff Schulwerk" (literally "Orff Schoolwork," but commonly called in this country "The Orff Method"). Designed for children in nursery schools, kindergartens and the first years of grammar school, it begins with clapping and speaking, progresses through children's chants on a minor third to elaborate ensemble work. Instrumental experience is provided with a set of specially constructed instruments — bells, xylophones and metallophones in several sizes. They have removable parts to facilitate a slow, gradual expansion from three-note tunes and *ostinato* accompaniments to pentatonic, diatonic and, finally, chromatic melodies and harmonies. Percussion instruments are added to help the children feel and understand rhythm.

During Orff's development of the Schulwerk, his other musical activities continued — composing, conducting, teaching. In 1937 he completed a major dramatic cantata, *Carmina Burana*. After its first performance he wrote to his publisher: "Everything I have written to date, and which you have, unfortunately, printed, can be destroyed. With *Carmina Burana* my collected works begin." Orff had found his idiom!

The success of *Carmina Burana* was followed by two comic fairy-tale operas, *Der Mond* (The Theft of the Moon) in 1938, and *Die Kluge* (The Peasant's Clever Daughter) in 1942. His *Antigonae* of 1949 and *Oedipus der Tyraan* of 1959, are more ambitious and more austere, largely because of the more dramatic nature of their text.

Orff's mature idiom is based on the use of rhythm as the form-building element of his music, as opposed to the Romantic's uses of harmony for this purpose. His rhythms are simple, often primitive; rhythmic patterns are repeated, oftentimes, with an intensity bordering on obsession. His melodies seem to be derived from the pattern of the rhythm, simple melodies, seldom — if ever — developed or varied. For contrast, the melodies and simple harmonies are shifted, sometimes shockingly, to different keys. The writing is strictly tonal, although sometimes in the contrapuntal texture two or more tonalities are in use at the same time. Since there is little thematic or contrapuntal elaboration, the impression is one of almost primitive force.

CARMINA BURANA

Introduction

The composer calls *Carmina Burana* a "dramatic oratorio"; for this reason it is frequently staged with sets, costumes, dancing and

A chorus of medieval monks in *Carmina Burana* intone their song: "O Fortune, variable as the moon, always dost thou wax and wane."

"In Springtime" follows. The people comment that "the bright face of spring shows itself to the world, driving away the cold of winter."

pantomime. It is scored for three choruses — a large and small one, plus a boys' chorus. The standard symphony orchestra is augmented by two pianos, five timpani and a large percussion group.

Orff selected the text from a group of famous 13th-century Goliard song texts and poems discovered in the old Bavarian monastery of Benediktbeuren in 1803, hence the name *Carmina Burana* — "Songs of Beuren." These secular song texts were written in a mixture of medieval Latin, low German and French by jesters and minstrels, vagabond poets and itinerant monks. They are a strange mixture of lyrics on springtime and love, dance songs, satires on church, state, society and the individual, and texts celebrating the sensual joys of food, drink and physical love.

In *Carmina Burana* Orff used a Latin text for the first time. His use of the language was quite different from Stravinsky's in the *Symphony of Psalms*. "Latin is a means to objectivity," said a friend of the composer, "but Orff considers it not as a dead language, but as the immediate and vital expression of living experience."

The composer has divided the cantata into three sections which are preceded by an "Introduction," an invocation to *Fortune,* the Empress of the World. This invocation is repeated at the end. The three sections are: "In the Spring," "In the Tavern" and "The Court of Love."

The forms used in the work are simple, mainly strophic. In spite of this "simplicity," the work is full of life. In *Carmina Burana*, Romantic tone-color is replaced by an orchestration forming blocks of sound. The melodies are folk-like and are set against and become part of a driving rhythm, frequently occasioned by the use of *ostinato* figures.

The "Introduction" is in two parts, the first — *O Fortuna* — is marked *Pesante* (Simply); the second — *Fortune plango vulnera* — is given a good, brisk tempo indication.

The accompaniment of *O Fortuna* is dominated by the bold, often harsh, pounding tones of the piano and timpani which hammer out the rhythm. After their first "stroke" the chorus enters *fortissimo* in stark chords:

O Fortuna,	*O Fortune,*
velut luna statu variabilis,	*Variable as the moon,*

The tempo now doubles; in unison octaves the chorus intones the text in a syncopated rhythm (Example 1) against a steady, ostinato bass in timpani and piano.

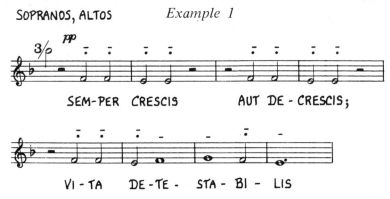

The melody of Example 1 is repeated; it is then heard a third time in the altos and basses while the sopranos and tenors (in unison octaves) harmonize with it in thirds.

Twice more the full chorus sing Example 1 in unison octaves; this is followed by two repetitions of the version harmonized in thirds.

Audaciously the sopranos leap to the higher octave; the full chorus in a unison spread over three octaves now intones Example 1. *O Fortuna* concludes with two repetitions of Example 1 as harmonized in thirds; this time it too, is spread over three octaves.

The text of *O Fortuna* begins:

O Fortuna,	*O Fortune,*
velut luna statu variabilis,	*variable as the moon,*
semper crescis aut decrescis;	*always dost thou wax and wane.*
vita detestablis	*Detestable life,*
nunc obdurat et tunc curat	*first dost thou mistreat us, and then,*
ludo mentis aciem,	*whimsically, thou heedest our desires.*
egestatem, potestatem	*As the sun melts the ice, so dost thou*
dissolvit ut glaciem.	*dissolve both poverty and power.*

The second part of the "Introduction" — *Fortune plango vulnera* — begins with a brief recitative for unison basses against a sustained D pedal.

An *ostinato* bass for low strings, piano and woodwinds then gives support to the men's chorus which announces the melodic figure of this movement:

Example 2

The tenors and basses repeat the melody of Example 1 as the sopranos and altos double an octave higher.

Verum est, quod legitur,	*now pregnant*
fronte capillata,	*and prodigal,*
sed plerumque sequitur	*now lean*
Occasio calvata.	*and sear.*

A brisk, loud and rhythmical eight-measure passage for full orchestra brings the first stanza to a close.

The second and third stanzas are set to a repetition of the music of the first.

XII

PAUL HINDEMITH (1895-1963) said that "the basis of all worthwhile composition must be, of course, inspiration and worthwhile musical ideas; after that comes technique. There seems to be an impression that there is today too much technique. It is my impression that there is not nearly enough technique."

This statement expresses very explicitly Hindemith's position in the contemporary stream of composers — an artist in whose works technique is everywhere in evidence. The results of his personal discoveries and experiments with technique led him to write two textbooks: *The Craft of Musical Composition* (1939) and *Elementary Training for Musicians* (1946). Based on the study of St. Augustine, Boethius and Sextus Empiricus, his philosophy of music and musical composition was espoused in a series of lectures given at Harvard College during the academic year of 1949-50 and published later by him under the title *A Composer's World.*

Paul Hindemith was born in Hanau, Germany, on November 16, 1895. Because his father objected to a musical career for him, he ran away from home when he was 11. He earned his living by playing the violin in dance orchestras, movie theaters (those were the days of "silent pictures"), cafés and night clubs.

Hindemith eventually enrolled in the Conservatory at Frankfurt. An unpublished *String Quartet* which won the Mendelssohn Prize in Berlin dates from this period. After securing a position as a violinist with the Frankfurt opera house, Hindemith wrote a brief biographical sketch. In it he said:

> As violinist, violist, pianist or percussionist I have 'tilled' the following fields of music: all sorts of chamber music, movies, cafés, dance halls, operetta, jazz band, military band. Since 1916 I have been concertmaster of the Frankfurt opera orchestra. As a

composer I have written mostly pieces that I don't like: chamber music in the most varied media, songs, piano works. Also three one-act operas which will probably be the only ones, since with the perpetual inflation of the cost of manuscript paper only small scores can be written.

His first fame outside of Frankfurt came from the performance of his chamber works at international festivals. His *Second Quartet* was played at the Donaueschingen Festival of 1921 and repeated the following year at the Salzburg Festival. In 1925 Hindemith first experimented with the jazz idiom. His *Concerto for Piano and Twelve Instruments* was performed at the Venice Festival that year, and an opera based on the jazz idiom, *Cardillac,* was presented at the Dresden Opera the next season.

In 1927 Hindemith was appointed professor of composition at the Berlin Hochschule. His aim, as already mentioned, was to produce versatile craftsmen in the sense of the 18th century, rather than the overspecialized virtuoso that had become popular in the late 19th century. He encouraged his students to learn to play a number of different instruments, to perform each others compositions, and to participate in as many varied musical activities as possible — solo work, small ensembles, orchestras, choruses, etc. Hindemith composed music for these students, *practical* music that fitted their needs both as to instrumentation and degree of difficulty. Some of it was band music, some unaccompanied choral music, some for solo instruments. Between 1936 and 1955 he composed sonatas for almost every instrument, including the tuba. Because of the useful nature of these works, it was called *Gebrauchsmusik,* literally "use-music." Musicians, teachers and critics in the United States were quick to attach this label to Hindemith's style. The composer seriously objected, for actually he was only doing the equivalent in the 20th century of what Bach did in writing cantatas for St. Thomaskirche or Haydn in composing symphonies for Prince Esterházy's orchestra. "It has been impossible to kill this silly term and the unscrupulous classification that goes with it," Hindemith complained. "Music that has nothing else as its purpose should neither be written nor used."

When the Nazi's came to power in Germany, Hindemith's days there were numbered. Although Hitler was eager to encourage artists of German blood, his taste in music (and philosophy, if such it can be called) stopped at the works of Wagner; nothing more modern than that! His Propaganda Minister, Josef Goebbels, accused Hindemith not only of "atrocious dissonance," but also of "cultural Bolshevism" and "spiritual non-Aryanism." His music was condemned as being "unbearable to the Third Reich."

Just before the outbreak of World War II Hindemith escaped and emigrated to the United States (of which country he later became a citizen) and accepted a position on the faculty at Yale University. After the War, in 1953, he retired to Zurich to live, although up until the time of his death in 1963 he continued to make many concert appearances throughout Europe and the United States.

Hindemith's most monumental works were two operas: *Mathis der Maler* (1934) based on the life of the 16th-century painter Mathis Grünewald, and *Die Harmonie der Welt* (1957) based on the life of the 16th-century astronomer Johannes Kepler. In both instances Hindemith created symphonies (bearing the same names as the operas) from the instrumental portions of them. His last stage work, *The Long Christmas Dinner* to a text by Thornton Wilder, was a more modest work. In the choral field, Hindemith probably excelled with his madrigals.

Hindemith's personal idiom in composition is best characterized by its perfection of style, the refined technique and the intellect behind its creation. He is a traditionalist when it comes to structure, his models being the great contrapuntal forms of the Baroque — concerto grosso, passacaglia, toccata and fugue. The symmetry and purity of the Classical sonata form are also cornerstones.

His use of harmony is more traditional than most other composers of his generation. His free use of the 12 tones always seem to be based around a tonal center. What daring sounds that do occur are usually the result of the contrapuntal texture. He held firmly to the principle of tonality with little use for Schoenberg's "Method." In the matter of rhythm, Hindemith is much more conventional than either Stravinsky or Bartók, and compared to his contemporary, Orff, Hindemith's rhythm is pale, conventional and unexciting.

"The Temptation of St. Anthony", one of the panels in the Isenheim Altarpiece of Mathias Grünewald , which inspired the third movement of *Mathis der Maler.*

MATHIS DER MALER

3. Versuchung des Heiligen Antonius

Mathis der Maler, as a symphony, was introduced in Berlin in 1934, four years before its production in Zurich as an opera from which the three movements of the symphony were extracted. Both the opera and the symphony are concerned with the most ambitious and extensive creation of the German religious painter Mathis Gothart Nithart (c. 1460-1528), known as Mathias Grünewald, whose paintings for the Isenheim Altar are among the greatest achievements of late Gothic art in Germany. The opera is a partly historical, partly fictional episode in his life. The action takes place in 1524-25, during the Peasant War and the early years of the Reformation. Hindemith represents Mathis as the universal creative artist torn between the call of his art and the claims made upon him by politics, economics and religion:

> He goes to war [Hindemith writes] and fights on the side of the rebellious peasants against the nobles and the church, and thus against his own master, Cardinal Albrecht of Mainz. There is a gross contradiction between his imaginary ideal of a fair combat and just victory, and the ugly realities of the Peasant's War. . . . In an allegorical scene he experiences the temptation of St. Anthony; all the promptings of conscience within his tortured soul rise to assail and plague him, and call him to account for his actions.[13]

The final movement of the symphony, "Versuchung des Heiligen Antonius"(The Temptation of St. Anthony) is in three sections. The opening or introductory one is based on two themes. The first is introduced immediately by strings:

Example 1

A passage based on this theme leads to a restatement of it by the strings, joined this time by the woodwinds.

The second theme appears in the strings; a rhythmical background is provided by the woodwinds.

Example 2

This theme (Example 2) then is taken over by the cellos; strings repeat it to a brass accompaniment. Next, Example 2 appears in the clarinet and French horn; the full orchestra accompanies it. The full brass — including the bass tuba — next takes it up.

A sustained tone by the flute, followed by two chords played by the full orchestra, leads to the bridge theme. It is a long, sustained melody played first by the oboe and repeated by the clarinet.

The clarinets play a figure which suggests Example 1; the full woodwind section then takes it up.

Full orchestra plays a descending, four-note figure. It is repeated by brass and woodwinds over an inversion of Example 1 in the strings. After an episodic passage, the four-note figure is played by the woodwinds in augmentation.

The cellos announce the theme of the middle section. It begins:

Example 3

This theme (starting with Example 3) is played by the violins; its after-phrase is repeated by the entire string section. This is an extended passage.

The four-note descending motive is heard three times: full

orchestra with trombones dominating, oboe and clarinet, and, after an episode, French horns.

The violas take up Example 3; the after-phrase is repeated by violins.

A variant of Example 2 appears in the trumpets and horns accompanied by woodwinds and strings. Brass and woodwinds drop out; the violins play the last portion of Example 2.

The score is now marked *Lauda Sion Salvatorem* (Praise Zion, the Salvation). An exact quotation of the Gregorian chant by that title is played by the flute:

Example 4

Example 4 is repeated.

A section marked *Alleluia,* a choral for brass instruments, follows. It begins:

Example 5

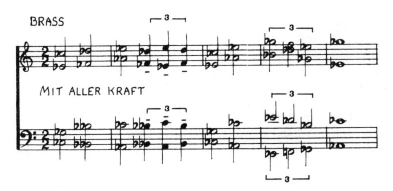

This choral brings the symphony to a close.

XIII

CARLOS CHÁVEZ (1899-   ) "is one of the best examples I know of a thoroughly contemporary composer," states Aaron Copland. "His music embodies almost all the major traits of modern music: the rejection of Germanic ideals, the objectification of sentiment, the use of folk material in its relation to nationalism, the intricate rhythms, linear as opposed to vertical writing, the specifically 'modern' sound images. It is music that belongs entirely to our own age. It propounds no problems, no metaphysics. Chávez' music is extraordinarily healthy. It is music created not as a substitute for living but as a manifestation of life. It is clear and clean-sounding, without shadows or softness. Here is contemporary music if ever there was any." [14]

Carlos Chávez was born on June 13th, 1899, just outside Mexico City, the seventh child of Agustín Chávez and Juvencia Ramírez de Chávez. On both sides, his ancestry included people of skill and learning: an inventor, a statesman, a scientist, an author, an outstanding patriot. Ethnically he is a *mestizo*, a person of mixed Spanish and American Indian blood.

Carlos Chávez was not the only musician in his family; he took his first piano lessons from his brother Manuel. He went on to study under a local piano teacher, and then worked with two of some skill: Ogazón and Ponce (known largely as the composer of *Estrellita*). With the former, Chávez acquired a wide knowledge of the classical and romantic literature; with the latter, he developed an interest in the hitherto neglected music of the Indians and the folk melodies of the *mestizo*.

In composition, Chávez was largely self-taught. He began to compose as a child, but his first work of independent merit was probably his *Symphony No. 1*, written in 1918. Within the three-year span after the creation of the symphony, he turned out a number of works for orchestra, piano, voice and chamber ensembles in a semi-classical style; few Mexican influences can be found in these works. This period culminated in his *String Quartet* of 1921.

The Mexican Revolution, which started in 1910 and swept on into the middle 1920's, did not interrupt the continuity of Chávez' life. It did, however, awaken in him a strong sympathy for the poor and humble peasants of Mexico. Profoundly affected by the social upheaval caused by the war, Chávez became intensely interested in the native Indian music of Mexico. He made numerous journeys into the remote regions of the country, and studied the melodies and rhythms of various Indian tribes whose civilizations had been least affected by the Spanish invaders centuries earlier.

A trip to Europe about this time led him to Berlin where he was disappointed in the stale, out-dated and academic music he found in vogue. On his return home he turned away from the European tradition to the folk-culture of his native Mexico for inspiration. He became, in the words of one of his biographers, "a nationalist, not in any narrow, jingoistic sense, but in the sense that he feels close to his land and its people, finds their music in his own blood, discovers the most complete liberation of his own talents in relation to Mexico's traditions rather than those of Europe."

In 1922 the Secretary of Education, who earlier that year had commissioned Diego Rivera to paint the now famous murals in the National Education Building, commissioned Chávez to write the music for the ballet *El Fuego Nuevo* (The New Fire). In this score there appears for the first time the seeds left in Chavéz by the Indian music with which he had been familiar since childhood, music he had heard during many visits to the ancient city of Tlacala.

Chávez stated his point of view clearly when he said: "The artist should belong to his time, and has but one means of doing so — by steeping himself in history in order to extract from it the experiences of past generations, and by knowing his own world with all of its developments and resources, so that he may be able to interpret its own fundamental necessities."

His second Mexican ballet, *Los Cuatro Soles* (The Four Suns -

1926) "one of his most delightful works," according to Copland, was based on an Aztec legend. In the music he amalgamated both Indian and *mestizo* elements. A year later Chávez completed *HP* which he described as "a symphony of the sounds around us, a revue of our times." The title was appropriate: *HP* for "horse-power."

It was during the 1930's and '40's that Chávez composed the music for which he is best known. The *Sinfonia de Antigona* (The 'Antigone' Symphony - 1933) had its origin in the incidental music written for Jean Cocteau's version of Sophocle's "Antigone" produced in Mexico City in 1932. The *Sinfonia India* (1936) was composed in New York during one of Chávez' many visits to this country. Its single movement is cast in the classical sonata form; its Principal Subject is a melody from the Huichole Indians of Nayarit, the Second Subject from the Yaqui Indians of Sonora. Chávez' *Toccata for Percussion Instruments* (1942) makes use of such native instruments as *claves* and *maracha*.

Works in traditional forms have always been created alongside more "nationalistic" works. In 1940, for example, Chávez completed both his *Piano Concerto* and *Xochipilli Macuilxochitl* (the Aztec god of music), a piece for an orchestra of native Indian instruments. By the 1960's Chávez' style had changed very little, although specific references to native themes no longer occurred. In *Tambuco* (1965) the rhythmic effects for gourds, rattles and rasping sticks reflected the native Amerindian element although specific themes were not borrowed or quoted in it. *II Invention*, a string trio written for the Third Inter-American Music Festival in 1964, is an atonal work.

In addition to his long career as a composer, Chávez has been equally active in the fields of music education, orchestral organization and conducting. In 1928 he founded the Orquesta Sinfonica de Mexico which he conducted until 1949, and from 1928 through 1934 he was the Director of the National Conservatory in Mexico City. Of his vast influence on the musical life of Mexico, the American composer Henry Cowell has said:

> To Chávez belongs the distinction of having changed Mexico, within a few years, from a country whose musicians were only locally known, to one of the most important centers of culture and activity. . . . He began with the premise that both musical composition and the presentation of music in Mexico should be

related to the life and musical needs of the Mexican people. . . .
He wished Mexicans to be proud of this splendid native product.[15]

TOCCATA FOR PERCUSSION INSTRUMENTS

3. Allegro un poco marziale

The *Toccata for Percussion Instruments* was written in 1942
and for a long time remained unpublished and unperformed. It was
not until August 13, 1948 that the work was programmed in a
concert of the Orquesta Sinfónica Nacional under the guest
conductorship of Eduardo Hernández Moncada. For the premiere
performance in the United States (Los Angeles, 1953) the composer wrote the program notes:

> This toccata was written as an experiment in orthodox percussion
> instruments—those used regularly in symphony orchestras—that is,
> avoiding the exotic and the picturesque. Thereafter it relies on its
> purely musical expression and formalistic structure.
>
> The thematic material is, for obvious reason, rhythmic rather than
> melodic. However, themes proper, integrated by rhythmic motives,
> are developed as I would have done with melodic elements. The
> form follows a given pattern and the course of the music follows a
> constantly renewed treatment of the basic thematic elements. . . .
>
> The third movement, *Allegro un poco marziale* (moderate, a little
> like a march) is built up in sonato form.[16]

The Principal Subject, in the timpani, is heard immediately in
Example 1 (see next page).

A six-measure passage in which a snare and bass drum join the
timpani leads to the Second Subject.

The Second Subject, 15 measures in length, is presented by
four drums: small Indian drum, Indian drum, side and tenor
drums. The timpani which accompanies this is eventually joined by
the bass drum; later the claves are added. The Second Subject
begins in Example 2.

Example 1

Example 2

Only claves and bass drum are heard; snare and side drums take over. Two bell tones are heard. "During the development . . . a section suggestive of Latin American rhythms appears." This section starts with the sound of a maraca; a snare drum soon joins it. Twice in succession a four-note figure for the bells is heard. A snare drum roll leads to a variant of the Principal Subject (Example 1) played by the timpani in counterpoint to a variant of the Second Subject (Example 2).

"A violent section (*Vivo*) derived from the basic thematic material" follows. A steady pattern of repeated 16th-notes on the small Indian drum is kept up throughout most of this section. The dynamic level builds to a *forte*; then in a *subito* passage the sound of a suspended cymbal is heard. The dynamic level starts to build again, leading to a *fortissimo* climax.

"At *Tempo primo*, a short recapitulation brings the work to a conclusion." First the unaccompanied timpani presents the Principal Subject (Example 1) in truncated form. A shortened form of the Second Subject (Example 2) is heard. The dynamic level becomes softer and softer, until a few pianissimo timpani strokes bring the work to a close.

XIV

DMITRI SHOSTAKOVICH (1906-   ) had the good fortune to become famous overnight, on May 12, 1926, when the Leningrad Philharmonic gave the first performance of his *Symphony No. 1*. The score was his graduation work from the Conservatory, and the 19-year old composer won the praise of public and critic alike. The Leningrad journal *Modern Theater* hailed Shostakovich as "one of the most brilliant of the younger Soviet composers." The Moscow magazine *Music and Revolution* said the symphony was "pleasing in its faultless technique and its sparkling talent." For once the critics were accurate when they said this work "was so engaging that the high expectations of the world seem amply justified," because it has remained so popular that 40 years later there are at least ten different performances of it available on phonograph records.

What had preceded the *Symphony No. 1* in Shostakovich's short life? The boy had experienced the ordinary childhood one would expect in a Russian intellectual family. His father, a chemist by trade, was interested in music and his mother had been a music teacher. Dmitri Dmitriyevich Shostakovich was born on September 25th, 1906 (new style calendar) in a house on the quiet Podolskaya Street in St. Petersburg. He was the first Soviet composer to

DMITRI SHOSTAKOVICH   BENJAMIN BRITTEN

grow up completely under the Communist regime, to know no other form of government.

Shostakovich, on the occasion of his 50th birthday, recalled for a Soviet magazine some interesting details concerning his youth:

> I grew up in a musical family. . . . There were, also, many music-lovers among the friends and acquaintances of the family all of whom took part in our musical evenings. I also remember the strains of music that came from a neighboring apartment where there lived an engineer who was an excellent performer on the cello and was passionately fond of chamber music. With a group of his friends he often played quartets and trios by Mozart, Haydn, Beethoven, Borodin and Tchaikovsky. I used to go out into the hallway and sit there for hours, the better to hear the music. In our apartment, too, we held amateur musical evenings. All this impressed itself on my musical memory and played a certain part in my future work as a composer.[17]

As a boy, Dmitri received his general education at Shidlov-skaya's Commercial School where he did well although he had some trouble with history and geography. At ten he was enrolled at Glyaser's School of Music in Petrograd, where, as a first-year student, he completed his first composition. In that troubled atmosphere of 1915-16, one saturated with wars and rumors of revolt, the boy's imagination turned to the theme that was uppermost in the minds of the adults around him. He composed a piece for piano called *Soldier* — "ever such a long piece," he says of it, jokingly, "with a mass of illustrative detail and verbal explanations (i.e. 'in this place the soldier shoots.')" The piece ended with the death of the soldier. A little later, in 1917, Shostakovich composed a funeral march in memory of the victims of the Revolution and even a revolutionary symphony. .

In 1919 Shostakovich entered the Conservatory as a piano student and won a Certificate of Merit at the first World Chopin Contest in Warsaw in 1927. Composition study was with a pupil (and son-in-law) of Rimsky-Korsakov. "After finishing the Conservatory," Shostakovich writes, "I was confronted with the problem — should I become a pianist or composer? The latter won. If the truth be told I should have been both, but it's too late now to blame myself for making such a ruthless decision."

During the latter-half of the 1920's, Russia again established contact with the outside world. Shostakovich now had the opportunity to hear such modern works as Stravinsky's *Les Noces* (The Wedding) and Hindemith's *Piano Suite "1922".* There were frequent concerts in Leningrad of Western music, including a performance at the opera house of Berg's *Wozzeck.* Hindemith, Bartók, Honegger and Milhaud were visitors in the U.S.S.R. Numerous articles and booklets on the works of Hindemith, Schoenberg, Berg and the French "Group of Six" as well as Stravinsky appeared. Modern Music Associations were organized in Moscow and Leningrad.

Now that he had heard contemporary music from western Europe, Shostakovich was inspired to write in the modern idiom himself, two works for the stage: first, an opera *The Nose* (1927); then, a ballet *The Age of Gold* (1929-31). The success of these two works— both based programatically on Soviet ideals and philosophy—helped his international reputation. He next turned to the creation of a complex, tragic opera, *Lady Macbeth of Mtsensk.* Performed in 1934 with great success in Leningrad, it was repeated many times in the next two years. Triumphant performances were also given in New York, Cleveland, London, Prague and Zurich.

Suddenly, on January 26, 1936, the official newspaper *Pravda* condemned the opera as "a mess instead of music." The editorial accused the composer of failing "to set himself the task of listening to the desires and expectations of the Soviet public. He scrambled sounds to make them interesting to formalist aesthetes who have lost all good taste." The opera was immediately withdrawn; Shostakovich simultaneously withdrew his *Symphony No. 4* on which he had been working.

The point in question was that of the Marxist-Leninist philosophy of classless art, of dialectical and historical materialism. It was derived from Lenin's esthetic of art:

> Every artist ... has the right to create freely according to his ideal, independent of everything. However, we are Communists and we must not stand with folded hands and let chaos develop as it pleases. We must systematically guide this process and form its results. [18]

In other words, Soviet composers were free to write as they wished as long as they allowed their idiom to be *systematically guided* and the *results formed* by the powers political!

After a period of stern self-examination, Shostakovich was reinstated when the Leningrad Philharmonic presented his *Symphony No. 5* in 1937. Across the score was written, "Creative reply of a Soviet artist to just criticism! " *Pravda* praised the "grandiose vistas of the tragically tense symphony with its philosophical seeking." Shostakovich did not venture into the world of opera again for 30 years.

The Nazi invasion of Russia inspired Shostakovich to new creative-patriotic efforts. "I volunteered for service at the front, and received the reply: 'You will be called when required.' So I went back to my duties at the Leningrad Conservatory" (where he was professor of composition). His *Symphony No. 7*, the "Leningrad," was inspired by the militant spirit of his native city in resisting the German invasion. "He rested his ear against the heart of his country," wrote the novelist Alexei Tolstoi, "and heard its mighty song."

In 1948, a conference of Soviet musicians was attended by General Zhdanov, representing the Politbureau, and a *Decree on Music* was issued by the Central Committee of the Party. Shostakovich, along with Prokofiev and others, was out of official favor again! Despite this second "official" rebuke, Shostakovich never lost his position in the hierarchy. In 1949 he represented the U.S.S.R. at the Conference for World Peace in New York. In four years his *Symphony No. 10* was praised both in Russia and abroad. In 1954 he was named People's Artist of the U.S.S.R., and on his 50th birthday won the Order of Lenin. The next year he became Chairman of the Composers Union. In 1966, on the occasion of his 60th birthday, Shostakovich stated his position bluntly. "Music appealing to millions, composed for man and in the name of man, is opposed to abstract, modernistic music, cut off from life and catering to the taste of the chosen few."

The Central Committee, in May of 1958, started a general "thaw" in Soviet policies and passed a resolution "correcting errors in the previous evaluations of operas." Shostakovich thereupon reworked his early opera, *Lady Macbeth of Mtsensk* and in 1962 successfully produced it as *Katerina Izmailova*. Three more symphonies date from the years 1957 to 1962, numbers 11, 12 and 13. The latter was a choral symphony based on poems of Yevtushenko, including his famous "Babyi Yar" denouncing anti-Semitism; when Premier Khruschev withdrew his support of Yevtushenko, Shostakovich's new symphony was also withdrawn!

In 1966 Shostakovich completed the sound track for Grigori Kozintsev's production of *Hamlet* in Boris Pasternak's translation. Shostakovich had first worked with Kozintsev more than 35 years earlier when, in 1929, he wrote his first of many film scores.

Shostakovich's musical style is a conservative one, firmly built on classical forms. "Shostakovich has decidedly rejected the idea that the tonal system of creative work has seemingly been exhausted," states his friend and fellow composer Dmitri Kabelevsky. "He refused to join those who supported the idea of atonalism! "

In talking about the *avant-garde*, Shostakovich has said:

> Dodecaphony, serial, pointillist and other kinds of music are one of the greatest evils of 20th-century art. Often as I have listened to the spurious works of the *vanguardists* to this day I cannot tell the difference between the music say of Boulez and that of Stockhausen, Henze and that of Stuckenschmidt. I am convinced that *vanguardism* is a screen for many composers to hide their lack of talent. Pioneering for the new music must proceed within the current of realism if that new art is to be progressive and

comprehensible to the people for whom art is in effect being created. In the West, many progressive musicians such as Britten, Milhaud, Hindemith, Orff, Samuel Barber, Aaron Copland and many others, who are vehemently opposed to *vanguardism*, have been producing splendid realistic works of music..... About myself I can say that my principal task for the present is to complete the opera I am now writing which is *And Quiet Flows the Don* based on Sholokhov's novel.[19]

THE AGE OF GOLD

3. Polka

Dmitri Shostakovich completed his ballet *The Age of Gold* in 1931 and then three years later extracted from it a suite of four movements. The ballet is a spoof of western society, which, in the eyes of the Soviets, is governed by the value and importance of gold. The story concerns the adventures of a Soviet football team in a foreign city during a World Fair. Music hall scenes alternate with scenes on the sports ground, the players being tempted away from the championship game with all the mystery of a detective novel.

The "Polka" occurs in one of the music hall scenes which bears the sub-title, "Once upon a time in Geneva." Actually the story is not the only comic element, for the music itself is a spoof of the polka.

The introduction is brief and humorous. The small, shrill E-flat clarinet plays a brief, awkward ascending pattern against a bassoon accompaniment. The French horns respond with repeated, harsh-sounding chords. The *pizzicato* strings then establish the basic pulse of the dance.

The xylophone introduces the principal melody, an awkward one filled with wide leaps:

Example 1

Two measures later the saxophone responds with another melody, one which is completed by the E-flat clarinet:

Example 2

After the solo saxophone is heard some more, the trumpet introduces a saucy tune:

Example 3

Accompanied by triangle and wood block, the upper wood-winds play a series of rhythmical but dissonant chords. The wood-winds repeat this passage.

The strings respond with a variant of Example 1; the wood-winds answer with a pert little melodic fragment. The trombone is heard, then the woodwinds again. A solo bassoon, unaccompanied, plays a figure that rises from its lowest tones.

The xylophone repeats the principal theme, Example 1. The trumpet immediately responds with Example 3, whose final measure is altered to lead to the few sharp, biting chords that end the "Polka."

XV

BENJAMIN BRITTEN (1913-   ) the English composer, was born in a house facing the North Sea, one buffeted by cold northeast winds during winter, a house close enough to the water's edge that the sound of huge breaking waves and screaming herring-gulls overhead could be heard on that raw November day on which the composer was born. Britten's fondness for sea and sail — bred of his childhood in Lowestoft — inspired his first opera, *Peter Grimes*, and led him to choose a home some quarter-century later that was also on the water's edge. For more than twenty years now Benjamin Britten has lived in Adelburgh. "Here in this hamlet by the North Sea, the composer found the peace denied him in London," wrote a commentator in the program notes for a 1967 revival of *Peter Grimes*. "In Adelburgh's salt air, Britten wrote the score for *Peter Grimes* which has been called a hymn to the sea. The composer's life in Adelburgh is a simple one. He usually rises at dawn, and by noon he has finished his day's creative work. In the afternoon he may wander along the shore pondering a new musical idea, play tennis or, like many of his neighbors, take to the sea to fish."

Britten was five when he began composing. "I remember the first time I tried," he later reminisced. "Hundreds of dots all over the page connected by long lines all joined together in beautiful curves. I am afraid it was the pattern on the paper which I was interested in and when I asked my mother to play it, her look of horror upset me considerably. My next efforts were much more conscious of *sound*. I had started playing the piano and wrote elaborate tone poems usually lasting about 20 seconds, inspired by terrific events in my home life such as the departure of my father for [a day in] London, the appearance in my life of a new girl friend, or even a wreck at sea. My later efforts luckily got away from these purely emotional inspirations."

There was always music around the Britten home. It was live music, for Benjamin's father, a dental surgeon, forbade radio or phonograph in the belief that these devices might prevent people from making music for themselves.

As a student, Britten excelled in mathematics, but he must have spent much time composing for there are large stacks of scores written during his student days, settings of poems by Shakespeare, Tennyson, Shelley and Kipling, selections from the Bible, bits of plays, and a few poems in French. Although his harmony lessons began when he was ten, he had no opportunity to hear 20th century works since there was no radio at home and music at South Lodge School was non-existent. His first experience with contemporary music occurred during a trip to the Norwich Triennial Festivel of 1924; he heard Frank Bridge conduct his own orchestral suite *The Sea*. Inspired by this "modern" work, Britten arranged to take lessons in composition from Bridge. "By the time I was 13 or 14 I was beginning to get more adventurous. Before then what I'd been writing had been sort of early 19th-century in style; and then I heard Holst's *Planets* and Ravel's *String Quartet* and was excited by them. I started writing in a much freer harmonic idiom."

At 16 Britten enrolled at the Royal College of Music in London and moved into an attic apartment where he could work on his compositions. The college provided little opportunity to expand his knowledge of contemporary music. He inquired there for a score of Schoenberg's *Pierrot Lunaire*. When he discovered there wasn't one in the college library, he wrote it down in their "suggestion book," a request that was turned down.

Britten later reminisced about his first years after graduation from college. He said:

> When I was nineteen I had to set about earning my living. I was
> determined to do it through composition; it was the only thing I
> cared about and I was sure it was possible. My first opportunity
> was the chance of working for a film company. This was much to
> my taste although it meant a great deal of hard work. . . . The film
> company . . . was a documentary company and had little money. I
> had to write scores for not more than six or seven players, and to,
> make those instruments make all the effects that each film
> demanded. I also had to be ingenious and try to imitate the
> natural sounds of everyday life. I well remember the mess we
> made in the studio one day when trying to fit an appropriate
> sound to shots of a large ship unloading in a dock. We had pails of
> water which we slopped everywhere, drain-pipes with coal slipping
> down them, model railways, whistles, and every kind of para-
> phernalia we could think of.[20]

In 1936 the Norwich Festival commissioned a work from
Britten. After the performance of the work, *Our Founding Fathers,*
Ralph Hawkes, a music publisher, approached the composer and
offered him a contract for anything that he wrote, a verbal
contract still valid today more than thirty years later. Soon
Britten's *Suite for Violin and Piano* was performed at the Barcelona Festival in Spain. A year later his *Variations on a Theme of
Frank Bridge* was played at the Salzburg Festival, a work which
within two years had been given more than 50 performances in
Europe and the United States and had established the composer's
international reputation.

Late in the 1930's the Britten family house in Lowestoft was
sold after the death of the composer's parents. Now restless and
rootless, and discouraged by the horrors of World War II which
had broken out in Europe, Britten decided to visit the United
States, a land he suspected was rich in opportunities for young
composers. In 1940, after his arrival in America, he composed
Sinfonia da Requiem in memory of his parents.

Although he considered the possibility of establishing permanent residence in the United States, the holocaust of war discouraged him, for he was a pacifist who felt lost and lonely far
from the land of his birth. Discouraged, he stopped composing.

Suddenly affairs changed. Britten writes:

> It was in California, in the unhappy summer of 1941. Coming
> across a copy of the poetical works of George Crabbe in a Los

Angeles bookshop, I first read his poem of *Peter Grimes*; and, at the same time reading a most perceptive and revealing article about it by E. M. Forster, I suddenly realized where I belonged and what I lacked. I had become without roots, and when I got back to England six months later I was ready to put them down. I have lived since then in the same small corner of East Anglia, near where I was born. [21]

To celebrate his first Christmas at home, he wrote one of his most popular choral works, *A Ceremony of Carols* (1942). After completing the equally beautiful *Serenade for Tenor, Horn and Strings,* Britten returned to Crabbe's poetry and in 1945 completed his first opera, *Peter Grimes.* This was followed by two more operas, *The Rape of Lucretia* (which Britten once told this author was not a success in spite of its title) and *Albert Herring* — like *Grimes,* an opera set in "a small market town in East Anglia."

One day when Britten and the tenor, Peter Pears, were traveling with the English Opera Group to the Holland Festival to give a performance of *Albert Herring*, Britten turned to Pears and said: "Why not make our *own* Festival? ....Why not an 'Aldeburgh Festival'? " And thus was born one of England's finest artistic endeavors. Over the years Britten has composed some of his finest music for this annual festival: the cantata *St. Nicolas* for the first festival in 1948; a short opera for children, *The Little Sweep* or *Let's Make an Opera* in 1949; a "Medieval miracle play" in 1958 — *Noye's Fludde*; a Shakespearean opera in 1960, *A Midsummer Night's Dream*; an adaptation of the form of a Japanese Nō play in 1964, *Curlew River*; two more "parables," *The Burning Fiery Furnace* in 1966 and *The Prodigal Son* in 1968.

Perhaps Britten's best-known orchestral work is his *Young Person's Guide to the Orchestra* written for an educational film based on the instruments of the orchestra. His largest choral work is the *War Requiem* completed in 1962 in memory of friends and artists killed in World War II. The composer's critics have suggested that the *War Requiem* shows up the weak points of Britten's "style," a largely eclectic and pragmatic one — one in which he borrows the most effective technique or method to best solve the musical need and purpose at hand. Perhaps the composer explained his own ideology best when he said:

I certainly write music for human beings — directly and deliberately. . . .

Almost every piece which I have ever written has been composed with a certain occasion in mind, and usually for definite performers, and certainly always *human* ones. . . .

I believe in roots, in associations, in backgrounds, in personal relationships. I want my music to be of use to people, to please them, to 'enhance their lives' (to use Berenson's phrase). I do not write music for posterity; in any case, the outlook for that is somewhat uncertain. I write music, now, in Aldeburgh, for people living there, and further afield, indeed for anyone who cares to play it or listen to it. But my music now has its roots in where I live and work. [22]

No living composer is more adept at setting the English language to music, be the form a song, chorus, opera, be the text medieval, Shakespearean or contemporary. "One of my chief aims," the composer has said, "is to try and restore to the musical setting of the English language a brilliance, freedom and vitality that have been curiously rare since the death of Purcell [in 1695]."

Britten is essentially a lyricist; even in his purely instrumental compositions the melodic line is a "singing" one. His approach is classical; form and structure are of greatest importance.

PETER GRIMES

Act II

"In writing *Peter Grimes*, I wanted to express my awareness of the perpetual struggle of men and women whose livelihood depends on the sea." The time is 1830; the Borough — a fishing village in Suffolk — is the setting. The original poem is the one by George Crabbe that Britten had read in a Los Angeles bookstore; the adaptation is by Montagu Slater.

Peter Grimes is the story of a lonely individual pitted against a hostile society. The village-folk themselves are the antagonists, for they misunderstand Grimes. He yearns for love, but foolish pride keeps him from accepting that love when Ellen offers it. He dreams of happiness and the sea, yet a horrible conflict within his nature drives him to destroy whatever joy and pleasure he might

The stormy North Sea at Adelburgh.

Peter Pears plays Grimes and Simon Large plays the boy John in Act II of *Peter Grimes*.

have hoped to attain. Doomed from the start, his futile attempts to escape his fate mark him for the desperate figure he is and lead him to a tragic suicide.

The Prologue takes place in Moot Hall where an inquest is in progress. The lawyer Swallow questions the surly old seaman Peter Grimes concerning the circumstances surrounding the death of his young apprentice at sea. Although the villagers present are clearly against Grimes, the boy's death is ruled accidental. Swallow suggests to Grimes that he not hire another apprentice until he has a woman to take care of the lad. As Grimes leaves the Hall, the widowed schoolmistress Ellen promises to help him in his quest for a better life.

Several days later, after life in the Borough has returned to normal, a storm erupts at sea. As Grimes' boat approaches shore, none of the fishermen will help him land it except for Captain Balstrode, a retired merchant skipper, and Ned, an apothecary and quack. Ned tells Grimes that he has found another apprentice for him at the workhouse. When no one else will go to pick the boy up, Ellen offers.

Later that evening Grimes waits at The Boar. It is a wild and stormy night, and the shutters of the tavern are closed against the storm. Finally Ellen — along with Hobson, a villager — arrives with the apprentice. Grimes immediately snatches the child from them and leads him away.

The second act opens outside the village church. It is Sunday and the sound of bells as well as pipe organ and choir can be heard from time to time during this scene. Ellen, along with John, the new apprentice, appear with the crowd in front of the church. She sings of the Sabbath:

Example 1

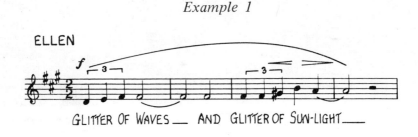

Glitter of waves and glitter of sunlight
Bid us rejoice and lift our hearts on high.
Man alone has a soul to save,
And goes to church to worship on a Sunday.

As the choir inside the church sings an anthem, Ellen sits beside John on the breakwater. She tries to talk with him, to question him about his days at the workhouse, but he is strangely silent. Ellen notices a tear in young John's coat. "Was that done before you came here? " she asks. (Unknown to Ellen, Mrs. Sedley — the village gossip — stops by on her way to church and watches this scene.) Ellen looks more carefully at the coat and tells John "that was done recently." The boy covers his neck with his hand. "John, what are you trying to hide? " She undoes the neck of the boy's shirt. "A bruise," she exclaims. "Well, it's begun! "

Grimes arrives and prepares to take John away immediately. Ellen questions the seaman about the bruise on the lad's neck. "He works for me, leave him alone, he's mine! " Grimes replies. Ellen tries to calm the enraged seaman, then asks, "Peter, tell me one thing, where the youngster got that ugly bruise? " "Out of the hurly-burly." Ellen suggests that it was perhaps Grimes' harsh ways that caused it. In the argument that follows, Peter cries out in agony and slaps Ellen when she tells him that they have failed in their dreams of a happier life. Grimes responds:

Example 2

Peter then drags the boy fiercely away with him. Ellen looks the other way weeping.

"What shall I do? " Ellen asks as the crowd starts to leave the church. They tell her to "speak out! " Musically, a large ensemble number follows. Ellen is heard first as she reminisces of her past hopes:

Example 3

ELLEN

FIGURE A

semplice ma marcato

WE PLANNED THAT THEIR LIVES SHOULD HAVE A NEW START, —

We planned that their lives should have a new start
That I as a friend could make the plan work
By bringing comfort where their lives were stark.

The Rector replies, "You plann'd to be worldly wise but your souls were dark." Ellen then finds the townsfolk arguing against her. Musically — throughout this ever more complicated involvement of solo voices — Ellen can be heard over it all with many melodic repetitions of Figure A.

Finally the church choir enters (both literally and musically) and boldly proclaims that he "who let us down must take the rap."

Example 4

CHORUS

ff

WHO LETS US DOWN MUST TAKE — THE RAP, —

Chorus and principals raise their voices in ever louder protests. They accuse Ellen of trying to be kind to a murderer. Finally Auntie, the proprietor of The Boar, leads Ellen away from the angry mob.

The Rector asks Swallow, "Should we go and see Grimes in his hut?" He replies that "popular feeling's rising!" Mrs. Sedley, the busybody widow, hints that she has some secret evidence against Grimes. "Now we'll find out the worst! " the crowd sings.

The Rector suggests that only the men go; the women must stay. Swallow asks Hobson to fetch his drum so that he can "summon the Borough to Grimes' hut! " Hobson sounds his drum and the men line up behind Swallow and the Rector. They all join in a lusty chorus:

Example 5

CHORUS, PRINCIPALS

NOW— IS GOSSIP PUT ON TRIAL,— NOW— THE RUMORS EITHER

FAIL, — OR ARE SHOUTED IN THE WIND SWEEPING FURIOUS THRO' THE LAND. —

The melody of Example 5 is repeated twice, the first time a whole step lower, the second time a fourth, then a fifth lower in pitch than the original statement.

After the men have left, Ellen and the rest of the women ask, "Do we smile or do we weep or wait quietly till they sleep."

An orchestral interlude, a *Passacaglia* connects the two scenes of the second act. Its seven-note theme is related to Grimes' phrase (Example 1) "So be it — and God have mercy upon me! " The *ostinato* bass pattern, announced *pizzicato* by cellos and basses, sounds ominous and portends of the disaster to come. Masses of sound are piled loudly on top of other masses of sound as the impending catastrophe approaches. The final measures — solo violin in its upper register against the celesta and sustained harmonics for the other strings — are haunting.

Peter Grimes' hut, an upturned boat beside the cliff over-looking the sea, is the setting for the second scene. The boy staggers through the front door as if thrust from behind. Peter follows in a towering rage. In a bold, descending cadenza-like phrase, Grimes tells the lad to "take those fancy buckles off your feet," and throws to the boy his sea boots, jersey, oilskin and sou'wester. As the lad cries softly, Peter shakes him. "Don't take fright, boy! Stop! " Grimes then outlines in a fast *Vivace* passage his solution to the taunts of the villagers:

> *They listen to money these Boro' gossips,*
> *Listen to money, only to money.*
> *I'll fish the sea dry, flood the market.*
> *Now is our chance to get a good catch,*
> *Get money to choke down rumour's throat!*

Grimes becomes calmer; he sings of marrying Ellen. Just as suddenly his mood changes again; he commands the lad to put on his coat. "We're going off to sea! " Once again the music becomes tranquil. Peter sings:

Example 6

PETER GRIMES

IN DREAMS I'VE BUILT MY-SELF SOME KIND- LIER HOME WARM__ IN MY

HEART AND IN A GOL-DEN CALM_____

> *In dreams I've built myself some kindlier home*
> *Warm in my heart and in a golden calm*
> *Where there'll be no more fear and no more storm.*

As Grimes finishes his aria, Hobson's drum can be heard in the distance as the men approach the hut. At first Grimes doesn't notice the sound as he is recalling that fateful day when his last apprentice died. Suddenly Grimes becomes aware of "an odd procession here. Parson and Swallow coming near. ....The Borough's climbing up the hill to get me! To get me! "

Angrily the men approach. To the melody of their march-tune, Example 4, they proclaim: "Now the liars shiver, for now if they've cheated we shall know." Hurriedly Peter starts to send the boy out the back door which leads directly down the cliff-side to his boat; he aims to be at sea by the time the men break down his front door. There's a knocking at the front door. While Peter is between the two doors, the boy loses his hold, screams and falls. Peter runs to the cliff door and climbs quickly out.

The men of the village enter the hut, calling for Peter Grimes. "Nobody here? What about the other door? " As the Rector looks out it he asks, "Was this a recent landslide? It makes almost a precipice. How deep? " Swallow answers "Some forty feet." "Dangerous to leave the door open! " the Rector replies.

After the men look about, Swallow comments that "here we come pell-mell, expecting to find out we know not what. But all we find is a neat and empty hut." The men all leave save for Captain Balstrode. He hesitates, looks round the hut, sees the boys' Sunday clothing lying around, examines them, then goes to the front door and shuts it. Balstrode leaves through the cliff door, hurriedly climbing down the way Peter and the boy went.

The Third Act, in two scenes, is short. At a barn dance the gaiety is interrupted as Balstrode enters with Ellen who carries the apprentice's wet jersey. The crowd cries for vengeance as Swallow orders Grimes' arrest.

A few hours later, as the villagers shout his name, Grimes staggers in alone. He does not notice the arrival of Ellen and Balstrode but hears the Captain tell him to sail his boat out to sea and sink it. Dawn breaks as the two men launch the boat; Balstrode leads Ellen away. The crowd gathers, having given up the search. Showing little interest in Swallow's report of a sinking boat, they begin their daily routine.

XVI

ALBERTO GINASTERA (1916-   ) is Argentina's most famous
composer, a creative artist who has earned an international reputation as a "nationalist" composer (although his two latest operas
are in a more universal musical idiom).

The "national" phase of Argentine music had actually been
founded around 1890 when Alberto Williams (1862-1952) returned
from his studies at the Paris Conservatory and wrote his first
composition that was inspired by the Argentine rural panorama.
This was a work for piano entitled *El Rancho Abandonado* (The

ALBERTO GINASTERA

"THE VIOLIN"   by Juan Gris.

Abandoned Ranch). It was followed by many other such works by Williams and his successors, among whom Juan Jose Castro (1895-   ) is perhaps the best known. By the decade 1930-1940 there existed a rather large body of Argentine *national* music, related in some way, either by subject, content, or by both, to the national environment: its history, its folklore, its landscape, its literature, its people.

Alberto Ginastera was a successor to this national tradition. Schooled at the Conservatorio Williams in Buenos Aires, he chose to follow the path of Alberto Williams and the nationalist group. "The word 'follow,'" Gilbert Chase tells us, "is misleading, since [Ginastera] actually went ahead and broke fresh ground. But it is correct to say that he walked within the national tradition in finding his way as an Argentine composer."

Actually Argentina is more "Latin" than most other countries we call "Latin American." Only a small remnant of the native Indian population has survived, and the Negroes — never very numerous in Argentina — have gradually disappeared. It is estimated that approximately 70 percent of the country's present population is of Italian descent, the balance largely of Spanish heritage.[23] The cultural influence during the nation's formative years was largely French, hence a truly "Latinized" country.

Alberto Ginastera's paternal grandfather immigrated from Catalonia, in Spain; his maternal grandfather from Lombardy, in Italy. Thus his parents, Luisa Bossi and Alberto Ginastera, were second-generation Argentines who had settled in the *gran aldea* (big village), Buenos Aires. There, on April 11, 1916, Alberto Ginastera was born.

No one in his family was musically inclined, but from about the age of five young Alberto showed an unusual interest in toy trumpets and drums. Two years later he started taking piano lessons, and at 12 he was enrolled in the already mentioned Conservatorio Williams where he studied for eight years. In 1936 he entered the National Conservatory of Music in Buenos Aires, studying composition first with a graduate of the Schola Cantorum in Paris, thus imbibing French influences of lasting effect.

During his student days Ginastera composed a large body of works in many different forms. He later destroyed most of them, claiming they were "immature." At this time he was most impressed by two contemporary works: Debussy's *La Mer* (The

Sea) and Stravinsky's *Le Sacre du printemps* (The Rite of Spring).

Ginastera's first published work was *Impressions of the Puna* printed in 1934; scored for flute and string quartet, its local color is derived from the northern highland region of Argentina where the surviving remnants of Indian tradition are found. In 1937 he completed *Panambi,* a "choreographic legend," based on an indigenous legend of the Guarnany Indians; it was successfully produced at the Teatro Colón three years later. Several piano works of this era likewise reflect the strongly national influence: *Argentine Dances* (1937), *Three Pieces* (1940) and *Danzas Criollas* (1946).

In 1941 Ginastera completed his second ballet, *Estancia,* based on scenes of Argentine rural life. It had been commissioned for the American Ballet Caravan which, because of the United States involvement in World War II, dissolved before producing it. A concert performance of the suite from *Estancia* was given at a Colón concert in 1943 and the ballet itself was finally produced on that stage in 1952. "With *Estancia* . . . Ginastera definitely established himself as a leader of the national movement in Argentine music."

Gilbert Chase goes on to say:

> Even in such ostensibly formal and non-associative scores as the *First String Quartet* (1948), the *Sonata for Piano* (1952) and the *Variaciones concertantes* for chamber orchestra (1953), there is a definite, though not necessarily overt, national character. Only in a small minority of works such as the setting of *Psalm XL* (1938), . . . the *Elegiac Symphony* (1944), dedicated "To the men who die for liberty," and the *Lamentation of the Prophet Jeremiah* (1946) . . . does one fail [by 1957] to discern any national elements, at least in the musical syntax (which does not mean that they may not be latent as a psychological factor).[24]

Ginastera was awarded a Guggenheim Fellowship in 1942, but because of the war he postponed his visit to the United States until 1946. He spent most of his time in New York and was commissioned to write several works while in this country. It was in 1947 that he completed the first of three works to which he has given the generic title of "Pampeana," derived from the word *pampas,* referring to the immense grassy plains of Argentina.

The composer returned to Argentina in 1948 and organized the Conservatory of Music and Scenic Art of the Province of

Buenos Aires, located in the city of La Plata, of which he became the director. Unfortunately he was removed from this position in 1952 by the Perón regime, just as the Peronistas had earlier removed him as professor of The National Military Academy in 1945. Fortunately, in 1956, after Perón's overthrow, Ginastera had the satisfaction of being named Interventor (Supervisor) of the Conservatory in La Plata.

Ginastera's music is colorful, often flamboyant, and appealing in a most uncerebral way. Although its vocabulary is modern (derived in his later works by serial procedures) its syntax is almost invariably familiar. "Music," he says, "must be expressive. All of the great composers have been expressionists in this sense: Mozart, Beethoven, Schubert, Mahler, Schoenberg, Berg." Ginastera asserts that "most modern composers have become frozen and sterile, especially the followers of Webern." As for electronic music, "Nothing of any significance has been done yet."

"Art for me," Ginastera has said in explaining his philosophy, "has an intellectual and spiritual function that comes out of order and control. The act of creation is possible only in a state of grace. No amount of craft is sufficient in itself. Nor can one be a saint in the morning and a devil in the evening! "

The music of Alberto Ginastera dominated the programs of many concerts in the Inter-American Music Festivals held in Washington, D. C. in the mid-1960's, but it has been the composer's two operas that have made his name well-known in the United States.

The first, *Don Rodrigo*, was given its North American première by the New York City Opera on the occasion of their move to Lincoln Center on February 22, 1966. *Don Rodrigo*, almost more a pageant than a drama, is based on an actual historical character in Spanish history. The music itself is eclectic, using some serial techniques, tone-clusters, chords in fourths, and is on the whole fairly conservative. "The appeal of *Don Rodrigo* to its first night audience perhaps was the idea of a contemporary opera that was attempting to be *grand* opera in the old style," stated one review. "For *Don Rodrigo* is that: it is big, noisy, full of pageantry, uncomplicated by 'psychology', with a Coronation Scene, battles, prophecies, love, dishonor, redemption, and all the conventional works."

One of the biggest scandals in many years was caused by

Ginastera's second opera, *Bomarzo*, which was banned because of its libretto by the Mayor of Buenos Aires! The story concerns Orsini, the 16th century Duke of Bomarzo, a hunchback, who seeks immortality as a foil for his thwarted life. "For me," states the composer, "Bomarzo is an anti-hero. He is a man of our times. The Renaissance was like ours. It too was an age of violence, of sex, of anxiety. Bomarzo is of our time and I had to compose music of our time."

The premiere of *Bomarzo* took place in Washington, D. C. in 1967. *Newsweek* headlined its review of the opera "Not for Squares," and referred to *Bomarzo* (because of its costuming) as "the topless opera." There can be no question, elementary passion is what the opera is all about. The musical setting is highly structured. Ginastera draws on nearly every contemporary orches tral and vocal technique imaginable. He partially employs a post-Webern serialism, as well as microtonalism, chromatic whole and aleatory (chance) forms. As for texture, the composer uses three different techniques: clusters, clouds and constellations. "Clouds," according to Ginastera, are sounds which are produced in an aleatory form and which stay suspended, slowly changing in color and form. "Constellations" are bright flashes of sounds which suddenly appear and disappear.

Bomarzo was probably best described in an earlier review of Ginastera's *Bomarzo Cantata*:

> It all sounded like something by Edgar Allen Poe, scored for Boris Karloff, dank tarn, and cask of Amontillado obbligato. Or it could be sketched by Charles Addams. The monologue of the vocalists is surrounded by an atmosphere of nightmare and hallucination. [25]

ESTANCIA

4. Malambo

The title *Estancia* could probably best be translated as "The Estate," for *estancia* is the term for the large ranches where cattle are raised in Argentina. It is the land of the *gauchos*, the hard-riding herdsmen of the *pampas* who traditionally play such an important role in Argentine history, folklore, legend and literature.

Ginastero has said of this countryside:

> Whenever I have crossed the pampa or have lived in it for a time, my spirit felt itself inundated by changing impressions, now joyful, now melancholy, some full of euphoria and others replete with a profound tranquillity, produced by its limitless immensity and by the transformation that the countryside undergoes in the course of the day. . . .
>
> From my first contact with the pampa, there awakened within me the desire to write a work that would reflect these states of my spirit. In some moments of my ballet *Estancia* the landscape appears as the veritable protagonist, imposing its influence upon the feelings of the characters. [26]

The story of the ballet *Estancia* is derived from one of Argentina's greatest literary masterpieces, *Martín Fierro* written in 1872 by José Hernandez, a bit of that country's *gauchesco* literature. The scenario of the ballet depicts the activity on an *estancia* from dawn to dawn, thus providing the composer with an opportunity for a succession of typical dances. The actual story itself must also have been close to the composer's heart, for it concerns a girl so enamored of rural life that she turns a cold shoulder to her city-bred suitor until he proves his mettle by mastering the difficult and dangerous skills of the gaucho.

In the orchestral suite derived from the ballet, the *finale* or fourth movement is a *malambo*, the most vigorous and typical dance of the *gauchos*. Gilbert Chase says that "with its tremendous rhythmic drive, [it] might be called the apotheosis of the *gauchesco* spirit in Argentine symphonic music"

The *malambo* is an agile, footstamping dance generally performed by a man alone, or by two men in competition with each other. The basic metrical pattern of six to the measure embodies the typical feature of the *malambo*, namely the zapateo (from the Spanish word *zapato*, "shoe"), the term applied to the energetic footwork of this virile and rustic dance.

The introduction to the *Danza final (Malambo)*—as the music is "officially" titled — is a brisk *Allegro* in 6/8 meter. Upper woodwinds, muted trumpets and strings (including the piano) are promiment in a 16-measure passage which establishes the rhythmic pulse of the movement. The violins and upper woodwinds then introduce the first melody of the dance:

Example 1

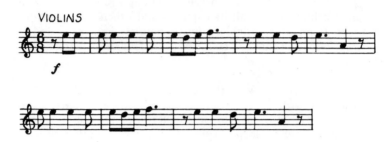

Soon a new, bolder melody is played in octaves by the violins:

Example 2

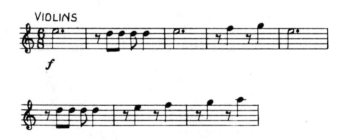

The following rhythmic passage contains measures sometimes divided into two, sometimes into three basic pulses (although the meter signature is always 6/8). The end of the passage is highly syncopated.

The opening rhythmic passage is repeated, followed by a restatement of Example 1 and its succeeding measures.

At the point of dynamic climax, the music is marked *Tempo di Malambo*. The upper woodwinds — piccolos, oboes and clarinets — introduce the principal theme, Example 3, which is twice repeated.

Example 3

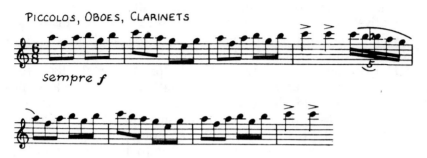

PICCOLOS, OBOES, CLARINETS

sempre f

The French horns boldly state a malambo motive of their own against a string accompaniment.

The upper woodwinds return to the principal tune, Example 3, playing it three successive times. The horns return to their motive. Once again the·upper woodwinds counter with statements of Example 3 — twice this time, but with some episodic passages added. The horns are now joined in their motive by trumpets, oboes and clarinets. The principal theme, Example 3, returns triumphant, boldly holding sway until the final climax of the dance.

XVII

PIERRE BOULEZ (1925-   ) "is the most gifted of the French composers of his generation," states a leading German music critic. He goes on to say:

In most of his pieces there emerges a fundamental musicianship which has the particularly French *spirituel* cast; he has the ability to think in terms of the whole, to pull things together formally; he is in control of his tone color and original ideas. The creative motivation of his art far outweighs the systematic and theoretical. Still today [1960] his music has no very large public, but no doubt his music can make its way in the course of the years. [27]

Pierre Boulez is not a prolific composer; the total number of his works is small. Just as they were in 1960, these few works are still relatively unknown to the general public. However, his name is widely known both as a talented composer and as an expert conductor of both modern and standard orchestral repertory.

The composer was born on March 26, 1925 in the little town of Montbrison in central France; his father was an industrialist. Although as a child Pierre dabbled in music and sang with his church choir, his father saw to it that he studied the "practical" subjects. Both at St. Etienne and Lyon, Boulez majored in mathematics as well as in music. When he went to Paris he intended to become a mathematician and took the entrance examination for the Polytechnic School. In the meantime he had met the composer Olivier Messiaen and in 1944 enrolled in Messiaen's harmony class at the Paris Conservatory; within a year Boulez had won the first prize in harmony.

In 1945 — the year of the harmony prize — Boulez heard for the first time a work by Arnold Schoenberg, and it made a profound impression on him. "I realized that here was a language of our time. No other language was possible. It was the most radical revolution since Monteverdi."

Boulez immediately made arrangements to study composition at the Conservatory with a young musician of Polish origin, René Leibowitz, who was an exponent of the 12-tone system. Within a year Boulez had completed three works, all in this idiom: *Sonatina for Flute and Piano, Piano Sonata No 1* and *Le Visage nuptial.*

The same year, 1946, Jean-Louis Barrault appointed Boulez the music director of the theater company that he and his wife, actress Madeleine Renaud, had organized. Free from financial concerns, Boulez now had an opportunity to perfect his conducting technique and to tour Europe, North and South America, and the Far East. Although a number of compositions date from his ten-year association with the theater, only one work was composed for the Barrault Theater itself, some incidental music for the production of Aeschylus' *The Oresteia* (1956).

Under the auspices of the Renaud-Barrault Company, Boulez organized in 1954 a series of concerts in the Petit Marigny Theatre; the following year the series took the name of Domaine Musical. In this series Boulez introduced the Parisians to many *avant-garde* works over the years. For the very first concert, Barrault himself

PIERRE BOULEZ   LUCIANO BERIO

appeared in a pantomime performance of Stravinsky's *Renard* conducted by Hermann Scherchen. Later Stravinsky appeared in person to conduct his own works: *Agon* in 1957 and *Threni* in 1958. Many 12-tone works were given first performances at Boulez' *Domaine Musical.* Schoenberg, Messiaen, Webern and Varèse were paid due homage, but works by Karlheinz Stockhausen, Henri Pousseur, Luigi Nono and Earle Brown were also performed.

On June 18, 1955, the International Society for Contemporary Music, having overridden the veto of its French delegation, sponsored the first public performance — given in Baden-Baden — of Boulez' *Le Marteau sans maître* (The Hammer Without a Master), a setting of poems by René Char. The success of this work established Boulez' international reputation as a composer. In addition to two commercial recordings, performances have been given in Paris, Vienna, Zurich, Munich, London, Aix-en-Provence, New York and Los Angeles.

Over the years, the compositions of Boulez have become more "serialized." At first the highly organized and restrictive *series* referred to only the melodic structure of his works. Gradually

Boulez brought the other constituent elements of music under similar rigid control.

One of the early works of 1946 already mentioned — the *Sonatina for Flute and Piano* — is in the Schoenberg idiom, the classic serial style. Soon rhythm became serialized. "How can this be achieved? " asks the composer.

> Paradoxically, [he answers] the point of departure will be to release polyphony from rhythm .... I accord equal importance to rhythmic structures and serial structures. My aim will be to create a reservoir of possibles in this domain too.
>
> The simplest case will consist of taking a series of [rhythm] values and having them undergo a number of permutations equal and parallel to that of pitches, by giving each note of the original series a permanent duration. [28]

In the *Piano Sonata No. 1* and *Visage nuptial* of 1946, such rhythmic and sonorous structures are added to the classic serial structure.

Boulez continued on his path of control. The cantata, *Le Soleil des eaux* and *Piano Sonata No. 2* of 1948, and the *Polyphonie X* of 1951, are works in which timbrel serial structure comes to join already existing structures of pitch and rhythm. Finally in 1955 the already mentioned *Le Marteau* was completed. "It is in this work," writes a French music historian, "that Boulez definitely conquers the integrality of sonorous space."

After this epitome of totally serial music, Boulez, "whose spirit cannot bear any stagnation, had to push ahead, always seeking to widen and deepen the domain of his art." Following certain experiments by John Cage and Stockhausen, Boulez made use of the revolutionary notion of *alea,* or chance, in his *Sonata No. 3 for Piano* and two *Improvisations sur Mallarmé.* In these works, in addition to a tight serial structure, the composer provides the interpreters certain opportunities of choice and improvisation in the course of performing a work:

> Being a function of duration, of its physical time of unfolding [says Boulez] musical development can allow 'chances' to intervene at several stages, on various levels of composition. In short, the result will be a linking, of greater probability, of aleatory events within a certain duration, itself indeterminate. This may appear

absurd in the context of our Occidental music, but Hindu music, for example, combining a sort of structural 'forming' with instantaneous improvisation, very easily accepts this sort of problem and solves it daily. [29]

Thus in the *Sonata No. 3*, within the framework of the most rigorous serial construction, Boulez indicates nevertheless several possibilities of interpretation and even of order of execution, presenting the different sections among which the interpreter may choose at the moment of performance!

It was only natural that when Boulez learned of experiments in electronic music he became intensely interested in them. "Rarely in the history of music," he writes, "could one have been witness to a more radical revolution, for one must understand that the musician finds himself facing an unprecedented situation, the creation of sound itself. . . .The composer . . . becomes the performer. . . .In a certain sense, the musician becomes a painter: he plays a direct role in the quality of his realization'"

In his *Two Studies*, Boulez attempted to apply total serialization to this highly mechanized music. Possibly because of the demands of his international career as a conductor, Pierre Boulez — who since 1954 has made Baden-Baden his home — has not offered the public a new work since *Eclats* in 1965, revised in 1966. "Conducting, for me," he says, "remains a stimulating contact with the mainstream of music, and it reflects favorably upon my own creative efforts."

In 1969 Boulez was appointed conductor of the New York Philharmonic Orchestra starting with the season of 1971-72; at the same time he will serve as chief conductor for the BBC Symphony in England.

LE SOLEIL DES EAUX

1. Complainte du lézard amoureux

Le Soleil des eaux (The Sun on the Waters) was originally presented in 1948 as a "poetic drama for radio" with text by the French "surrealist" poet René Char and incidental music by Pierre Boulez. The drama depicted the revolt by fishermen of the Sorgue

River country in France against the installation of a factory that poisoned the river.

In 1959 Boulez reworked his music for the radio drama into a cantata, using two poems by Char (the second was not part of the original script) as his text and incorporating the original orchestral interludes. The cantata is scored for three soloists (soprano, tenor and bass), a three-part chorus (sopranos, tenors and basses) and a standard orchestra augmented by much percussion: xylophone, vibraphone, glockenspiel, timpani, gong and cymbals. The first of the two poems, *Complainte du lézard amoureux* (Lay of the Lizard in Love), is set for soprano soloist, while all soloists and chorus join in the second poem, *La Sorgue.*

The first movement is in the form of a free dialogue between the solo soprano and the orchestra. The soloist's lines are for the most part unaccompanied, and the orchestral interjections are very brief but extremely concentrated. Although the music is serial, based on the tone row system, it is powerful and evocative. Because the tone row of this work is characterized by a preponderance of major thirds, giving it a "whole-tone" aura, (see Example 1) the melodic line seems to be descended from Debussy. Because the soprano text is frequently set in the song-speech style or *Sprechstimme*, the vocal line seems to be descended from Schoenberg. As the individual tones of the melody are assigned to different instruments, a style known as *Klangfarben,* the timbre is suggestive of Webern.

Complainte du lézard amoureux is a gentle song which captures the atmosphere of a lazy, warm summer's day, an atmosphere admirably evoked by the shimmering music of the orchestra which alternates with the improvisatory effect of the soprano's music (marked *comme improvisé* and *non mesuré*).

The orchestra immediately states the tone row, which, as has been stated, contains a preponderance of major thirds. Overlapping entries and sustained notes give the statement an echo-like effect, again suggesting the "impressionistic" aspect.

Example 1

[Note 1: The tones of Example 1, played by various instruments (*Klangfarben*), are assigned as follows:

1 xylophone	7 cellos
2 harp	8 2nd violins
3 harp	9 2nd violins
4 vibraphone, xylophone, harp	10 1st violins
5 vibraphone	11 1st violins
6 xylophone	12 2nd violins

Note 2: The use of the row does not adhere to the principles established by Schoenberg, rather it is subjected to various permutations. For example, the F-natural in the lower part, No. 6, starts the next statement of the row, a transposed permutation split up like the first between two parts.*]

When the soprano enters, her melodic line, incorporating some *Sprechstimme* denoted by the *X*'s on note stems, extends into a permutation of the row and its retrograde 1-2-3-4-5-6-10-7-8-11-9-12 and 12-11-10-8-9-4-6-5-7-3-1-2 (See Example 2).

*Furthermore, for the analytically minded, the last note of the previous row, C-sharp, is the first note of the upper part. Starting on F the permutation reads 1-2-3-4-5-10-6-8-7-11-9-D-sharp-12. The foreign D-sharp starts a further statement, a permutation of the retrograde, transposed up a minor third.

Example 2

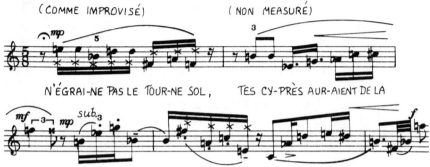

N'ÉGRAI-NE PAS LE TOUR-NE SOL,   TES CY-PRÈS AUR-AIENT DE LA

PEI-NE, CHAR-DON-NE-RET, ___ RE-PRENS TON VOL ET RE-VIENS À TON NID DE LAI..(NE)

N'égraine pas le tournesol,	*Do not pick at that sunflower,*
Tes cyprès auraient de la peine,	*Your cypress trees would be most disturbed,*
Chardonneret, reprends ton vol	*Goldfinch; fly off again*
Et reviens à ton nid de laine.	*And return to your woolly nest.*

The orchestra interlude at this point is extremely brief. They continue on then to accompany the soloist in the second stanza.

Tu n'es pas un caillou du ciel	*You are not a pebble of the sky*
Pour que le vent te tienne quitte	*So that the wind has no power over you,*
Oiseau rural; l'arc-en-ciel	*Bird of the countryside; the colors of the rainbow*
S'unifie dans la marguerite.	*Become one again in the daisy.*

The third stanza is sung without instrumental accompaniment:

L'homme fusille, cache-toi;	*Man is out shooting, so hide yourself;*
Le tournesol est son complice.	*The sunflower is his accomplice.*
Seules les herbes sont pour toi,	*Only the grass is on your side,*
Les herbes des champs qui se plissent.	*The grass of the field as it folds.*

The most extensive of the orchestral interludes occurs at this point. It is based on several repeated patterns (see Example 3); only the timbre changes. Figure A repeats itself every three tones; Figure B lasts only five, and its more subtle line is sometimes split into two pairs of eighths as indicated; Figure C is an underlying rhythmic *ostinato,* shared by several instruments, and repeated incessantly; Figure D is played by viola, flute, bassoon and trumpet.

Example 3

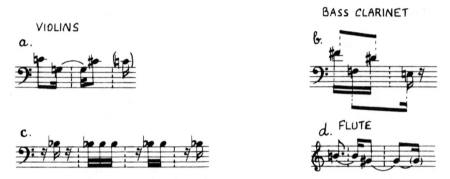

In addition, a simple rhythmic canon — Example 4 — is heard; it is also a melodic canon by inversion. Perhaps the composer was trying to represent musically the last line of the previous stanza which speaks of grass folding in on itself.

Example 4

The orchestral interlude concludes with repeated tones on the large gong. Next, the soprano sings again without accompaniment:

Le serpent ne te connaît pas,	*The snake takes no notice of you,*
Et la sauterelle est bougonne;	*The grasshopper grumbles away to herself;*
La taupe, elle, n'y voit pas;	*As for the mole, she can't see a thing;*
Le papillon ne hait personne.	*The butterfly hates no one.*
L'écho de ce pays est sûr.	*The echoes of this countryside have a safe sound.*
J'observe, je suis bon prophête;	*I am keeping watch; I am a good prophet;*
Je vois tout de mon petit mur,	*I can see everything from my little wall,*
Même tituber la chouette.	*Even the owl as she staggers forth.*

The orchestra enters boldly, almost "staggering forth" like the owl. The soloist continues:

Il est midi, chardonneret.	*It is midday, goldfinch.*
Le séneçon est la qui brille.	*The small yellow weed is still there;*
Attarde-toi, va sans danger:	*Go on, take your time, the danger is past;*
L'homme est rentré dans sa famille!	*Man has gone home to his family!*

This interlude is gentle, enchanting, suggesting a dream-like trance of luminous beauty; trills — perhaps of would-be birds — are heard. In the final stanza the soprano sings two lines unaccompanied, then the orchestra joins her.

Qui, mieux qu'un lezard amoureux	*Who better than a lizard in love*
Peut dire les secrets terrestres?	*Can tell the secrets of the earth?*
O leger gentil roi des cieux,	*Oh sweet and airy king of the heavens,*
Que N'as-tu ton nid dans ma pierre!	*Would that your nest were in my rock!*

Beatle Paul McCartney and friend Paul Asher talk with composer Luciano Berio.

XVIII

LUCIANO BERIO (1925-   ) has been one of the leading figures in contemporary Italian music since the 1950's. He was born in Oneglia (now Imperia) on the Italian Riviera. He is the third generation of composers in his family as his father and his grandfather were church organists and composers. Young Berio began his musical studies with his father and, like his father, completed his training at the Conservatory of Milan.

The composer later said with ire (referring to Mussolini's regime):

> It was not until 1945 that I first had the opportunity to see and hear the works of Schoenberg and Stravinsky, Webern, Hindemith, Bartók and Milhaud. I was already 19 years old! Of that crucial period let me simply say that among the many thoughts and emotions aroused in me by those encounters, one is still intact and alive within me today: anger — anger at the realization that Fascism had until that moment deprived me of knowledge of the most essential musical achievements of my own culture.[30]

While carrying on his Conservatory studies he was employed as coach and accompanist for the classes of two well-known opera stars. Before graduating in 1950, Berio gained a wider practical experience as pianist-coach, conductor (and occasionally timpanist) for a small touring opera company which played in northern Italian provincial cities and towns. The year after his graduation from the Conservatory, a Koussevitzky Foundation Fellowship enabled him to travel to the Berkshire Center at Tanglewood to study composition with his compatriot, Luigi Dallapiccola.

On his return to Italy, Berio joined the staff of the Italian radio, where in 1954 he established a Studio Di Fonologia for study of and experimentation in electronic music. The following year he launched a series of concerts of contemporary music which he called *Incontri Musicali* (Musical Encounters) and edited a progressive music magazine of the same name. He also became active as conductor (chiefly of his own music) at La Scala in Milan, the Teatro Fenice in Venice, the Rome Opera, and he has conducted the Chicago Symphony and the New York Philharmonic Orchestras as well.

Berio's compositions include, among the larger works, a *Magnificat* of 1949; *Variations for Chamber Orchestra,* 1953; *Nones,* for orchestra, five variations on a poem, "The Ninth Hour" by W. H. Auden, 1954; and two *Alleluias,* 1955 and 1957. Among the purely electronic compositions of this period are *Mutations* and *Perspectives.* His smaller works include *Chamber Music* of 1952 for voice and three instruments on some poems of James Joyce; *El mar la mar* in 1953 for voice and five instruments; *String Quartet* in 1956; and, a *Serenata No. 1* in 1958 for flute and fourteen instruments. This latter work, the *Serenata,* has proven to be one of Berio's most frequently performed chamber works.

Concerning the *Serenata,* Berio said in a letter to a friend:

> I wrote it in 14 days for the Domaine Musical, so I didn't have time to think about the possible choices but wrote what I had in my head (ears included). A sort of stream of consciousness if you will. . . .[It was one of] the first postwar serenades; it seems to me, that is, that [it] represented the first example of serial music which smiles a bit. . . I have always heard the strains of old nocturnal serenades in it. [31]

In 1950, Italy. like most of Western civilization, had a small group of enthusiasts for contemporary art, while the rest — as elsewhere — ignored it. With this lethargic public Berio achieved a notoriety by his daring broadcasts and modern compositions.

> "A new, vital personality," one critic said of Berio and his music. "If one considers his writings on music, or his radio talks, there is no question that here is a profound thinker. A penetrating examination of his scores reveals an intelligence and imagination which are unquestionable. "[32]

One of Berio's most outstanding compositions dates from 1958, *Thema: Omaggio a Joyce* (Theme: An Homage to James Joyce), a fine example of *musique concrète.** How much of the work was inspired by Berio's first wife, the American soprano Cathy Berberian, only the composer knows. Her unusual artistic talents must have suggested to the composer new possibilities in sound, speech and music.

In *Thema,* the only sound source used is that of the soloist's voice. The text is the beginning of the eleventh chapter of James Joyce's *Ulysses,* a passage that concerns Mr. Bloom's afternoon in the Ormond Bar, Dublin.

The first part of *Thema* is a recitation by the soloist of the original Joyce text. Then follows, after a slight pause, a prepared tape recording. Berio has built the performance tape entirely out of sounds recorded during an earlier reading of the text by the soloist.

The composer comments:

> All transformations are accomplished through superimposition of identical elements with varying time relationships (phrase shifting, especially where Joyce is concerned with musical onomatopoeia), through wide frequency and time transpositions and through 1/3 octave filtering. Though at certain points it would have been a simple matter to extend the transformations by introducing electrically produced sounds, this was not done because the original intention was to develop a reading of Joyce's text within certain restrictions dictated by the text itself.[33]

---

* *musique concrete* is constructed from recorded natural sources of sound (the voice, gongs, crowd noises, ocean's roar, etc.) in contrast to *electronic music* which is constructed from sounds produced electrically (sine waves, square waves, white noise, etc.)

Berio goes on to say, "With *Thema* I attempted to establish a new relationship between speech and music, in which a continuous metamorphosis of one into the other can be developed."

In support of his technique employed in *Thema*, Berio has written:

> Verses, prosody and rhymes are no more an assurance of poetry than written notes are an assurance of music. We often seem, in fact, to discover more "poetry" in prose than in poetry itself and more "music" in speech and noise than in agreed upon musical sounds. It is with this general perspective that *Thema (Omaggio a Joyce)* must be approached. [34]

Berio's last work before leaving the Studio di Fonologia, written in 1961, was *Visage* for magnetic tape, based on the voice of a soloist *and* electrically generated sounds.

> *Visage* is purely a radio-program work [states the composer], a sound track for a "drama" that was never written. Consequently its destination is not really the concert hall but rather any conceivable medium for the reproduction of words. . . . *Visage* does not present meaningful speech but the semblance of it. Only a single word is pronounced and repeated: the word *parole,* meaning "words" in Italian. The vocal events from inarticulated or articulated *speech,* from laughter to crying and to singing, from patterns of inflections modeled upon specific languages to *aphasia,* etc., are constantly related to electrically produced sounds. . . For me, *Visage* also constitutes a tribute to the radio as the most widespread disseminator of useless words. [35]

During the 1960's Berio traveled widely; his travels included many trips to the United States. He held composition classes in Darmstadt and Dartington, and in the United States at Mills College and at Tanglewood. At the latter, his *Circles,* a Fromm Foundation commission, received its first performance. His other works of the period include the opera *Passagio,* and a choreographic play with voices, orchestral instruments and magnetic tape recorder, *Esposizione.*

In 1965 Berio was appointed to the staff of Juilliard School of Music at Lincoln Center in New York. "I used to live in Italy, coming to the United States often," the composer jokingly told a reporter. "Now I live in the United States and go to Europe *very* often."

The composer's main interest seems to be in the musical theater. "Opera is dead for me now. I regard composers writing new operas for the opera houses as completely nonsensical. ... As a musico-dramatic form, opera is completely useless." Casting traditional opera aside, Berio finds the brightest possibilities in a more flexible musical theater "because music and theater are the most valuable tools today to help people transform themselves and things. Good theater demands a kind of organization in terms of actions and the meaning of words which to a certain extent can be seen analogous to musical structure. I do not believe in the sharp dichotomy between music and theater, for music has a strong dramaturgical connotation for me."

Berio's *Laborintus II* of 1968 provides an insight into this line of reasoning, an example of his theory of multiple ideas. It is a work involving three areas: dance, language (singers and chorus), and instruments — all to be carefully lighted for total effect. "This is certainly neither an opera nor a ballet. It is in between things as a fusion of different elements."

More recently Berio has become involved in what he calls "a kind of interdisciplinary approach" to different media. He has tried working out combinations of tape and light performance coordinated with instruments or voice. "I am interested in those aspects of sound that are too often disregarded as nonmusical; that is, the richness of the human voice — the speaking voice. It is as important to integrate this aspect of sound into the musical structure as it once was the singing voice. The key to all this is Schoenberg's *Pierrot Lunaire,* which explored the no-man's land between the speaking and singing voice for the first time."

Berio has also shown great interest in large instrumental groups which he refuses to call orchestras because

> They have very precise historical connotations. They are still an extension of the polyphonic distribution of acoustical courses based on choral writings. I wish eventually to reconsider the orchestra in terms of what has been done by Schoenberg and Webern; that is, to develop it as a multiplication of the soloistic type of writing, reconstituting it under new acoustical considerations. For me the great line historically of this new development is through Debussy, Stravinsky, Schoenberg, and the new generation of composers.[36]

The composer goes on to state that "the most important development in music now is to integrate the new things to be heard in new environments. But I object to the term *avant-garde,* which is too often used in the United States. Anything I do of certain value will be experimental. This is really the only avant-garde aspect of my work."

SINFONIA

Part 3

When Luciano Berio conducted the world première performance of his *Sinfonia* on October 10, 1968, at Lincoln Center with the New York Philharmonic Orchestra, public and critic alike sat up and took notice. *Time* magazine called *Sinfonia* "a white-hot musical experience that invokes the malaise of the times better than all the sit-ins, beards, beads and clubbings that wrench contemporary life." A West Coast music critic who headlined his review *Excitement at N. Y. Philharmonic,* called the new work "amazing" and "adventurous."

Sinfonia was one of 18 compositions commissioned by the New York Philharmonic in 1966 to honor its 125th anniversary. The title *Sinfonia* means nothing classical, but simply refers to the sounding together of voices and instruments in it. This — in the case of both the 1968 première performance and the release of the recording the following year — meant the Swingle Singers* plus the full-sized New York Philharmonic Orchestra.

Berio supplied the program notes for the first performance. He said:

> The four sections into which *Sinfonia* is divided are not analogous to the movements of the classical symphony. The title, in fact, must be taken only in its etymological sense of "sounding together." Although their expressive characters are extremely

---

* The *Swingle Singers* are an eight-member Paris-based group led by American Ward Swingle. They have popularized Bach scores by performing them to the accompaniment of a jazz rhythm section, singing the themes in wordless scat syllables *(ba ba do ba dee).*

diversified, these four sections are generally unified by similar harmonic and articulatory (duplication and extended repetition being among the most important) characteristics.

The text of the first part consists of a series of short fragments from *Le Cru et le ·cuit* by the French anthropologist Claude Levi-Strauss. These fragments are taken from a section of the book which analyses the structure and symbology of Brazilian myths about the origins of water and related myths characterized by similar structure.

The second section of *Sinfonia* is a tribute to the memory of Dr. Martin Luther King. Here the vocal part is based on his name, nothing else.

The main text for the third section includes excerpts from Samuel Beckett's *The Unnamable,* which in turn prompt a selection from many other sources, including Joyce, spoken phrases of Harvard undergraduates, slogans written by the students on the Sorbonne walls during last May's insurrection [1968] in Paris (at which I was present), recorded dialogues with my friends and family, snatches of *solfège* and so on. Meant to be adjusted to the particular performance, this part of the text is to be put into the language of the audience and certain portions altered to fit the occasion.

The text for the fourth section, a sort of coda, is based on a short selection from those used in the three preceding parts. ...

Section III of *Sinfonia,* I feel, requires a more detailed comment than the others, because it is perhaps the most "experimental" music I have ever written. It is another homage, this time to Gustav Mahler, whose work seems to bear within it the weight of the entire history of music; and to Leonard Bernstein for his unforgettable performance of the *Resurrection* Symphony last season. The result is a kind of "voyage to Cythera" made on board the 3rd movement of Mahler's Second Symphony. The Mahler movement is treated like a container within whose framework a large number of references are proliferated, interrelated and integrated into the flowing structure of the original work itself. The references range from Bach, Schoenberg, Debussy, Ravel, Strauss, Berlioz, Brahms, Berg, Hindemith, Beethoven, Wagner and Stravinsky to Boulez, Stockhausen, Globokar, Pousseur, Ives, myself and beyond. I would almost say that this section of *Sinfonia* is not so much composed as it is assembled to make possible the mutual transformation of the component parts. It was my intention here neither to destroy Mahler (who is indestructible) nor to play out a private complex about "post-Romantic music" (I have none) nor yet to spin some enormous musical anecdote (familiar among young pianists). Quotations and references were chosen not only for their real but also for their potential relation to Mahler. The juxtaposition of contrasting elements, in fact, is part of the whole point of this section of *Sinfonia,* which can also be considered, if you will, a documentary on an *objet trouvé.* As a structural point of reference, Mahler is to the totality of the music of this section what Beckett is to the text. One might describe the relationship between words and music as a kind of interpretation, almost a *Traumdeutung* [literally "dream interpretation"], of that stream-of-consciousness-like flowing which is the most immediate expressive character of Mahler's movement. If I were to describe the presence of Mahler's "scherzo" in *Sinfonia,* the image which comes most spontaneously to mind is that of a river, going through a constantly changing landscape, sometimes going underground and emerging in another, altogether different place, sometimes very evident in its journey, sometimes disappearing completely, present either as a fully recognizable form or as small details lost in the surrounding musical presences.[37]

Berio's use of words and text in *Sinfonia,* according to one critic, "makes a highly emotional impact. Somehow Berio's use of words, his painting with texts which are half-perceived through collages and overlays,—disturbs and arouses the listener to a constant awareness, a heightened sensitivity to the musical events and flow."

The greater portion of the quotations in the spoken collage of Part III come from Samuel Beckett's* *The Unnamables,* which begins (in the English translation by the author):

Where now? Who now? When now? Unquestioning. I, say I. Unbelieving. Questions, hypotheses, call them that. Keep going, going on, call that going, call that on. Can it be that one day, off it goes on, that one day I simply stayed in, in where, instead of going out, in the old way, out to spend day and night as far away as possible, it wasn't far. Perhaps that is how it began.[38]

---

* Samuel Beckett was born in Ireland in 1906 and served for a time as secretary for James Joyce, whose "stream of consciousness" style he emulates. Since 1945 Beckett has written exclusively in French. He is best known for his play *Waiting for Godot* of 1952.

Sinfonia is scored for 24 violins divided into three equal sections, eight each of violas and cellos, six string basses, piccolo, three flutes, three clarinets, an E-flat clarinet, two oboes, English horn, alto saxophone, tenor saxophone, two bassoons, a contrabassoon, four horns, four trumpets, three trombones, bass tuba, harp, piano, electronic harpsichord, electric organ and percussion. Concerning Section III of *Sinfonia,* Berio has said:

> It is mainly based on harmonic transformations whose starting point is always Mahler's *Scherzo.* With the exception of a very few moments, there are always *at least* two different musics superimposed and transforming each other. The number of references, from Bach to Pousseur (and myself) would make an endless catalogue. I consider this section of *Sinfonia* also an exercise on "relativity" of perception of music history.[39]

A crashing chord opens the third movement; it is followed by a collage of spoken quotations:

> Peripetie. Nicht eilen, bitte. Recht gemä − sehr gemälich, nicht eilen. Le jeux des vagues. Quatrième symphonie, deuxième partie. Deuxième symphonie, première partie. Quatrième partie, troisième partie. In ruhig fliessender bewegung. Where now? Who now? What now? And now? Keep going. (Do mi re do si la.) Peripetie. Where? Nothing more restful than chamber music − than flute − than two flutes. (la re fa la sol, do mi do si si re si la, t. k. ... a i a i.)[40]

The repetitive bass pattern, Example 1, of the Scherzo from Mahler's *Symphony No. 2* emerges from the lower depths of the orchestra. This motive establishes itself as the rhythmic foundation and "beat" of most of the Berio movement.

Example 1

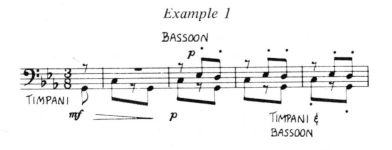

Soon the thematic exposition of Mahler's Scherzo unfolds. The violins are heard first with the basic melodic idea:

Example 2

Another melody emerges from Example 2, one at once both new and derivative:

Example 3

Other motives from the Mahler Scherzo are heard as the collage of voices becomes more prominent:

Example 4

PICCOLO
CLARINET

OBOES
CLARINETS

OBOE

CELLOS
BASSES

After an extended and somewhat rambling section based on previously heard materials, the sound of castanets is heard for the first time; it is followed by loud crashing sounds from the huge Chinese gong. Solo bits from a saucy little French folk song are sung by the treble voices of the Swingle Singers.

The basic rhythmic pattern, Example 1, returns briefly; then, out of a confusion of orchestral sounds, comes a more serene quotation from the *Trio* of Mahler's Scherzo:

Example 5

A brief excerpt from one of the waltz themes in Richard Strauss' *Der Rosenkavalier* is heard:

Example 6

Following a hint of Ravel's *La Valse,* a quotation from the Rose Presentation Scene of the Strauss' opera is made by the treble voices of the Swingle Singers and the orchestral strings.

Suggestions of Example 2 are heard as it emerges from the orchestra much as a stream emerges from flowing undergound. The underlying pulse of Example 1 provides a foundation for the collage of music, voices, interjections and rambling fragments in another extended section.

The dynamic level subsides. Only a single voice is heard: "And after each group disintegration the name of Miakowski hangs in the clean air."

A dynamic climax with crashing chords follows. A suggestion of Debussy's *La Mer* is heard:

Example 7

Example 7 is followed by the Introductory Section of the Finale from the Mahler *Symphony No. 2* with its forceful chords. *Doo-bee-doo's* of the Swingle Singers are heard in the mixture; introductions of the singers by name are made.

The spoken voice breaks clearly through: "There was even for a second a hope of Resurrection*". The intensity of the music subsides; the movement comes to a quiet conclusion as the resounding timbre of the gong is heard.

---

* Mahler's Scherzo from the *Symphony No. 2*, subtitled "The Resurrection", is a transformation into symphonic music of one of the composer's songs: *Die Fisch-predigt des Heiligen Antonius* ("Saint Anthony's Sermon to the Fish"). The words of the song, full of sarcastic pessimism, are taken from "Das Knaben Wunderhorn," a famous collection of German folk ballads. Saint Anthony, desiring to preach and finding the church empty, decides to address himself to the fish. They all come swimming towards the shore and are very pleased with the sermon. But as soon as he finishes, everything is again as it was before: the pikes remain thieves, the eels love too much, the carp eat too much, the crayfish crawl backwards, etc.; in short, everyone remains unchanged.

The actual title, "Resurrection Symphony" comes from the Finale based on Klopstock's "Resurrection Hymn."

HANS WERNER HENZE   KARLHEINZ STOCKHAUSEN

XIX

HANS WERNER HENZE (1926-   ) is a strange figure in the annals of contemporary German music. In 1946, following Germany's overwhelming defeat in World War II, the country started on its long road to recovery. It was a nation and a people anxious to see a rebirth of culture in their land as well as a renaissance of economic prosperity. In casting about for young artists on whom to pin hopes for the future, they discovered Hans Werner Henze. This 20-year-old German-born youth became, to quote one critic, "by all odds the most successful (and very probably the most gifted) among the postwar German composers."

But, Henze — if anything — is unpredictable! In 1953 he turned his back on his fatherland and moved south to Italy. He first took up residence in Forio on the isle of Ischia (near its sister island of Capri, off the coast of Naples) and later purchased a country house at Castel Gandolfo near Rome where he now lives when not off on an international conducting or lecture tour.

His compositional style or technique has likewise undergone a major transformation. He was originally hailed as one of the leaders of the "Darmstadt group," that informal association of radical young composers who were given their strongest moral and material support by performances of their music at the International Holiday Courses for New Music given in the German city of Darmstadt. These young men were dedicated followers of the 12-tone method and pointillistic style of Anton Webern.

Henze's highly successful opera of 1949, *Boulevard Solitude,* was composed in this newly developing post-Webern pointillistic vein. But just then a change in Henze's style started to take place. The exact date of the complete transformation is difficult to discover. As late as 1956, in a piece written for Pierre Boulez' concerts in Paris, *Concerto,* Henze employed some of the effects of pointillism. Yet two years later, in his ballet score *Ondine* for the Royal Ballet of London, he employed the most conventional and old-fashioned means: *ostinatos,* sequences, common chords and triads, tonality, modulation and regular phrases and periods.

Just who is this controversial, puzzling and contradictory figure in music?

Hans Werner Henze was born at Gütersloh, a small town in the German province of Westphalia, on the 1st of July, 1926. There he received his early training. Later he studied at the State School of Music in Brunswick; that is, until he was drafted into the German army of World War II. His first post-war job was as chorus master for the Bielefeld State Theater; he augmented his income by playing the piano at ballet schools.

"My real music studies began in Heidelberg in 1946 when I became a pupil of Wolfgang Fortner," Henze relates. "To him I owe a thorough grounding in traditional methods of composition, strict counterpoint and fugue. At the same time, he introduced me to modern music and its esthetic problems."

Two years later Henze went to Paris to study for a time with René Leibowitz, from whom he learned the workings of the

12-tone method and came to understand how he could apply this method to his own artistic needs. He then became the artistic director of the ballet at the Wiesbaden State Theater, working there and in Paris on his first full-length opera, the previously mentioned *Boulevard Solitude,* "a delicately-colored, sadly poignant variation on the subject of Manon Lescaut."

New compositions poured from his pen during the years 1947-51: the ballets *Jack Pudding, Labyrinth,* the *Idiot* and others; three symphonies, two concertos, chamber music. Each new work was hailed with cheers by the "progressives" and with groans (and often boos and catcalls) by the traditionally minded.

Then followed Henze's move to Italy and the change in his musical idiom. "The free, happy post-war years were over. Everything in public life pointed toward restoration." The opera, *King Stag* (1956), was the first evidence of this new (or was it old?) musical vocabulary. In it the 12-tone method was forsaken for a style that employed tonal, bitonal, polytonal and serial procedures in a nonsystematic, nonschematic way. A major role was now assigned to melody, "this pure source of illumination which can only be discovered in a childlike rapture."

King Stag was followed by such divergent works as the operas *The Prince of Homburg* (1960), *Elegy for Young Lovers* (1961), *The Young Lord* (1965, a comedy), and *The Bassarids* (1966); the ballets *Dance Marathon* (1957, with jazz elements), and the previously mentioned *Ondine* (1958); works for voice and orchestra such as *Five Neopolitan Songs* (1958); and choral works, among which *Muses of Sicily* (1967) is one of major importance.

In 1968 Henze caused a scandal of quite another kind, this one of a political nature. The composer, who has strong sympathies to the political left, wrote an oratorio — *The Raft of Medusa* — dedicated to the memory of the Cuban revolutionary leader Che Guevara. Scheduled for its world premiére in Hamburg, a hugh photograph of Guevara decorated the back stage wall. When the composer insisted that a red flag be placed above the stage, the entire chorus refused to sing. "At the same time," according to the newspaper account, "noisy left wing students with flags and banners entered the auditorium demanding that 'mink collars' of the 'establishment' leave the hall at once." The noisy half-hour scene was broadcast live throughout northern Germany. Finally the deputy director of the north German radio station cancelled the performance and assured the patrons that they would get their money back.

It may be said that Henze is an eclectic composer, drawing his inspiration and style from a number of sources. His roots are as much in Stravinsky as in Schoenberg, for in addition to basing his early works on the "method of composition with 12 tones related only one to another," he has always shown a preference for "natural" note relationships in the style of early Stravinsky. "Henze recognizes," one writer has said, "the hierarchy of note relationships. Fifth and fourth make up the constructive framework, third and sixth fill out the sound and thus produce the characteristic euphony, second and seventh add spice."

Henze also has shown a proclivity for various metric-rhythmic peculiarities of Stravinsky's idiom as well as his weakness for parody. His earliest actual "model" however, was Alban Berg's *Violin Concerto.* Small wonder, then, that one of Henze's earliest compositions and his first employing serial techniques was his own *Violin Concerto* of 1947.

Henze has said:

Since the premiere of *King Stag* in 1956 my 'position' has become unclear. I have been accused of treason to the cause of New Music and many seem to think that in turning away from serial methods of composition I have taken a decisive step toward the artistic abyss.

My alleged lack of 'position' stems from my unwillingness to go on using means which I have already explored. . . . I do not believe there is a single binding musical language of our time. . . . I *am* inconstant and 'positionless,' however, to the extent that when I begin work on a new piece I never have a set plan, a preconceived opinion or a theory. I do not hold such a low opinion of music as to imagine that I know more than music itself. With each new composition everything is difficult and problematic until I have found a possibility − a technique, if you like − through which I can express myself clearly. But the value of this technique ceases to exist when the work is finished. . . . Every new piece is my first. . . . [41]

SYMPHONY NO. 5

III Moto Perpetuo

Throughout the later compositions of Hans Werner Henze — theatrical works as well as the purely instrumental — there is a blending of the German and Italian influences. The Germanic love for form, for order, for logic is always in evidence. It is only on occasions that the Italian *cantabile* style — that love for a long, singing melody — breaks through. This is particularly true of his Symphony No. 5, whose pages would provide a music analyst many hours of dissection and rewarding research. Yet, for the general public it is the tuneful and memorable passages of the work that endear it to the heart.

Henze's *Symphony No. 5* was commissioned by the New York Philharmonic Orchestra in celebration of its opening season in the Lincoln Center for the Performing Arts. The work is dedicated to the conductor of that concert, Leonard Bernstein. Apropos of the structure and form of the work, Henze has said:

> For the past fifty years and more the symphony, as it was understood in the nineteenth century, has no longer existed. Between Stravinsky and Webern, all works still termed 'symphonies', appeared to be either a replica, an elegy or an echo. It is as though the musical language of today is no longer in command of the old forms, or as though the old forms no longer possess any power over the new language. Be that as it may, I have forbidden myself to take the pessimistic view all too easily engendered by that thought. . . .

> In my world the old forms strive to regain significance, even where the modern timbre of the music seldom or never allows them to appear on the surface. While it may be true that the emotional power which alone can master those forms is insufficient in modern man and that the constructive capacity and tonal material of present day music produces only illusions of the old forms, I use them, nevertheless, and in spite of such afflictions, for the representation of the things that make up my world. . . . Ancient forms appear to me as classical ideals of beauty, no longer attainable, but visible from a great distance, arousing memories like dreams. . . .

> In the *Fifth Symphony* (1962). . . the Finale (Moto Perpetuo)
> could be regarded as a Rondo, but consists, in fact, of thirty-two
> variations on the Arioso material of the second movement.[42]

Unless one were to spend hours with the study score of the
Moto Perpetuo, it would be impossible to discover all 32 variations. And, if it is difficult to locate them by reading the score, it
is next to impossible for the average or the experienced listener to
delineate them in a half-dozen listenings to the movement. Therefore, rather than dissect the music measure by measure, section by
32 sections, a broader overview — what one hears "at a glance" —
is given.

The Theme of the variations is an exact quotation of the flute
melody of the Arioso or second movement. It has been transposed
up a half-step for the Finale, and the octave in which some of its
tones appear has been changed. Because it employs nine of the 12
tones, makes awkward jumps between some of them, and divides
its initial appearance between different instruments, it suggests the
post-Webern serialism and pointillism without, in fact, being related
to it.

The Theme as initially presented in the Finale by divided
violas and cellos is as follows:

Example 1

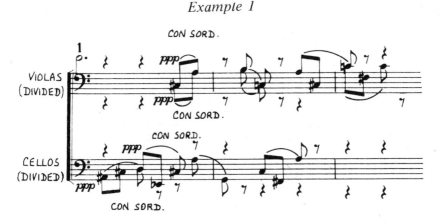

As the movement gets under way, Example 1 is heard as a
low rumbling in the divided, muted violas and cellos. Gradually
higher strings take over, some first violins playing harmonics.

A "morbid" variant of the Theme appears very softly in the timpani, accompanied by the sustained chords of the flutes and harps.

A gradual crescendo from the depths of the strings builds up to a high-pitched climax augmented by loud brass chords. It dies away again in the depths of the soft strings.

The pianos become prominent in a brief variation, followed by one for pairs of oboes and English horns. The variant of the timpani returns briefly. Next comes the Theme in a variant of fast triplets played by four flutes.

Now the trombones — to the accompaniment of two pianos — play their variant of the theme. Four trumpets take over *"con grazia,"* (with grace); the accompanying chords by violins *piano* are lost against the four trumpets. As soon as the trumpets drop out, the first violins play a sustained, legato form of the Theme accompanied by staccato figures for woodwinds and other strings.

Muted trumpets and stopped horns enter with sustained chords, each of which makes a crescendo. A variant of the Theme is buried in the lower, staccato strings. Loud trombones take over with their rhythmic variant of the Theme.

An ascending passage for the pianos leads to a new variant for the timpani, this time *fff.* A low, rhythmic figure for trombones is prominent in the accompaniment. As the passage fades away to a *pppp,* the flutes take up a little accompanying figure in half-steps. The French horn plays a soft, sustained thematic variant to this accompaniment. An oboe takes over, accompanied only by harps, alto flute and some muted strings. It is followed by the alto flute which now takes up a sustained form of the Theme.

Arpeggios for the pianos lead to the next variation in which one variant of the Theme in eighths is played by flutes and harps as an accompaniment for a sustained variant played by the oboe.

Strings enter legato; two ascending and descending arpeggios for the pianos follow. The flute, to a harp and string accompaniment, plays a variant. The violins are heard next as the upper woodwinds and lower strings become active with eighth-note figures.

A passage similar to the opening of the Moto Perpetuo follows: against a soft roll on the timpani, a rumble is heard in the low strings. It is Example 1, *con sordino* (muted). It builds to a *fortissimo* climax. There is a measure of complete silence.

A lengthy concluding passage begins with *sforzando* chords for the brass. Soon the full orchestra joins in. Rising arpeggios for trombones, then trumpets and finally timpani are heard in the complex texture. The rhythmic figures and sustained chords built up out of variants of the theme predominate to the end.

XX

KARLHEINZ STOCKHAUSEN (1928-   ) is one of the most controversial European composers of significance today. Musicians are divided in their reactions to his creations. Are they truly musical compositions or just interesting and amusing experiments or hoaxes? Was his "progress" from post-Webern pointillism to complete serialism, finally arriving at totally electronic music an honest search after a valid means of musical expression, or was it rather his search for sensationalism and notoriety, the act of a charlatan?

He has often been accused of having to explain his compositions with wordy prefaces that are many times longer than the pieces of music themselves. One writer has accused the composer of less than honesty in all this when he says: "Stockhausen [has] explained his new techniques in profusion; informed criticism exposed some of these techniques as verbal bluff." In contrast, a newspaper correspondent has written: "Stockhausen seems to have had a precise idea of his purpose in each of his works and to be able to formulate it in words. . . .What he does can be understood rationally, and defended rationally."

Stockhausen was born in Mödrath, Germany, near the Rhenish city of Cologne, on August 22, 1928. Reared in that city under the trying conditions of World War II, he entered the Cologne Conservatory of Music after the war. Following three years of routine study Stockhausen was delighted when Frank Martin, the distinguished Swiss composer, joined the faculty. For a

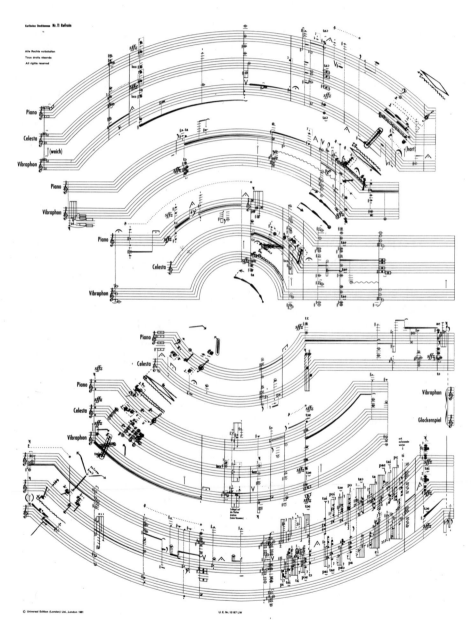

First page of *Refrain* by Stockhausen.

full year Stockhausen, under Martin's tutelage, studied the 12-tone method of composition.

After completing his studies at the Conservatory in Cologne, Stockhausen moved to Paris to take up study with French composers Darius Milhaud and Olivier Messiaen, the latter being well-known for his predeliction for the art of the Orient. In addition to his studies, Stockhausen participated with a group of instrumental and vocal musicians that met regularly to study and perform Asiatic music, principally Balinese and Tibetan. The composer has said:

> I became aware, that even in the smallest question of selection of sound material I would have to decide whether to hold myself strictly to our central-European tradition or make a music whose tradition is the music of the entire world. . . . It seems to me that I decided for the latter, without losing awareness of the high degree of richness and complexity in the Viennese school (i.e., in the music of Schoenberg, Berg and Webern). [43]

From Paris Stockhausen returned to Cologne, working at the West German Radio Studio and simultaneously studying the science of acoustics at the nearby University of Bonn, specializing for three years in work at Werner Meyer-Eppler's Institute of Phonetics and Communication-Theory within the University.

Stockhausen's first compositions were written for conventional instruments: *Crossplay* in 1951 for clarinet, piano and percussion; *Piece* in 1952 for orchestra, and later that same year a *Percussion Quartet* for piano and three timpanists. Next came the composer's interest in *alea,* * music of chance. *Chance* in music was not something completely new, for musically, everything which is not "written in the notes" is within the aleatoric sphere. A composer oriented in the music of western civilization had always to leave certain factors to the interpreter of his music. The performer had to decide just how loud the *forte* passage was to be, how fast the *Vivo* section. (Although the interpreter had to move within certain limitations: e.g., the *forte* passage *had* to be more intense than the *piano* passage, the *Vivo* faster than the *Lento* section.) In the eastern culture on the other hand, particularly in

---

* *alea,* literally "dice", hence dealing with chance or random occurrence

Hindu music, chance had always been an important factor. It had always combined a kind of structural "formant" with instantaneous improvisation.

One of Stockhausen's first efforts in aleatoric music was his *Klavierstücke XI* (Keyboard Piece No. 11) of 1958. The printed sheet of music comes in a roll contained in a cardboard carton, and the purchase price includes a flimsy wooden stand to be put on the piano. The music itself (which has an annoying way of falling down) is 37 x 21 inches and consists of 19 bits or fragments. These are to be played in any conceivable order, with any of six different speeds, dynamics and types of touch (staccato, legato, etc.), thus giving the possibility of an astronomic number of different versions, or compositions.

In reviewing the first performance of the piece at the Darmstadt International Holiday Courses for Music in 1958, the music critic Everett Helm wrote:

> David Tudor played Stockhausen's *Klavierstücke* brilliantly. He then repeated it with the bits in a different order and with different dynamics and tempos. It is an interesting experiment, and time will tell whether or not it is more than a trick.[44]

One of the gravest problems facing contemporary composers is that of notation, the attempt to use accepted symbols to convey to the performer the composer's musical intentions. When aleatoric music involves more than one performer, it becomes increasingly difficult to indicate to the musicians what is expected of them. In his *Refrain* for piano, celesta and vibraphone, Stockhausen has solved the problem by having a transparent plastic strip (see illustration) that pivots around the center. The symbols on the strip alter the musical text, depending on its position. The curved staffs have no significance other than to make feasible the use of this rotating strip. The forms of the note-heads indicate duration (more or less by size); notes beamed together (as at the lower right) must be played as quickly as possible. The syllables above and below the parts are to be spoken by the players.

In addition to experiments in alea, Stockhausen has from his earliest days at the Cologne Radio Studio experimented with electronic means of music construction. "Among the sound-sources in the Cologne Studio were electronic music-instruments — a melocoard and a trautonium — which served in some experiments as sound-sources, but which were soon discarded when the idea of sound-synthesis asserted itself."

Sound-synthesis is the creation of a musical tone from scratch by purely electronic means. Its opposite function, sound-analysis, had been known by scientists for years. Sound technicians in a laboratory had been able to take a musical tone* (any pitch played by an instrument) and break it down, analyzing it so that its *fundamental* and numerous *overtones* — the individual "pure" components — could be noted. Stockhausen's idea was to reverse the process. In other words, instead of analyzing or breaking a musical tone down into its pure components, he would put the pure components together to create or synthesize a musical tone. The discovery of the sine-wave generator — the main source of "pure" tone — made all this possible. Thus was born *electronic music.*

Herbert Eimert, the director of the Cologne Radio Studio where Stockhausen had done his early work has said:

> Electronic music is, and remains, part of our music and is a great deal more than mere 'technology.' But the fact that it cannot be made to take over or imitate the functions of traditional music is clearly shown by the unequivocal difference of its material from that of traditional music. . . .
>
> Electronic music is based on the composition of electrically generated sounds made audible by a generator, i.e. recorded on tape without recourse to any instrument or microphone. Electronic music exists only on tape (or on record) and can only be realized in sound by means of a loudspeaker system. . . .
>
> The composer's equipment consists of a sound generator, a loudspeaker, tape recorder and filter; all this apparatus is to be found in any well equipped radio station. . . . The composer determines each note by its pitch, duration and intensity. Only he no longer has only 70-80 pitch levels at his disposal (this is the average number utilized in instrumental music; Bach's *Well-*

---

* A *natural* musical tone (as opposed to one created electrically) consists of a *fundamental* — that pitch which we perceive — and a series of *overtones* (higher and softer pitches than the fundamental) indistinguishable by the human ear as separate pitches. It is these overtones, though — along with attack and release — which give a musical tone its quality or timbre and helps one distinguish a middle C played by a trumpet from a middle C played by a clarinet.

Tempered Clavier utilizes 50-55 different pitches), only 6 or 7 intensities from *pp* to *ff* and only half-notes, quarters, eighths, dotted and syncopated values. He now has at his disposal the entire range of frequencies from 50-15,000 c.p.s., 40 or more precisely calculated dynamic levels and an infinite number of durational values, measured in centimeters on tape. None of this material can be adequately notated by traditional means. . . .

The multiplicity of forms of electronic elements far exceeds the possibilities of graphic notation. It is thus necessary to notate differentiations, which are unknown to traditional music, in a way which corresponds to acoustical phenomena. This cannot be effected by an extension of traditional notation; it is better to present the sound procedures of electronic music graphically in the form of an 'acoustical' diagram. [See the sample page from Stockhausen's *Study II.*] Thus 'scores' of electronic compositions resemble precise acoustical diagrams with their coordinates, frequency (cycles per second), intensity level (measured in decibels) and time (cm.p.s.). The composer is required to have a certain amount of acoustical knowledge. [45]

One of Stockhausen's first major works in this medium, now considered *the* classic of electronic music, was *Gesang der Jünglinge* (Song of the Youths), first performed in 1956. For his text Stockhausen selected part of the canticle *Benedicite, omnia opera Domini;* it was sung and spoken on tape by a 12-year old boy using his normal voice. Then the tape was manipulated. All phonetic properties of the text, all the timbral components that together constitute speech, were analyzed, isolated, classified, and then "serialized." Other aspects were also organized serially, such as varying degrees of intelligibility of the words, the range of modes of rendition from speech to singing, the apparent distance of the sounds (near of far, echo effect, etc.) as well as their horizontal position (right and left), and all dynamics, speeds, pitch levels, etc. In addition, the taped voice was superimposed upon itself to form ensemble effects, crowd murmurs and shouts, canonic structures (spoken and/or sung) and speech-clusters. All other sounds − those that did not originate in the boy's throat − were produced electrically. Many of these have deliberately contrasting "inhuman" tones.

The work was designed for five loudspeakers surrounding the audience. "I attempted," says the composer, "to form the direction and movement of sound in space, and to make them accessible as a new dimension for musical experience. The five loudspeakers should be placed around the listeners in the hall. From which side, by how many loudspeakers at once, whether with rotation to left or right, whether motionless or moving — *how* the sounds and sound groups should be projected into space; all this is decisive for the comprehension of the work."

Stockhausen's next composition was *Kontakte,* the first work in which the composer combined instrumental and electronic music. It is scored for electric sounds, piano and percussion. In performance, a four-track tape of electronic music is played back over loudspeakers while two instrumentalists are performing. The tape continues through the work, from start to finish. "My original plan," the composer relates, "was to let the musicians react to the electronic music in a way that would vary from one performance to another."

In the summer of 1964, Stockhausen composed two works. The first piece was called *Mixtur,* a composition for orchestra and ring-modulators.* "During the performance of it the sounds from five instrumental groups, together comprising a normal orchestra, are picked up — each one independently — by microphones; the microphones are connected with ring-modulators, in which the sound is modulated in timbre, rhythm, dynamic level and pitch by means of sine-wave generators, which are operated by musicians according to indications in the score; the result is played back over five loudspeaker groups, simultaneously with the original orchestral sound."

The other composition of that summer of 1964 was *Mikrophonie I* which is discussed in detail in the next section. This was followed by *Mikrophonie II* for choir, Hammond organ and ring modulators. In it the composer "attempted a synthesis of vocal and electronic music." To accomplish this, a transformation of the vocal sounds was made by means of electronic equipment *during* the performance in contrast to the procedure used earlier in *Gesang der Jünglinge* in which the transformation was made on tape *before* the concert.

---

* *Ring modulators* are analog multiplier circuits used to combine signals in such a manner that the output consists of sums and differences of all the input frequency components.

Stockhausen has been criticized many times for perpetrating a gap between the *avant-garde* music he creates and the general, concert-going public. "The new music is not for a clique! " he retorts. "Many more people should be able to respond to it. But they must understand that there is no difference between music for study and music for enjoyment. We are not writing mere entertainment. Those who wish to learn about this music must study constantly, must listen to every disc they can get. The distance between contemporary music and the public is a sign of this society's decadence."

MIKROPHONIE I

Karlheinz Stockhausen's *Mikrophonie I* * for tam-tam (large Chinese gong), two microphones, two filters and potentiometers** received its premiere performance in Brussels on December 9, 1964. The steps which led up to its creation as well as its structure are best described by the composer himself. Stockhausen says:

> Several years ago I bought a large tam-tam for my composition *Momente* and had set up this instrument in my garden. During the summer of 1964, I undertook an experiment in which the tam-tam was excited with various objects that I found around the house — objects of glass, cardboard, metal, wood, rubber, synthetics. At the same time, I held and moved with my hand a directional microphone that was connected first to an electronic filter with a potentiometer for volume control, and then to an amplifier and loudspeaker. In so doing, I used the microphone to listen to the tam-tam the way a doctor examines a patient with a stethoscope. Meanwhile, a technician, who was sitting in the living room, freely altered the adjustment of the filter and potentiometer. The result was recorded on tape. The tape recording of this experiment represents a discovery of greatest importance to me.
>
> It was on the basis of this experiment that *Mikrophonie I* was

---

* pronounced mi-kráw-fun-nie

** Potentiometers are devices used for the precise measurement of voltages by comparison of an unknown voltage with a reference voltage. They serve the purpose of volume control on audio equipment. The expression potentiometer is frequently abbreviated "pot."

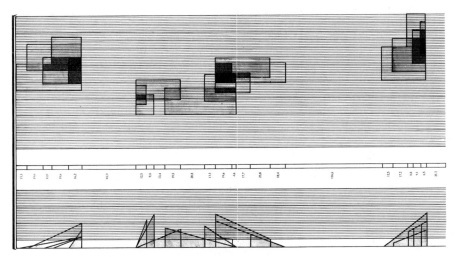

A page from *Studie II* by Stockhausen.

composed. With various materials, two players excite the tam-tam; two other players pick up the vibrations with directional microphones. Distance between the microphone and tam-tam (which influences the dynamics and timbre), relative distance between the microphone and the point of excitation on the tam-tam (influencing pitch, timbre, and above all determining the spatial impression of the sound, ranging between distant, echoing and extremely close), and rhythm of microphone movement are prescribed in an appropriate notation. Each of two or more players activates an electronic filter and potentiometer. They again shape the timbre and pitch (through a combination of filter adjustment and volume control) and the rhythm of the structures (through metrically notated alteration of both instrument settings).

In this way, three independent, interacting, yet, at the same time, autonomous sound structuring processes are bound together. These were then composed to function synchronously or independently, homophonically or as polyphony of up to six parts.

The score consists of 33 independent musical structures which may be combined for a given performance by means of a prescribed 'connection scheme.' This scheme determines the relationships between the structures. There are two groups of players; three musicians (one tam-tam player, one microphonist and one filter and potentiometer player) form a group, and at a given time play one of the thirty-three structures. At a particular point, they give the cue for the second group to begin with the next structure. After a specific interval of time, the second group returns the cue for the first group to begin with the next structure, and so forth. The relationships between structures are determined in three ways: (1) with respect to a given structure, the ensuing one is either similar, different, on contrary; (2) this relationship either remains constant, increases, or decreases; (3) the ensuing structure (which usually begins before the end of the given structure) either supports, is neutral to, or destroys that structure.

Thus, the "connection scheme" determines three relationships for every connection between two structures. For example, a structure may be followed by one that is *similar* to it, *and* whose relationship remains *constant, and* that *supports* it; or a structure may be followed by one that is *contrary* to it *and increasingly destroys* it; or by one that is *different* and becomes *decreasingly neutral,* etc. According to these criteria, the musicians choose the order of the structures, which are themselves composed in respect to these same characteristics. Although the relationships (between structures) composed into the "connection scheme" remain fixed for all versions (in order to guarantee a strong and directional form), the *order* or structures may vary considerably from version to version. [46]

FOOTNOTES

1. Myers, Rollo H. *Erik Satie* (New York, 1968).
2. Stevens, Halsey. *The Life and Music of Béla Bartók* (New York, 1964).
3. Stravinsky, Igor, and Robert Craft. *Dialogues and A Diary* (New York, 1963).
4. Stravinsky, Igor. *An Autobiography* (New York, 1962).
5. Stravinsky, Igor, and Robert Craft. *Op. cit.*
6. Krenek, Ernst. "Anton Webern: A Profile" in *Anton Webern; Perspectives* (compiled by Hans Moldenhauer, ed. by Damar Irvine) (Seattle, 1966).
7. Webern, Anton. *The Path to the New Music* (Ed. by Willi Reich, Eng. trans. by Leo Black) (Bryn Mawr, Pa., 1963).
8. *Ibid.*
9. Stravinsky, Igor. *Die Reihe* (ed. by Herbert Eimert and Karlheinz Stockhausen) Vol. 2 "Anton Webern."
10. Willi Reich quoted in *Orchestral Music: An Armchair Guide* by Lawrence Gilman (New York, 1951).
11. Milhaud, Darius. *Notes Without Music,* (English trans. by Donald Evans) (London, 1952). All quotations of Milhaud in this sketch are from this autobiography.
12. Copland, Aaron. *The New Music: 1900-1960* (New York, 1968).
13. program notes by Paul Hindemith quoted in *Music Through the Centuries* by Nick Rossi and Sadie Rafferty (Boston, 1963).
14. Copland, Aaron. "Composer from Mexico: Carlos Chávez" *New Republic* May 2, 1928, revised in *The New Music: 1900-1960* (New York, 1968).
15. Cowell, Henry. "Chávez" in *The Book of Modern Composers* (Ed. by D. Ewen) (New York, 1950).
16. program notes by Carlos Chavez reprinted on cover for Columbia recording MS 6447.
17. Shostakovich, Dmitri. "A Contemplation of the Road Traveled" in *Sovetskaya Muzyka* (No. 9, 1956).
18. Lenin, Vladimir Ilyich. *O Kulture i Iskusstve* ("About Culture and Art") (Moscow, 1957).
19. Shostakovich, Dmitri. "Music and the Times" *Music Journal* (XXIII/1; Jan. 1965).
20. Holst, Imogen. *Britten* (New York, 1965).
21. Britten, Benjamin. "On Winning the First Aspen Award" *Saturday Review* (Aug. 22, 1964).
22. *Ibid.*
23. Davies, Howell (ed.). *The South American Handbook* (London, 1956).
24. Chase, Gilbert. "Alberto Ginastera: Argentine Composer" *Musical Quarterly* (XLIII/4; Oct. 1957).
25. Margrave, Wendell. "Current Chronicle" in *Musical Quarterly* (LI/2; Apr. 1965).
26. program notes for the recording of *Pampeana No. 3* by the Louisville Symphony Orchestra.
27. Worner, Karl H. "Current Chronicle" (trans. W. Wager) *Musical Quarterly* (XLVI/2; Apr. 1960).
28. Boulez, Pierre. "Eventually" *Revue musicale* (1952) quoted in *Notes of an Apprenticeship* (trans. H. Weinstock) (New York, 1968).
29. Boulez, Pierre. "Alea" *Nouvelle Revue francaise* (No. 59; Nov. 1, 1957).
30. Berio, Luciano. "The Composer on His Work" *The Christian Science Monitor* (60/195; July 15, 1968).

31. letter to Massimo Mila.
32. Brindle, Reginald Smith. "Current Chronicle" *The Musical Quarterly* ·(XLIV/1; January, 1958).
33. Berio, Luciano. *Poesia e Musica: un' esperienza* (Milan, 1958).
34. Berio, Luciano. "Program Notes" for TMK(s) Vox Productions, record TV 34046S.
35. *Ibid.*
36. Berio, Luciano. *Program Notes* (New York, n.d.).
37. Berio, Luciano. "Sinfonia" *Notes On The Program.* (New York, 1968).
38. Beckett, Samuel. *The Unnamable* (trans. by the author) (New York, 1965).
39. letter to Nick Rossi
40. *Ibid*
41. Henze, Hans Werner. "The Composer on His Work" *The Christian Science Monitor* (60/188, July 8, 1968).
42. Henze, Hans Werner. From a lecture given at the Technical University, Berlin, on January 28, 1963, reprinted in *Henze: 5 Symphonien* (Hamburg, 1966).
43. Stockhausen, Karlheinz. *Donaueschinger Musiktage* (trans. by Joshua Rifkin) October, 1965.
44. Helm, Everett. "Current Chronicle" *The Musical Quarterly* (XLV/1; Jan. 1959).
45. Eimert, Herbert. "What is Electronic Music?" (trans. by Hans G. Helms) *die Reihe* (No. 1, 1955).
46. Stockhausen, Karlheinz. *Music of Our Time,* (New York, 1966).

MUSIC OF THE UNITED STATES

Front cover of Victor catalogue issued in March of 1917, advertising the world's first jazz phonograph record. The advertisement shows Nick LaRocca's all-white band with Billy Jones on piano, Larry Shields on clarinet, LaRocca on trumpet, Emile Christian on trombone and Tony Sbarbaro on drums.

PART II

MUSIC OF THE UNITED STATES

Although the United States is geographically separated from Europe by a vast expanse of water, it has never been able, in music, to separate itself very far from cultural and artistic developments of the old world. Art in the United States has pretty much followed patterns and periods established on the continent.

The first composer to write music on this side of the Atlantic was Conrad Biessel (1690-1768), an immigrant German mystic. Having settled in Germantown, Pennsylvania, he composed over 1,000 hymns. The first native-born composer was Francis Hopkinson (1737-1791) who served as a Judge of the Admiralty for Pennsylvania and later signed the Declaration of Independence. In music he was only an amateur, but he had talent and composed a quantity of songs and keyboard works.

The first composer in this country of unique talent was William Billings (1746-1800), a tanner by trade and self-taught in music. Deeply religious, he published six different books of *Anthems, Fuges and Chorusses in several Parts* (to use his quaint spelling), hundreds of tunes which were naive but fresh, full of vitality and gusto for use in church. He believed that such singing should be a pleasure, not a chore. The tunes he wrote are forceful and moving, and have great appeal even today.

Following the Revolutionary War, professional musicians started coming to the United States from Europe, some as immigrants, others only to visit while on professional tours. The oldest musical organization in this country was the St. Cecilia Society founded in Charleston in 1762 with private subscription concerts. The trend then swung northward as New York, Boston and Philadelphia formed musical organizations of their own.

Lowell Mason (1792-1872) proved to be a major figure in the music of the United States in the 19th century. In addition to composing many hymn tunes, he was responsible for introducing music into the curriculum of the public schools in 1836. The most gifted musician of 19th-century America was Stephen Foster

(1826-1864), some of whose melodies have never been surpassed in beauty and originality in this hemisphere, and can find their equal only in the songs of Schubert elsewhere in the world.

Born in New Orleans and educated in Europe, Louis Moreau Gottschalk (1829-1869) was a fine concert pianist in the flamboyant style of Franz Liszt. He was also a composer. Because of his international concert tours as a keyboard artist, he was able to introduce European audiences to some of his own compositions, the first works most had ever heard by a composer from the United States. Gottschalk's pieces were based on his own Creole background and his experiences with the tunes and rhythms of the Caribbean.

Except for rare talents like Billings and Foster, the most significant music of the United States during the 18th and 19th centuries came not from individuals — largely European educated — but from various sub-cultures or societies. In 1741 a Moravian Colony was established in Bethlehem, Pennsylvania; shortly thereafter a number of composers developed, creating music for their religious services, compositions that are only now being "rediscovered" and subsequently republished in new editions.

Music was one of the featured components of camp meetings sponsored by traveling revivalists. The "revivalist songs" were in a more popular idiom than the older, staid hymns of the church. A religious group known as the *Shakers* was founded near Mt. Lebanon, New York shortly after the Revolutionary War. The beauty of their indigenous, simple tunes led to the re-publication in 1940 of many of these tunes in a collection called, *The Gift to Be Simple.* The title song of the book was used by Aaron Copland in his ballet *Appalachian Spring.*

Negro spirituals rose into prominence after the Civil War. The black people had brought with them from Africa a tradition of singing and a love of music. Toiling long hours on the plantations of the South, their only diversion from work was singing. One of the first spirituals to be published was *Roll, Jordan, Roll* in 1862. It proved to be a great favorite in the North as did *Blow Your Trumpet, Gabriel.*

Late in the 19th century, native born composers finally started to establish for themselves a place — even if temporary — in the symphonic literature of the United States. The pattern was almost always the same: a basic music education was obtained in the United States, followed by graduate work in composition at one or more of the European music centers. John Knowles Paine (1839-1906) was one of the earliest and established the "Boston" or "New England" group of composers which included George W. Chadwick (1854-1931) and Horatio Parker (1863-1919). Occasionally a work by one of these men is revived in deference to "American history and tradition" in the arts, but while a few of their compositions are of interest, the works are in spirit, second-class European pieces.

Edward MacDowell (1861-1908) was the first American composer to gain fame and a reputation in Europe as well as in the United States. His late 19th-century German Romantic training, however, permeated all his compositions. Even though he might call a work his *Indian Suite,* except for the timbre of the tom-tom or American Indian drum in it, the composition would make much more sense to a German musician than to a native American Indian. (Just when all of MacDowell's music seemed to have sunk slowly into oblivion, a *Concerto* of his was revived for the Inauguration Concert of President Nixon in 1969.)

As the 20th century dawned, the United States seemed to be ready for full participation in the mainstream of music. Its period of training and apprenticeship was behind it. The future looked bright.

I

JAZZ is a unique phenomenon of the United States. Nothing like it has ever evolved elsewhere. No other music of the United States has so swept the world and been the symbol of a nation and its culture.

Jazz is new. Jazz is music of the 20th century. Jazz is music of the United States. Jazz is the enslaved and harried black man's contribution to the life, pleasure and culture of his forcefully adopted homeland.

One noted authority has claimed that if the Renaissance era was dominated in music by the Netherlands, the Baroque era by Italy, the Classic by Austria-Bohemia and the Romantic by Germany, "we can find persuasive evidence that we are now in the midst of what the future musical historians may well designate the Afro-American Epoch."

To find the origins of jazz we must look back into the forced migration of great numbers of west Africans to various parts of the Americas. These people brought with them the heritage of a highly developed and important folk music. In Africa they had known a wide variety of instruments, and there had been "professional musicians" in many of the tribes. They had music for a wide assortment of activities, including entertainment. For example, the Bahutu of Ruanda had at least 24 different types of social songs, including, according to one authority,

> those played by professional musicians for entertainment, songs for beer drinking, war homage to a chief, hunting, harvesting, and general work; songs sung at the birth of a child or to admonish erring members of the society, to recount a successful elephant hunt, to deride Europeans; songs of death, vulgar songs, and others.[1]

Once in the United States, these black slaves were affected by the music of their white masters. From them they learned some songs; others they learned from missionaries or from neighbors in the cities. Some of these songs

> were sung in styles indistinguishable from those of the whites, but on most of them the Negroes imposed some stylistic traits from Africa. They presumably also continued to sing African songs and to compose new songs in the African styles, but this was problematic because the slaves did not have a common language and tribal groups were purposely broken up by the slave traders.[2]

Perhaps the most important element of their heritage from Africa was the sense of rhythm; they frequently used percussion instruments in a rhythmic accompaniment. A second influence was the call and response pattern of many of the African songs, with a leader asking a question in the song while the chorus replied. The Africans loved instruments, and this probably led the early slaves to devise inexpensive instruments of their own: the washtub or gutbucket, washboards used as scrapers and placed on baskets for resonance; frying pans, cowbells, bottles, wood or bone clappers. They also quickly adopted and adapted a variety of European-devised instruments, including the harmonica, fiddles and brass instruments.

In adopting instruments from the middle-European culture, the blacks, of necessity, had also to adopt the major scale around which these instruments were designed. In changing from the five-tone pentatonic scale, the blacks encountered difficulties of pitch with the two new scale tones, the third and the seventh. In all of their subsequent music — blues or jazz — one of the chief melodic characteristics came to be the somewhat lowered pitch of the third and seventh of the scale.

The blues may be related to spirituals. The so-called *field blues* were simply short calls and wails, repeated by field hands communicating with each other in the cotton fields. As in Africa, so in the United States individual song makers came forth to create original songs out of a style already in existence. Perhaps the first great "blues composer" was Lead Belly — whose real name was Huddie Ledbetter (1888-1949) — a Texas convict. The typical form of his song, also adopted by the early jazz bands that played the blues, was three part: the third part was the one of contrast. This form can be observed in the *St. Louis Blues*.

In addition to the flattened or slightly lowered third and seventh degrees of the scale in the blues, it is also typical that the main melody have short phrases, separated by long pauses, long enough for an answering countermelody (as in the call-and-answer patterns of the tribal ceremonies of West Africa).

Because original jazz, like folk song, was an aural tradition, it was difficult to trace its history and evolution until the phonograph had been perfected to the point where it could faithfully record this aural art. Concerning the birth of jazz, Gunther Schuller has said in his excellent book, *Early Jazz: Its Roots and Development:*

> It is impossible to establish the exact beginnings of jazz as a distinct, self-contained music. Some historians use the year 1895 as a working date; others prefer 1917, the year that the word *jazz* seems to have become current and the year that the Original Dixieland Jazz Band made what are generally considered the first jazz recordings; still others prefer dates in between. But whatever

Jelly Roll Morton's *Red Hot Peppers* during a recording session in Chicago early in the 1920's for the Victor label. Andrew Hilaire on drums, Kid Ory on trombone, George Mitchell on trumpet, Johnny Lindsay on bass, Morton on piano, Johnny St. Cyr on banjo and Omer Simeon on clarinet.

"King" Oliver's *Creole Jazz Band* in 1923 with Honore Dutrey on trombone, Baby Dodds on drums, Louis Armstrong on cornet, Joe Oliver "clowning" with a "slide trumpet," Lil Armstrong on piano, Bill Johnson on banjo and Johnny Dodds on clarinet.

date is picked, it is safe to say that in purely musical terms the earliest jazz represents a primitive reduction of the complexity, richness and perfection of its African and, for that matter, European antecedents.[3]

One of the first of the jazz musicians was named Ferdinand Morton (1885-1942). His composition, *Jelly Roll Blues,* was so popular and famous that he came to be known more by the appellation Mr. Jelly Roll than Mr. Morton. In any event, he claimed that he invented jazz in New Orleans in 1902. This boast is denied by all other participants in the development, but it could just as easily have been true because of his background and the great artistic contributions he *is known* to have made to jazz. He represented the strange mixture of cultures, societies and castes that merged to form jazz. Morton was a proud descendant of French-speaking Creoles, in close contact with the white masters and professional men of Southern society, with French opera and Spanish dance music. As a musician, he worked with many darker, illiterate blacks, who brought into the cities a crude but lively and distinctive heritage from the plantations, with remnants of their varied heritages from West Africa.

During this early period, from the turn of the century until the first phonograph recordings of jazz were made, it is difficult to surmise what the music really sounded like. As Schuller said:

Even if we could find isolated examples of great enduring jazz in this formative period, we would still have to admit that early jazz represents, speaking strictly musically, a relatively low point in the Negroes' musical history. Indeed, how could it have been otherwise? Circumstances such as segregation and extreme race prejudice forced the music to be what it was. That it was as much as it was, and that it had enough strength to survive and eventually grow into a world music, is abundant proof of its potential strength and beauty.[4]

The names associated with these early years — the period of the "original" New Orleans style jazz — include, in addition to Morton: Buddy Bolden, Bunk Johnson and Emanuel Perez. These bands of black musicians worked in the Storeyville or "forbidden quarter" of New Orleans; they played in the roughest places in town: cabarets brothels and gambling houses. Under the conditions in which they worked, no white man could or would have survived. The pay was next to nothing and personally they were treated as scum. But it was a form of living. Here jazz developed.

The sheer sound of a jazz band — its peculiar timbre — was probably a more important characteristic than its rhythmic syncopation or cross-rhythms, more novel than its harmony or primitive and informal counterpoint. Ordinarily these bands consisted of trumpet and/or cornet, trombone and clarinet, all supported by the "rhythm section" — a piano, plucked bass viol, banjo and various drums and cymbals.

When the United States entered World War I in 1917, the Navy ordered Storeyville closed. The municipal government of New Orleans was forced to revoke the licenses of gambling halls and brothels alike. That left many jazz bands out of work. A few of the black musicians migrated northward, but the great color barrier that existed forced most of them to stay in their own area and seek other kinds of employment. Morton, for one, traveled north, but could never establish himself in a regular musical career. He earned more as a pool player than as a musician!

Actually in the 1920's it was largely the white musicians who made money and fame in the field of jazz, all on what they had learned from the black founders of jazz. The first recording of jazz — *Dixie Jass Band One-Step* — was recorded on the old Victrola label in 1917 (the same year Storeyville closed) by the Original Dixieland Jazz Band, a group of young white musicians from New Orleans led by Dominic James La Rocca (1889-   ).

As jazz bands arrived in New York, groups such as the Original Dixieland Jazz Band and Morton's Red' Hot Peppers started to make changes in their structure. Three saxophones were now included in jazz groups. Playing chords in close position, their sound formed a sustained background against which the trumpet, trombone or clarinet solos could be set off.

On November 12, 1925, the Okeh Company recorded in its Chicago studios a little five-piece ensemble of black musicians for the first time: Louis Armstrong's *Hot Five,* a group that eventually made a great number of recordings. Armstrong (1900-   ) thereby linked his earlier jazz experience playing in "King" Oliver's band in New Orleans during the late 1910's to the Chicago jazz style of the mid-1920's. His long and successful career was eventually to form links with the New York jazz of the 1930's, followed by the international jazz world of the 1950's.

Among the Hot Five was a pianist named Lillian Hardin who was not only Armstrong's wife, but a composer for the ensemble. An analysis of one of her compositions recorded by this original group of 1925 — *Hotter than That* — suggests such characteristics of jazz at that time as unique syncopation and phrasing, sweeping progressions of melody and unexpected accents:

> An introduction, played by the whole ensemble with trumpet as principal voice, consists of the last eight measures of the 32-measure tune. It leads immediately to the first "chorus," in which the trumpet is accompanied only by chords of the piano and guitar. Here Armstrong presents, as the basis for variations, a version of his wife's melody already loaded with as much syncopation as Morton or Oliver would have used for a climax after three or four choruses. Then Armstrong rests, giving the second chorus to Johnny Dodds, clarinet. Dodds's melody is conceived as a counterpoint to the basic tune, full of broken chords; it makes sense over the chordal accompaniment, in the absence of the tune, but its meaning is best appreciated by listeners who can imagine the tune in the background. For the third chorus Armstrong sings nonsense syllables, again varying the basic melody. Then in a static interlude of eight measures, he sings fragments, answered antiphonally by John St. Cyr, guitar. Then the trombone, "Kid" Ory, begins a solo, but halfway through this chorus the whole group joins, with trumpet dominating in an astonishing simplification of the main melody on straining high notes. A coda, for guitar, makes a beautiful surprise ending on a diminished seventh chord. The total form of this performance, like the "hot" rhythm, uses symmetrical convention as a foil for novel adventures. Yet the climax is the moment closest to tradition, when the whole ensemble joins in counterpoint.[5]

If Louis Armstrong was responsible for the expansion of the role of the soloist in jazz, then Duke Ellington (1899-   ) was equally responsible for the development of the ensemble. Together, these two trends led away from the more folk-like qualities of early jazz. While Armstrong featured high notes, tricky figures, involved syncopations and motivic developments, Ellington was known for music characterized by rich chords, chromatic progressions, varied, lush and frequently contrasting sounds. However, neither style ignored the other. Armstrong in his solos never departed altogether from the jazz ensemble, and Ellington, in his

JELLY ROLL MORTON   LOUIS ARMSTRONG

ensemble work, never failed to leave room for the spontaneous
solos contributed by individual players.

A song by Ellington, *It Don't Mean A Thing If You Don't
Have That Swing,* provided the name for the jazz style of the
1930's — "swing" — just as Armstrong's favorite epithet — "hot"
— was used to distinguish the style he represented in the 1920's. In
swing there is a relaxation of the hot jazz rhythm, a conscious
move away from loud dynamics, high pitched tunes, much vibrato,
blue notes and rhythmic drive. The bands grew in size, now usually
numbering between 10 and 29 players. They generally included
three to six saxophones, clarinets (sometimes these were "doubled"
or played by the sax men), three or more trumpets, three or more
trombones, and a rhythm section which included a piano, plucked
bass viol, assorted drums and perhaps guitar, banjo or vibraphone.

Duke Ellington (Edward K. Ellington) has been one of the
central figures in the development. of jazz. Asked how he went
about composing music for his band, he answered quite simply, "I
just write something one night and we play it the next." He
humbly adds with a smile on his face, "There have been a lot of
nights. Over four decades of them." Ellington has told his story:

The first thing I ever wrote was *Soda Fountain Rag.* I was fourteen. I worked as a soda jerk in Washington. That was my home. I also had a job as a piano player. I worked for 75 cents a night. I got other jobs — with bands. Then I organized my own band.

I studied some. But I could hear people whistling and got all the Negro music that way. You can't learn that in any school.

I was going to be a painter. I won a scholarship in Fine Arts at Pratt. I planned to go there — after one more year. But I got mixed up in this music. And I was doing all right. At 18 I had bought a car and a house. . . .

I have always had a band to play what I wrote. I could always hear it. It would be terrible not to hear what you've written. . . .

I have no idea how many things I've written. Thousands I guess. A lot of them have been "head" things, things we've done at rehearsal, or on a job, or in a recording studio. Someone thinks of a phrase, a lick, a theme, we work it around, change it, develop it. Pretty soon we have a new tune and a new arrangement. That's why you sometimes see names of various members of the band listed as composer with mine. Of course the name was mainly Billy Strayhorn for a long time. He was with me 28 years — till his passing in May, 1968. He and I had such communication.[6]

The *swing* style of the 1930's was followed in the 1940's by another off-shoot of jazz. It all started at Minton's Playhouse, a night club in Harlem. Several young black musicians who were tired of "swing music" used to get together. As one writer has said:

It was becoming urgent to get a little air in a richly decked-out palace that was soon going to be a prison. That was the aim of trumpeter Dizzy Gillespie, pianist Thelonious Monk, guitarist Charlie Christian (who died before the group's efforts bore fruit), drummer Kenny Clarke, and saxophonist Charlie Parker. Except for Christian, they were poor, unknown and unprepossessing; but Monk stimulated his partners by the boldness of his harmonies, Clarke created a new style of drum playing, and Gillespie and Parker took choruses that seemed crazy to the people who came to listen to them. The bebop style was in the process of being born.[7]

This lively group that used to gather at Minton's for jam sessions had gotten into the habit of referring to the arrangements they developed by simple onomatopoetic titles that imitated the initial rhythmic figure of each, such as *be-bop, re-bop,* and *oo-bop-shbam.* Later, these nicknames for a new kind of jazz caught on and it became standard practise to call the music of the 1940's *bebop,* or simply *bop.*

There was one group of jazz musicians, though, that did not go along with Parker and the bop style. The lead was set by a young saxophonist, Lester Young. In contrast to the "hot" jazz style of the decade from 1925 to 1935, Young's new style came to be known as *cool.* Among its adherents are both black and white musicians: Miles Davis, J.J. Johnson, Stan Getz and a number of others. The cool style, in a general way, represents a striving toward a certain conception of musical purity. As Hodier analyzes it,

> this effort, which implies a rejection of the hot way of playing and its most typical procedures, finds it justification in the new element it contributed, a kind of modesty in musical expression that was not to be found in jazz before. Even when the performer seems to be letting himself go most completely (and cool musicians. . .cultivate relaxation), a sort of reserve, by which we do not mean constraint, marks his creative flight, channeling it within certain limits that constitute its charm. It may be said that cool musicians have brought a new feeling to jazz. With them, jazz becomes an intimate art.[8]

During the early 1950's another off-shoot started to gain attention, probably best characterized by the title *progressive jazz.* It brought the movement full circle. Originally jazz had become known in Paris around the 1920's by way of imported phonograph records. Europeans, especially composers, were fascinated by what they heard. Debussy, Stravinsky, Ravel and Milhaud all made use of jazz characteristics in their own compositions. By World War II Debussy and Ravel were dead and Stravinsky and Milhaud were in California. One of Milhaud's pupils in composition at Mills College was a young white jazz musician, Dave Brubeck. The young student got the idea of imposing some of the techniques of so-called "classical" music onto jazz, a sort of "harmonic liberation" for the popular style. Among a large following, the Dave Brubeck Quartet became famous and remained popular until he disbanded the Quartet in 1967.

A similar idea of mixing the classic techniques with the popular — only this time on a large scale — was reflected in the work of another west coast artist, Stan Kenton. He called this "liberated" harmonic style *progressive jazz*, and developed a large almost symphonic band to play it.

By the 1950's the pendulum started to swing in the opposite direction. The movement was back to the simpler, more common triadic harmonies, which was reflected in a plain, unembellished melodic line backed by an elemental, primitive and powerful "beat." It was *rock 'n' roll*, rooted, according to Austin, "in blues and Negro church music." Elvis Presley was one of the first to exploit this style commercially. Even though rock 'n' roll seemed to be much more a development of white musicians, Henry Pleasants claims that "a sharp ear for musical style will find traces of African influence. . . in the explicit beat of seminal rock-and-roller Elvis Presley."

In the 1960's rock 'n' roll was followed by an import from England, the sound and the style of The Beatles. Their arrival, says Ned Rorem, "has proved one of the most healthy events in music

Duke Ellington listens as the President of the United States plays *Happy Birthday* on the piano in the East Room of the White House.

since 1950." He then goes on to elaborate what he means. "By healthy I mean alive and inspired – two adjectives long out of use. By music I include not only the general area of jazz, but those expressions subsumed in the categories of chamber, opera, symphonic: in short, all music."

The Beatles have not really added anything new, but "simply brought back excitement" in the music. Except for their talent, the excitement originates in their "absolutely insolent – hence innocent – unification of music's disparate components – that is, in using the most conservative devices of harmony, counterpoint, rhythm, melody, orchestration, and making them blend with a contagious freshness."

As the Beatles became more popular, hundreds of similar groups sprang up, not only in the United States, but all across the face of Europe. Some were original and have survived, others were crass commercial imitations and have fallen by the wayside. Bit by bit the phenomena of electronic music entered into the psychedelic sound and light shows such "mod" groups developed. Even "serious" composers started experimenting with mixed media. Morton Subotnick, Director of Electronic Music at The Electric Music Circus in New York and a faculty member of New York University, states that "the need to create something to be performed spontaneously and witnessed 'live' in contrast to phonograph recordings of electronic music has led me to experiment in the development of a new presentational institution – mixed media."

The pros and cons of "popular" music (referring to jazz and its derivatives) as compared or opposed to "serious" or "classical" music (referring to music composed for the traditional forces: symphony orchestras, chamber ensemble, opera stages, etc.) has been a lively issue since 1950. The distance between "classical" and "popular" music has varied over the centuries, but today the borderline is less distinct than ever before, due to the interpenetration of ideas and techniques such as the electronic materials now so readily available to all. There are many more styles being developed in both categories, from the most simplistic to the most complex, and some common interests are to be found: Berio admires the Beatles, and vice versa, while The Mothers of Invention quote Varèse.

"As for popular music versus serious music," boldly states composer Mischa Portnoff, "a significant development in our culture in the past quarter of a century has been the breakdown of the false boundary separating them."

The signs of the times do not seem to indicate, however, that "popular" and "classical" will join forces to provide us with only one stream of music. David Hamilton puts it well when he says:

> The future of music hardly seems to lie in the grand amalgamation of everything into one universal style now advocated in certain quarters, but rather in the encouragement of valid tendencies at all levels. Whatever the history of the arts has taught us (and we may well wonder, looking around us), it suggests that immediate success is no necessary criterion of enduring quality.[9]

II

CHARLES IVES (1874-1954) was both one of the most unusual and one of the greatest of the American composers. Leonard Bernstein refers to him as "Our first really great composer . . . our Washington, Lincoln and Jefferson of Music." Henry Cowell has said that "Ives can, in fact, be shown to be one of the four great creative figures in music of the first half of the 20th century. The others are Schoenberg, Stravinsky and Bartók."

It was around 1945 that Arnold Schoenberg singled Ives out for special recognition. Up to this time Ives was known only to a small number of music lovers, mostly professional musicians. On the surface this did not seem to concern the composer very much for he always appeared to be rather apathetic to either praise or criticism. When his *Symphony No. 3* (completed in 1904) won the Pulitzer Prize in 1947 the typical Ives reaction was "prizes are the badges of mediocrity." He immediately proceeded to give the money away.

In his book, *Music and Society,* Wilfrid Mellers comments:

CHARLES IVES   EDGAR VARÈSE

Ives is a genuine American type, a man of immense physical
energy and competence in practical affairs, and of a vigorous
originality and independence. Between 1890 and 1910 he had
effected the revolutions of atonality and the exploration of
polyrhythms and polyharmonies which afterwards came to be
associated with the most advanced composers of central Europe,
and his discoveries ranged, indeed, much further than any European composer had ever dared to go.[10]

Charles Ives was also one of the most successful insurance
executives the United States has ever produced, a man who made
millions in the field, a man who wrote one of the most important
books on the subject. He helped found the firm of Ives and Myrick
in New York City, and by the time of his retirement in 1930, it
was the largest insurance agency in the United States.

Paradoxically, this business executive came home from the
office at the end of the day and spent his evenings writing music
at his desk because he enjoyed it. As he filled the sheets of
score-paper, he tossed them onto the floor. When the piles of
music became too high, he packed them in cardboard boxes and
hauled them out to the barn for storage.

Always planning to look over these disordered boxes of manuscripts, he did, during the fall of 1949, do some rummaging around. He found a few dusty sheets which turned out to be his *Symphony No. 2*, written in 1897. Painstakingly individual parts for the performers were copied out. A few months later Leonard Bernstein and the New York Philharmonic Orchestra gave the world premiere of the symphony 54 years after it had been written. Since it was the first time one of Ives' symphonies was to be performed by a major orchestra, Bernstein invited the composer to be his guest at the premiere. When the composer declined, Bernstein offered to conduct a rehearsal of it at any hour and date that would suit Ives. Furthermore, Bernstein would leave the auditorium dark so that no one would know that the composer was present. When Ives refused even this offer, the best the conductor could do was to have Mrs. Ives as his guest of honor for the premiere.

When she returned home after the concert she told her husband how successful the work had been and how much the public had liked it. Ives sneaked down to the kitchen a week later and listened to a broadcast performance of it on the maid's radio. This was his only experience hearing one of his major works professionally performed!

Charles Ives was born in Danbury, Connecticut, not far from where his forbears had settled shortly after the landing of the Pilgrims. His father had been a band director in the army during the Civil War, his mother a music teacher in Danbury. Once out of the service, the elder Ives continued his interest in music by playing the piano for dances, the organ for the Sunday church services, and by leading the town band and occasionally arranging music for them. Charles' father was also an experimenter, always trying to find new sounds and learn how to use them effectively. He even built an instrument with 24 violin strings stretched over a clothes press so that he could play quarter-tone music.

As a boy, Ives attended many outdoor camp meetings and heard countless revival songs. Stephen Foster had been a friend of his father, so the boy heard many of Foster's immortal tunes. When he was eight, his father discovered him thumping out rhythms on the family piano, trying to make it sound like the percussion section of a marching band. Father Ives promptly took the boy down to the barber shop and turned him over to the

German barber who was also the drummer in the town band. By the time he was 12, Ives was the drummer in the Danbury Town Band. His father also saw to it that the lad had lessons in piano, violin, cornet, sight-reading, harmony and counterpoint. By the time he was 11, Ives had started organ lessons and two years later was the organist at the Congregational Church of Danbury, playing two Sunday services and giving frequent recitals.

Several years earlier Ives had begun to compose, the first work being a *Dirge for Chin Chin,* the family cat. His father's band performed one of his pieces, but for that performance Charles begged out of playing. As the band marched down his street loudly blaring forth the melody of his composition, the lad played handball against the side of the house and appeared to completely ignore it all.

At 20, Ives enrolled at Yale to study composition with Horatio Parker. As far as can be determined, Parker seems to have ignored the daring new compositions that Ives was writing and looked only at the standard harmony exercises required of the students. While at Yale he wrote music for a theater orchestra for amusement, played on the football team and was a member of the baseball team. Ives' *Symphony No. 1* dates from his college days, a work filled with dissonances and written in many tonalities simultaneously.

As Ives approached the time for graduation he determined that he wanted a full and comfortable life, and although his marriage was still eight years away, he decided that a musician simply didn't earn enough money to support a family in such style. He therefore chose a career in insurance. After graduation he started by working for the Mutual Life Insurance Company at $5 a week. The job was in New York City, so he moved there and shared a small apartment with several other young men, a place they dubbed "Poverty Flat." His already-mentioned *Symphony No. 2* was composed there.

During these busy years at the insurance office he wrote music every evening, works that included *Washington's Birthday* (1909), *4th of July* (1912), *Three Places In New England* (1914) and *Concord Sonata* (1915). Almost none of his compositions were ever performed. A violinist friend had tried over a few works for that instrument. Ives did send off movements of two different symphonies to the two most influential conductors in the United

States at that time — Damrosch and Mahler — hoping for a possible performance. Damrosch lost the music that was sent to him and Mahler died before he had a chance to look over the other. Ives' only support in his musical endeavors came from his loyal and faithful wife.

About the time of World War I Ives ceased to compose. He said:

> [My] things [were] done mostly in the 20 years or so between 1896 and 1916. In 1917 the war came on and I did practically nothing in music. I did not seem to feel like it. We were very busy at the office at this time with the extra Red Cross and Liberty Loan drives, and all the problems that the war brought on. As I look back [1928] I find I did almost no composing after the beginning of 1917.[11]

By the end of the war diabetes made it impossible for Ives to hold a pen. No longer able to write, he turned to having the music he had already written published. He paid for the printing costs himself and distributed copies free of charge to anyone that made a request. Three volumes were issued, and for many years this was all of Ives' music that was known to the public. The first major presentation of his music was on the series *Evenings On the Roof* in Los Angeles. During the 1944-45 season, most of his chamber works and several songs were performed. Two years later his *Symphony No. 3* was premiered by the New York Little Symphony Orchestra, 20 years after he had written it; the work won for Ives the aforementioned Pulitzer Prize.

After his retirement in 1930, Ives led a secluded life. Too shaky to hold a razor by that time, he grew a beard. Heart disease bothered him, and in his last few years he developed cataracts over both eyes which could not be removed because of his diabetic condition. He died in 1954, just four days before the biography of him by his friend Henry Cowell was published.

There can be little doubt that Charles Ives has made a profound contribution to contemporary musical literature in general and to modern music in the United States in particular. Perhaps Arnold Schoenberg best epitomized a tribute to Ives when he stated:

There is a great man living in this country — a composer. He has solved the problem of how to preserve one's self and to learn. He responds to negligence by contempt. He is not forced to accept praise or blame. His name is Ives.

SYMPHONY NO. 4

II Allegretto

Charles Ives' *Symphony No. 4* is a most unusual composition by one of the world's most unique composers. The performance of it requires three conductors for the massed forces: the usual symphony orchestra plus chorus, a small brass band, two pianos (in addition to the solo piano with the orchestra), celesta, pipe organ, five timpani and assorted percussion. Some of the writing is in the quarter-tone* idiom. Musical quotations are made from more than two dozen other musical compositions, works ranging from hymn-tunes like *Beulah Land* and *Martyn* to *Yankee Doodle* and *Turkey In the Straw.*

It is interesting to compare the relative position of Ives' interest in quarter-tone music to that of other composers, all European. Ives first mature experiments with quarter-tone music** date from 1903 to 1913, and the writing of the *Symphony No. 4* occupied the years 1909 to 1916. Alois Hába, a Czech who is generally acknowledged to be the "developer" of quarter-tone

---

*   A quarter-tone is half a semitone, the latter being the smallest interval ordinarily used in Western music.

** In *Essays Before a Sonata and Other Writings* by Charles Ives, the composer tells how his father became interested in quarter-tone music. He says:

> "One afternoon, in a pouring thunderstorm, we saw him standing without hat or coat in the back garden; the church bell next door was ringing. He would rush in to the house to the piano, and then back again. 'I've heard a chord I've never heard before — it comes over and over again but I can't seem to catch it.' He stayed up most of the night trying to find it on the piano. It was soon after this that he started his quarter-tone machine."

George Ives' "quarter-tone machine" was a device made with twenty-four or more violin strings that could be tuned in various ways. He used to pick out quarter-tone melodies on this device and try to get his family to sing them. But, as Ives relates, "he gave that up except as a means of punishment — though we got to like some of the tunes."

music, wrote his first quarter-tone work in 1919, a *String Quintet*, published his first essay on the system in an encyclopedia in 1920, and printed his own treatise on it in 1925.

During this period of Ives' work in this idiom, roughly 1903 to 1913, the following works were completed by other composers:

1903	Debussy	*La Mer*
1909	Schoenberg	*Erwartung*
1909	Debussy	*Images pour orchestre*
1910	Stravinsky	*The Firebird*
1911	Stravinsky	*Petrouchka*
1912	Schoenberg	*Pierrot Lunaire*

In his autobiographical memo of 1932, Ives says concerning the composition under discussion:

> Fourth Symphony. This was started with some of the Hawthorne movement* of the second piano sonata around 1910-11 [changed to 1909-10]. . . It was all finished around the end of 1916 . . . Some of the things in it were from other things that I had been working on before or at that time . . . The second movement . . . is in some places an orchestration of the 'Celestial Railroad' idea from the second movement of the *Concord Sonata.*[12]

Speaking of Hawthorne's short story, *The Celestial Railroad* — a fantasy, Henry Bellamann says in his program notes of 1927, based on conversations with Ives:

> The aesthetic program of [the Symphony No. 4] is the searching question of What? and Why? which the spirit of man asks of life. This is particularly the sense of the Prelude. . . The succeeding movement, [the second] is not a scherzo . . . It is a comedy in the sense that Hawthorne's 'Celestial Railroad' is a comedy. Indeed this work of Hawthorne's may be considered as a sort of incidental program in which an exciting, easy, and worldly progress through life is contrasted with the trials of the Pilgrims in their journey through the swamp. The occasional slow episodes —

---

* In his *Piano Sonata No. 2* Ives subtitled each of the four movements, naming them after great New England personalities: "Emerson" (the opening sonata-allegro movement); "Hawthorne" (a fantastic scherzo), "The Alcotts" (a simple, religious slow movement); and as a finale, "Thoreau."

Pilgrim's hymns — are constantly crowded out and overwhelmed by the former. The dream, or fantasy, ends with the interruption of reality — the Fourth of July in Concord — brass bands, drum corps, etc.[13]

The music of the second movement is extremely complex in sound. At points it assaults the ear both from the "on-stage" orchestra and the other instrumental ensembles placed about the concert hall. "When one tries to use an analogy between the arts as an illustration, especially of some technical matter, he is liable to get in wrong," Ives writes in the conductor's score just before the second movement. He then goes on to say: "But the general aim of the plans under discussion is to bring various parts of the music to the ear in their relation, as the perspective of a picture brings to the eye. As the distant hills, in a landscape, row upon row, grow gradually in the horizon, so there may be something corresponding to this in the presentation of music. Music seems too often all foreground even if played by a master of dynamics."

The second or "comedy" movement opens with two great sighs in the bass viols; this is overlaid with the sounds of the full orchestra, *pianissimo,* "as of an awakening city."

This is followed by an eerie quarter-tone hymn* for unaccompanied strings and solo piano:

Example 1

VIOLINS I AND II (*div.*)   SQUARE SHAPED NOTES = QUARTER TONES   ($\frac{1}{4}$ #)

---

*   It is interesting to note the *sound* of this passage if one is not accustomed to quarter-tone music. Instead of triads, Ives uses four tones in each chord. He has said that a quarter-tone triad "to most ears, I imagine, sounds . . . out of tune," while with four tones "we have a balanced chord which, if listened to without prejudice . . seems to establish an identity of its own."

The hymn gives way to a growing bustle, a strongly rhythmical passage, which culminates in *Tramp, Tramp, Tramp* ("In my prison cell I sit. . .")

Example 2

This episode quickly builds to a dynamic climax, and suddenly disappears.

The tempo changes to *Adagio;* a quarter-tone setting of *In the Sweet By and By* is heard, Example 3. It persists beyond a brief, loud *Allegro* fracas.

Example 3

Again a growing bustle, quite a rhythmical passage, leads to *Tramp, Tramp, Tramp,* Example 2, played by the trombones *fff*. Busy episodes based on fragments of *Hawthorne* follow, but it is so noisy that they are hardly recognizable.

The brass finally break through with *The Red, White and Blue* (which also started the final phantasmagoria in Hawthorne):

Example 4

The dynamic level subsides. The somewhat quieter section which follows is, according to Ives, "a take off here on polite salon music . . . pink teas in Vanity Fair social life." First violins are prominent, then the deeper, more resonant tone of a solo viola takes over. A lone trumpet, *piano,* enters with a syncopated figure. The texture becomes more dense and the pianos become the most prominent instruments in the tonal palette; a flute doubles the pianos' right hand melody.

As the flute drops out, the left hand part of the solo piano is barely audible as it plays an irreverent version of the "human-faith-melody" from *Hawthorne*:

Example 5

The trumpets (or, as Ives specifies in the score, "Alto sax or cornet with paper over bell) play a variant of *Long, Long Ago.*

An extended episode leads to a repetition of the ragtime figures.

Trumpets (with help from the tuba) play a theme from *Hawthorne,* a profane version of Beethoven's motive from the opening of his *Symphony No. 5;* in counterpoint the trombones play *Beulah Land*, the cornets the phrase "Down in the Cornfield" from Foster's *Massa's in de Cold, Cold Ground,* and the piano, *In the Sweet By and By.*

Example 6

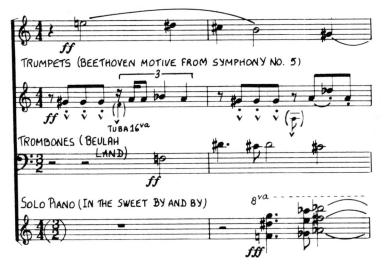

After a loud dynamic climax, all but strings, solo piano and celesta drop out. The violas take up the old hymn-tune *Martyn:*

Example 7

The trombones respond with *Beulah Land* from Example 6. After another dynamic climax, a variant of *Martyn* (Example 7) is heard, *pianissimo,* in an extended passage played by the first violins and accompanied by a quarter-tone piano and strings. This all leads up to the *Country Band March,* played first by the trumpet:

Example 8

TRUMPET

The sound of the music now becomes a mass of tune on top of tune, a veritable three-ring-circus of melodies. In addition to the *Country Band March,* Example 8, other melodies heard include: *Yankee Doodle,, Marching Through Georgia, Turkey In the Straw, Long, Long Ago, Reveille* and *The Irish Washerwoman.*

The final burst – *fff con fuoco* (with fire) – "dissipates [without slowing down] and immediately disappears like a hallucination."

III

EDGAR VARÈSE (1883-1965) has been one of the most unusual composers America has known. Born and trained in Europe, Varèse spent most of his creative life in the United States. He was most influential in fostering first performances during the 1920's of new music by native U.S. composers through the International Composers Guild which he founded in New York. He also taught, at one time or another, a great many young American composers. Except for these activities (according to his friend and fellow-composer Henry Cowell) "Varèse's own music has nothing in particular to do with America." Cowell then goes on to say concerning Varèse's style:

> It was originated in Europe under the influence of his teacher, Busoni, and was also affected by the Italian 'futurist' school of percussionists. However, his best work, *Arcane*, was written in

America, and his longest work is called *Amerique,* indicating very well just what the work is — a Frenchman's concept of America! [14]

As Henry Cowell has said, it was in the United States that Varèse's major compositions were first performed. It was in this country that his works were first ridiculed. It was in America that Varèse gave up composing in 1937, discouraged, convinced that his fellow musicians would never understand his music. And, it was in this country that Varèse became a "musical hero" after World War II when the youngest generation of composers — electronically oriented ones — discovered that back in 1939 Varèse had said, in a lecture at the University of Southern California:

Personally, for my conceptions, I need an entirely new medium of expression: a sound-*producing* machine (not a sound-*reproducing* one). Today it is possible to build such a machine with only a certain amount of added research.

If you are curious to know what such a machine could do that the orchestra with its manpowered instruments cannot do, I shall try briefly to tell you: whatever I write, whatever my message, it will

EDGAR VARÈSE and
HEITOR VILLA-LOBOS

Varèse studio

reach the listener unadulterated by 'interpretation.' It will work something like this: after a composer has set down his score on paper by means of a new graphic notation, he will then, with the collaboration of a sound engineer, transfer the score directly to this electric machine. After that, anyone will be able to press a button to release the music exactly as the composer wrote it — exactly like opening a book. [It is interesting to note that the first primitive tape recorders did not become commercially available for more than seven years after the date of this lecture; electronic sound genesis followed by 14 years].

And here are the advantages I anticipate from such a machine: liberation from the arbitrary, paralyzing tempered system; the possibility of obtaining any number of cycles or, if still desired, subdivisions of the octave, and consequently, the formation of any desired scale; unsuspected range in low and high registers; new harmonic splendors obtainable from the use of sub-harmonic combinations now impossible; the possibility of obtaining any differentiation of timbre, of sound-combinations; new dynamics far beyond the present human-powered orchestra; a sense of sound-projection in space by means of the emission of sound in any part or in many parts of the hall, as may be required by the score; cross-rhythms unrelated to each other, treated simultaneously, or to use the old word, 'contrapuntally,' since the machine would be able to beat any number of desired notes, any subdivision of them, omission or fraction of them — all these in a given unit of measure or time that is humanly impossible to attain.[15]

After many heartaches and a hiatus of 20 years in his composing, Varèse went on to achieve this dream. For the Brussels World's Fair of 1958, the architect Le Corbusier was asked to design the pavilion of the Philips Radio Corporation (then Europe's largest such firm). Le Corbusier in turn, asked his friend Edgar Varèse to compose the music.

Le Corbusier designed the pavilion in the shape of a three-peaked circus tent externally and (to use his own analogy) in the shape of a cow's stomach internally. This provided a series of hyperbolic and parabolic curves from which Varèse could project his 480-second long composition. Along these curves, placed with infinite care, were 425 loudspeakers operating from an 11-track tape. The sound itself was accompanied by a series of projected images chosen by Le Corbusier, some of them photographs, others montages, paintings, printed or written script. No synchronization between sight and sound was attempted by the two artists; part of the effect achieved was the result of a discordance between aural and visual impressions and part the result of their not infrequent accidental concordance. The audience, some 15 or 16,000 people daily for six months, evinced reactions to Varèse's *Poème électronique* almost as kaleidescopic as the sounds and images they encountered — terror, anger, stunned awe, amusement, wild enthusiasm.

The life of the composer of this arresting piece of Organized Sound (he rejects the expression *musique concrète* for his own works) started in Paris on December 22, 1883. He spent his childhood there as well as in Villars, a village in Burgundy where his mother's family lived. When he was nine, his father, an engineer, moved the family back to his birthplace, Turin, a city in the northern Piedmont region of Italy. Of his youth Varèse later wrote:

> When I was 11 I wrote an opera on Jules Verne's *Martin Paz,* in which I was already involved with sonority and unusual sounds. I detested the piano and all conventional instruments, and when I first learned the scales, my only reaction was, 'well, they all sound alike.'

> Up to then I had studied entirely by myself; my father was against my studying music and wanted me to go into mathematics and physics at the Polytechnic in Zürich. He even locked the piano at our house so that I couldn't touch it. But when I was 17, Bolzoni, the head of the Turin Conservatory, became interested in me and encouraged me to go back to Paris (my birthplace). There I went first to the Schola Cantorum, where I studied with Roussel and d'Indy. d'Indy was typical petty nobility, calling himself "le Victome d'Indy," an anti-Semite . . . and a terribly pedantic musician . . .

> So I left the Schola after a year and went to Widor, a magnificent, open-minded musician and a marvelous organist. . . . By that time I was already disenchanted with the tempered system, though, and could never understand why we should be limited to it when our instruments can give us anything we want, and why it should be imposed as a prescriptive, as if it were the final stage of musical development. In other fields, like chemistry or physics, the basic assumption is that there is always something new to be discovered. So I left the Conservatoire as well after a couple of years

(although the immediate cause for leaving was a rather nasty exchange of unpleasantries with Fauré who, as administrator of the Conservatoire, kicked me out).[16]

By the time Varèse was 20 he had written quite a quantity of music, including one work, *Gargantua,* at the encouragement of Romain Rolland, and a song, *My Light,* on a poem by Goethe. "At that time Goethe was very important to my thinking, as was Hoéné Wronsky, an officer in Napoleon's army, who was also a physicist and philosopher, who created a phrase I never forgot: 'Music is the corporealization of the intelligence that is sound.' "

That statement was to remain with Varèse a lifetime as both his credo and his goal.

Varèse's youthful heroes in music were Debussy, and then Strauss and Busoni, both of whom were very influential in his career after he went to Berlin in 1905:

> Above all I admired Debussy, primarily for his economy of means and clarity, and the intensity he achieved through them, balancing with almost mathematical equalibrium timbres against rhythms and textures — like a fantastic chemist.[17]

The "essential touchstone" for Varèse, though, was to be the pianist-composer Busoni's book, *Sketch of a New Esthetic of Music:*

> Imagine my excitement on reading these words of his [he once told a college audience] : 'Music was born free; and to win freedom its destiny.' Until then I supposed no one but myself held such a theory. When I took Busoni my scores, he was at once interested and in spite of the great difference of age [Varèse was 22, Busoni 39] a friendship developed during the remaining years I was in Berlin.[18]

After the outbreak of World War I Varèse returned to Paris to serve in the French Army. On the eve of 1916, having been discharged from the service because of ill health, Varèse arrived in the United States. All his compositions up to this date had been destroyed by a fire. The very word, America, had meant to him since childhood, "all discoveries, all adventures . . . the unknown." And in this symbolical sense, "new worlds on this planet, in outer space, and in the minds of man," Varèse gave the first work he wrote in this country the title of *Amériques* (1918-22).

In 1921 Varèse founded the International Composers Guild in New York to foster performances of new and unperformed compositions. During the six years of its existence, Varèse, as its chairman with the active assistance of Carlos Salzedo, was responsible for the world or American premieres of works by such composers as Bartók, Berg, Chávez, Cowell, Hindemith, Kodály, Milhaud, Ravel, Respighi, Satie, Schoenberg, Still, Stravinsky and Webern.

These were also busy years of creation for Varèse, the composer: *Offrandes* (1921) for soprano and chamber orchestra; *Hyperprism* (1922) for winds and percussion; *Octandre* (1923) for winds and double bass; *Intégrales* (1924), the largest of his ensemble pieces; *Arcana* (1925-27) for symphony orchestra; *Ionisation* (1930-31) for 13 percussionists [and reviewed in the next section]; *Ecuatorial* (1933-34) for bass voice (later revised for a chorus of basses), four trumpets and trombones, piano, organ, two Theremins (an early electronic instrument) and six percussionists; and *Density 21.5* (1936) for unaccompanied flute solo (written at the request of a flutist for the inauguration of his platinum flute; 21.5 is the density of platinum).

Throughout all these works there is evidence of a fresh, new approach to composition. Melody, when Varèse uses it, is often characterized by wide skips, broken sometimes by chromatic passages, sometimes by repeated tones. His metrical indications show his concern for the intricacies and subleties of rhythm, for he marks one work 3/4 and a half, another 1/4 and a half, and still another 4/4 and a half. The extra one half represents in each case an added half-beat or eighth-note at the end of the measure. He relies heavily on percussion, because (according to Cowell) "it is perhaps [a] desire to focus the interest on harmonies of sound-quality alone — without the distraction of harmonies of pitch — or on chords of rhythm."

There followed a period of 17 years without a composition from the pen of Varèse. "The situation really seemed hopeless," he told a friend, "I'm afraid I developed a very negative attitude toward the entire musical situation. . . . The frustration of having my music ignored was only part of it . . . . I wanted to work with an electrical engineer in a well-equipped laboratory. . . . I tried in [New York] and in Hollywood, but no doors opened. It is, however, not exact to say that I deliberately stopped composing. I kept working on a score that I called *Espace,* but I would tear up at night what I had written during the day or vice versa."

When at last Varèse was given a chance to compose electronically, it came through friends. Through the efforts of the painter Alcopley, an Ampex model 401A tape recorder and accessories was given anonymously to Varèse. He then completed *Déserts* (1949-54) for winds, percussion and electronically organized sound. This was followed by the commission for the Brussels World's Fair already mentioned, *Poème électronique,* created at the Philips Laboratories in Eindhoven, The Netherlands. His final work, left incomplete at the time of his death in 1965, was *Nocturnal* for voices and instruments.

IÒNISATION

Ionisation requires an ensemble of 13 musicians who play a total of 37 different instruments of percussion and friction. For 1931 — when the work was first performed — it was a daring experience for a composition to be exclusively a study in the sonorities and rhythms of percussion instruments.

The instruments used fall into three groups: those of a definite pitch; indefinite pitch; and continuous pitch. Those of a definite pitch (and, of necessity tuned to the hated tempered scale): tubular chimes, celesta and piano. Among those of indefinite pitch — except for a sense of "high" and "low" — three sizes of bass drum, snare drums, tenor and side drums, cymbals, gong, tam-tam, triangle, slapstick, Chinese blocks (three sizes), cowbell, sleighbells and anvil. Varèse also calls for a number of exotic percussion instruments: bongos (West Indian drums), castanets, tambourine, a Basque drum, a guiro (a Cuban gourd with one side serrated; it is scratched by a wooden stick), claves (Cuban sticks of hardwood), maracas (Cuban rattles). In the third group of instruments, those of continuous pitch, are two sirens (one high, one low) and a lion's roar (a medium size wooden barrel with a parchment head through which a rosined string is drawn, the sound being produced by rubbing the string with a piece of cloth or leather).

Each section of *Ionisation* is identified by its own combination of instruments or range of sonority, and each important change in the sonority is also a demarcation in the form. The rhythm of the work, according to the composer, "derives from the simultaneous interplay of unrelated elements that intervene at calculated, but not regular, time-lapses. This corresponds more nearly to the definition of rhythm in physics and philosophy as 'a succession of alternate and opposite or correlative states'."

Although it is musically exciting to listen to *Ionisation* as a total work, it is also revealing to go back, listen several times and discover how the work is put together, for there is a definite form built up out of sonorities and rhythms.

Introduction. A characteristic figure ♫♩ is sounded by two bass drums. The sirens, one high and one low, enter in rotation, starting from *ppp* and swelling to *mp*. The snare drum enters in the seventh measure, starting a tremendous *crescendo* of the *metal* group (gongs, tam-tam, cymbals, triangle). The *crescendo* ends abruptly.

The First Subject is played by the military drum accompanied by the bongos:

Example 1

WITH FELT-COVERED MALLETS

Four measures reminiscent of the Introduction are heard. It is followed by an episode involving snare drum and Chinese blocks.

The First Subject, Example 1, is repeated for two measures, then the bongos enter in strict imitation of the Subject, continuing in its free counterpoint.

After a Codetta played by Chinese blocks, the snare drum is heard. It is followed by a syncopated figure for the claves. Once again the Chinese blocks are heard. A gradual *crescendo* (for 10 measures) leads to the Second Subject played by bongos, military drum, Chinese blocks, maracas and snare drum.

Example 2

A rather long passage follows for the metals — anvils, cymbals, gongs, tam-tam and triangle, accompanied by sirens. There is a *fermata*. This is followed by another outburst of sound, followed by a *pianissimo* passage and then another outburst.

The First Subject, Example 1, returns in the military drum, but the accompanying bongo figure is different.

The Second Subject, Example 2, returns, now in two figures of quintuple 16th-notes, all building in a tremendous *crescendo*, leading to the Coda.

The tuned instruments — piano, celesta and tubular chimes — enter for the first time in the Coda. The First Subject, Example 1, is restated by the military drum. The Chinese blocks are heard, followed by a solo for the snare drum. Bits of the First Subject, Example 1, are heard again. The conclusion is *pianissimo* on a long *fermata*.

IV

WALTER PISTON (1894-   ), is an arch-conservative in music compared to either Charles Ives or Edgar Varèse. Piston spent 36 years teaching composition at Harvard and has authored four outstanding books in the field: *Harmony* (1941), *Counterpoint* (1947), *Principles of Harmonic Analysis* (1933) and *Orchestration* (1955). With such a background it is no wonder that Aaron Copland can say of him:

> His music has a characteristic way of going straight to the point. He knows what he wants to say — and says it, without elaboration. The formal design of each movement is likely to be rather conventional, though worked out, of course, with a sure hand. There is fairly certain to be more than enough counterpoint, since the composer has a special fondness for fugal forms, due, perhaps to his academic background. Piston's work is most daring, however, in its harmonic aspect. It is this side of his music that is

most original, despite the fact that the chords in themselves are by origin rather eclectic; the more astringent and complex harmonic entities have no terrors for him. One can recognize the Piston touch most easily because of his boldness in handling these harmonic textures of every kind.[19]

Walter Piston was born in Rockland, Maine, where his grandfather, an Italian sailor named Antonio Pistone, had settled, married and dropped the final *e* from his name. Walter's father was a bookkeeper and cared very little about music. When Walter was nine, the family — father, mother and four boys — moved to Boston where the children grew up. It was several years after this move before the boys' father got around to buying Walter a violin and one of his brothers a piano. Lessons were started on the violin right away and Piston was soon playing in the school orchestra at Mechanic Arts High School.

Upon graduation in 1912 Piston became a draftsman for an elevated railway company. Then, having had a strong interest in art for some time, he enrolled in the Massachusetts School of Art. Fortunately there was no tuition. He earned his board and room by playing the violin and piano in dance halls.

As the United States became involved in World War I, Piston decided to enlist in the Navy as a musician. Since the naval band would have no use for violinists or pianists, he learned how to play the saxophone out of a manual. He served during the war in a band stationed at the Massachusetts Institute of Technology; his rating of "musician, second class" was, according to Piston, "purely technical! "

After the war Piston worked for a time as an artist, but felt that he didn't have an adequate education. He enrolled at Harvard as a music major; he earned enough money to support himself and his wife (he had married shortly after being discharged from the service) by playing in dance halls and cafés once again. He graduated "with honors" in 1924.

As an incipient composer, Piston rebelled against the standardized academic routine which taught harmony and counterpoint according to outmoded and unimaginative textbooks. He determined to continue his study of composition in an atmosphere more conducive to creative writing. To this end he moved to Paris, and, for two years, studied with Nadia Boulanger at the American Conservatory at Fontainebleau. It was an exciting experience.

WALTER PISTON (1894-   ) author of books on harmony, counterpoint, orchestration and principles of harmonic analysis, and one of America's most distinguished composers of the conservative tradition.

Satie, Stravinsky and the Group of Six were all active at the time in Parisian music circles. At the Conservatory, Piston's classmates included Aaron Copland, Virgil Thomson and Roy Harris.

After completing his studies with Mme. Boulanger, Piston returned to the United States and joined the Harvard Music Department faculty in 1926. He was appointed a full professor in 1944, and in 1951 was named Naumburg Professor of Music. Thus Piston stands as a teacher of singular distinction in his own right. Among his more gifted students have been Elliot Carter, Leonard Bernstein, Harold Shapero and the late Irving Fine.

With the exception of the amusing and very popular ballet score, *The Incredible Flutist,* the spirited *Carnival Song* for men's chorus and brass, and the gay *Tunbridge Fair* for band, Piston's compositions have been almost wholly instrumental works cast in the so-called absolute forms: symphony, prelude and fugue, toccata, suite, quartet, sonata, etc. This could suggest that his compositions might be "dry" and uninteresting, but such is certainly not the case. From the standpoint of structure, as Copland earlier pointed out, Piston's mastery of form, polyphonic line and instrumentation is absolute. Yet there is within it all an expressive content; it can be by turns virile and tender. There is, thus, a beautiful balance between heart and head, of form and content — an aim which Piston has expressed as his foremost objective as a creative artist.

As a full-scale symphonist, Piston made his mark (with the *Symphony No. 2,* given the New York Music Critic's Award in 1943) somewhat later than the other major American composers of his day. Roy Harris's *Third,* Samuel Barber's *First* and William Schuman's *Third* were already established as major American works in this form by the time Piston hit his symphonic stride. His *Symphony No. 3* won the Pulitzer Prize in Musical Composition in 1947, and his *Symphony No. 4* as premiered in 1951 by Anatol Dorati and The Minneapolis (now the Minnesota) Symphony Orchestra won the Naumburg Recording Award. His *Symphony No. 8* is his most recent contribution to this genre.

In retirement Piston lives with his artist wife in Belmont, Massachusetts, in a New England home designed by Mrs. Piston. It has two wings that branch out from the living quarters on opposite sides. One is the composer's studio filled with scores and books; on the opposite side is his wife's studio filled with easels and canvases.

Often asked if he composes "American" music, Piston has stated his own philosophy well when he answers by saying:

> Ours is a big country and we are a people possessing a multitude of different origins. We already have a large literature of music by native composers. The outstanding characteristic noticeable in this music is its great diversity. If a composer desires to serve the cause of American music he will best do it by remaining true to himself as an individual and not by trying to discover musical formulas for Americanism.

SYMPHONY NO. 3

IV Allegro

Walter Piston's *Symphony No. 3* was commissioned by the Koussevitzky Music Foundation (established by the former music director of the Boston Symphony Orchestra, Serge Koussevitzky, in memory of his first wife). The composer completed the work at Woodstock, Vermont, during the summer of 1947, and Serge Koussevitzky conducted its first performance with the Boston Symphony Orchestra on January 9, 1948.

For the occasion, Piston supplied the following program notes for the fourth movement:

> *Allegro* (4/4) A three-part form similar to that of a sonata form movement. There are two themes, the first being developed fugally in the middle section.

> The second theme is march-like, first heard in oboes and bassoons, over a staccato bass, and later played by full brass at the climax of the movement. Tonality C.

The music gets off to a rousing start immediately. The full orchestra announces the bold and rhythmic Principal Theme:

Example 1

OBOES, CLARINETS, VIOLINS.

FIGURE A

The Principal Theme is repeated *fortissimo*.

Woodwinds are heard, *mezzoforte,* in a bridge passage.

A four measure passage, full of crisp rhythms played by the French horns, introduces the Second Theme — a "march-like" tune — played by oboes and bassoons over a pizzicato bass:

Example 2   (Second Theme)

The Second Theme is repeated at a higher pitch by all the woodwinds and French horns. Trumpets join in the last measure.

A loud, rhythmic passage on the pitches C and G, played by the timpani and reinforced by bassoons and low strings, leads to the fugal Development section.

The Subject (Example 3) of the fugal section is derived from the opening of the Principal Theme (Example 1). The Subject is stated by bass clarinet and cellos:

Example 3 (Subject)

BASS CLARINET, CELLOS

Subsequent entrances of Example 3 are as follows:

> bassoons and violas (on the dominant — F-sharp)
> English horn, clarinet, 2nd violins (on D-flat)
> flute, oboe, 1st violins (on E-flat)

An eight-measure episode, rhythmically reminiscent of Figure A, leads to the closing section of the fugue which is in stretto (the entrances overlapping). The Subject, Example 3, is heard, in stretto, as follows:

> French horns
> trombones
> lower woodwinds and lower strings
> upper woodwinds and upper strings

Five measures based on the rhythmic pattern ♩ ♫♫ leads to the Recapitulation of this sonata form.

The Principal Theme, Example 1, is heard exactly as it appeared the first time.

The bridge is quite similar to its antecedent, but this time it does not modulate.

A rhythmical, four-measure passage for French horn again introduces the Second Theme, Example 2, this time started by the muted trumpets and completed by the woodwinds. The Second

Theme is repeated by full brass fortissimo.

The Coda is based on Figure A from Example 1 played by the full orchestra, *fortissimo,* bringing this energetic finale to a conclusion.

WILLIAM GRANT STILL (1895-   ) is proud of the fact that he is an American.

In speaking of music, Still believes that every American composer should be well acquainted with jazz no matter how much or how little of it he uses in his compositions, for "jazz is one of the few idioms developed by the United States that can be said to belong to no other people on earth." Proud of his black heritage, Still early in life decided to use Afro-American titles for most of his compositions and to embody in his works the distinctive features of such music. He made history for the Afro-American when he was the first to conduct an all-white radio orchestra in New York City and first to write a symphony. He also made history when he conducted the Los Angeles Philharmonic Orchestra in two of his own compositions at a Hollywood Bowl summer concert in 1936, for it was the first time in the history of the country that a black person had ever led a symphony orchestra. In 1955 he conducted the New Orleans Philharmonic Orchestra, becoming the first black person to lead a major symphony orchestra in the deep South.

William Grant Still was born in Woodville, Mississippi. Both his parents were accredited teachers and musicians; both were talented and brilliant. His father's musical education on the cornet had been gained by making a 75 mile trip for each lesson! Later his father founded and conducted a brass band in Woodville, the only one in town; he also tried his hand at composition. Unfor-

WILLIAM GRANT STILL

HOWARD HANSON

tunately, he died when his son was six months old.

The lad's mother then took him with her to Little Rock, Arkansas, where she obtained a job teaching school. About five years later she married a postal employee, Charles B. Shepperson, who was a fan of operatic music. He spent a large share of his meagre income buying phonograph records of arias performed by the outstanding stars of that period. This gave the boy an opportunity to hear music that pleased him more than anything he had heard before.

At 16 Still graduated from high school as first honor bearer and class valedictorian. When the question of college arose, his mother tried to steer him away from a course in composition, for she felt that there was no future for a "serious" musician, especially for a black one. He therefore enrolled at Wilberforce University where he took a Bachelor of Science degree. Nevertheless, he played in the University string quartet and made arrangements for their band. The first concert of his compositions was a recital which he gave at Wilberforce.

Within two months of graduation, Still left the university. Lean days followed. He married, worked at odd jobs, played oboe and cello with various orchestras, starved, froze, joined the United States Navy. All this time he wondered how he could continue the professional study of his music. Through a legacy from his father, he studied at Oberlin College in Ohio. Then, because of the merit of his work, he was given a scholarship to study composition privately.

W.C. Handy, the "father of the blues," gave Still his first job as an arranger. He toured with Handy's Band from New York through the South. Now that he could afford it, Still applied to study composition with George W. Chadwick who, because of Still's talent, wanted to teach him free of charge. This was followed by a scholarship to study with the revolutionary French-American composer Edgar Varèse.

Still then performed in pit orchestras for vaudeville and New York musicals. He played banjo in the orchestra of the Plantation Nightclub on Broadway. When its conductor left, he advanced to that position. He also made musical arrangements for Sophie Tucker, Earl Carroll's *Vanities* and later for Paul Whiteman. When CBS started, Still was arranging for Donald Voorhees for the network broadcasts, and, later, turned to NBC as an arranger for the Maxwell House Hour. When its conductor left, some of the men in the orchestra suggested that Still become their conductor. The management agreed and William Grant Still became the first black to conduct an all-white radio orchestra in New York.

One of Still's earliest successes was a composition for three voices and chamber orchestra, *From the Land of Dreams,* which was performed by the Composer's Guild in New York in 1925. It raised a storm of protest because it was discordantly loud and ultra-modern in style. The composer then realized that he was working in a fashion that was unsuited to him, one that did not allow his own distinctive musical abilities and inspiration to shine through. He made up his mind to adopt an idiom derived from his own black heritage.

Still is known for five symphonies (including the *Afro-American Symphony),* a quantity of orchestral works including *In Memoriam: The Colored Soldiers Who Died for Democracy, Poem for Orchestra, From the Black Belt, California* and *The American Scene* — a "suite for young Americans." He has also written works for band, for the accordian, and a number of piano solos. He has composed six operas, some on Afro-American themes. His catalogue of works include numerous songs and works for chorus. Of his four ballets, *Sahdji* has been widely performed by Howard Hanson and the Eastman-Rochester Symphony Orchestra.

AFRO–AMERICAN SYMPHONY

III Animato

The very first words printed in the conductor's score of the *Afro-American Symphony* indicate the composer's profoundly religious nature: "With humble thanks to God, the source of inspiration." It is his philosophy that, "he who develops his God-given gifts with a view to aiding humanity, manifests truth."

The *Afro-American Symphony* was composed in 1930 and first performed by the Rochester Philharmonic Orchestra in 1931 under the baton of Howard Hanson, who later conducted the work in Berlin, Stuttgart, and Leipzig. The audience in Berlin broke a 20-year tradition to insist upon an encore of the *Scherzo;* later an audience in Budapest did the same thing when Karl Krueger conducted the symphony there.

> At the time the symphony was written, [Still says] no thought was given to a program for the *Afro-American Symphony*, the program being added after the completion of the work. I have regretted this step because in this particular instance a program is decidedly inadequate. The program devised at that time stated that the music portrayed the 'sons of the soil,' that is, that it offered a composite musical portrait of those Afro-Americans who have not responded completely to the cultural influence of today. It is true that an interpretation of that sort may be read into the music. Nevertheless, one who hears it is quite sure to discover other meanings which are probably broader in their scope. He may find the piece portrays four distinct types of Afro-Americans whose sole relationship is the physical one of dark skins. On the other hand, he may find that the music offers the sorrows and joys, the struggles and achievement of an individual Afro-American. Also it is quite probable that the music will speak to him of moods peculiar to colored Americans. Unquestionably, various other interpretations may be read into the music.

> Each movement of this Symphony presents a definite emotion, excerpts from poems of Paul Lawrence Dunbar being included in the score for the purpose of explaining these emotions. Each movement has a suggestive title: the first is *Longing,* the second *Sorrow,* the third *Humor* and the fourth *Sincerity.* In it, I have stressed an original motive in the blues idiom, employed as the principal theme of the first movement, and appearing in various forms in the succeeding movements, where I have tried to present it in a characteristic manner.

> The *Afro-American Symphony* represents the Negro of the days not far removed from the Civil War.

> When judged by the laws of musical form, the Symphony is somewhat irregular. This irregularity is in my estimation justified since it has no ill effect on the proportional balance of the composition. Moreover, when one considers that an architect is free to design new forms of buildings, and bears in mind the freedom permitted creators in other fields of art, he can hardly deny a composer the privilege of altering established forms as long as the sense of proportion is justified.[20]

The composer has subtitled the third or Scherzo movement: *"Humor,* expressed through religious fervor." In the score he quotes the following lines of the great black poet Paul Lawrence Dunbar (1872-1906):

> "An' we'll shout ouah halleluyahs,
> On dat mighty reck'nin' day."

"The harmonies employed in the Symphony," the composer states, "are quite conventional except in a few places. The use of this style of harmonization was necessary in order to attain simplicity and to intensify in music those qualities which enable the hearer to recognize it as Negro music. The orchestration was planned with a view to the attainment of effective simplicity."

The tempo of the Scherzo is marked: *Animato* (♩ =126). The brief introduction (some seven measures in length) is based on variants of Figure A of the Principal Theme, Example 2. A timpani roll is heard; the motive of Figure A is played first by low winds and strings:

Example 1

The violins take up the Principal Theme of the movement; the tenor banjo is prominent in the accompaniment.

Example 2

Strings and clarinets play a variant of Example 2, accompanied by a syncopated figure in the upper woodwinds.

The second theme, Example 3, is derived from the Principal Theme, Example 2; it is played by upper woodwinds and strings, reinforced at times by the trumpet.

Example 3

The dynamic level subsides; the oboe, over a pizzicato string accompaniment, plays the Principal Theme, Example 2, in a saucy manner. The flutes start to play it, but quickly abandon the theme.

In a transitional passage, the trombones are prominent:

Example 4

An ascending passage of four measures for strings and wood-winds is heard; it grows in dynamic intensity.

In the following measures, a "call and answer" pattern is established between the combined strings and woodwinds, and the brass. (It is based, rhythmically, on the second variant of Figure A from Example 1.)

Example 5

The "call and answer" idea is carried on between the low woodwinds and strings, and the low brass.

A melodic variant of Example 2 is started by the flutes and continued by the oboe. Soon the strings take up a motive derived from Figure B of Example 2.

The muted trumpets, in a passage full of rhythm, are heard with a variant of Figure A from Example 2; they are answered by the other brass. The full orchestra then takes up the antiphonal "call and answer" pattern; this passage is based on Figure B from Example 2.

The dynamic level subsides; violins play a melodic variant of Example 2. (The banjo is prominent in the accompaniment throughout this section.) Next, the woodwinds play their variant of Example 2.

The violins are now heard with Example 3.

A bridge passage leads to the Coda; it is based on a variant of Figure C for Example 4.

The strings, *fortissimo,* play a syncopated melodic variant of Example 2; the trumpets accompany this with a transformation of the "blues theme" from the first movement of the *Symphony*:

Example 6

The music quickly builds to a dynamic climax; the brief Scherzo is over.

VI

HOWARD HANSON (1896-   ) has been composer, conductor, educator, administrator and cultural consultant to the government. Of these many roles, he probably will be remembered best for his efforts in behalf of native American composers. No other individual in the second quarter of this century has done as much for the budding young composers of the United States as Howard Hanson.

As a composer he will be liked and honored by those who also enjoy the music of Sibelius and Grieg and the late-Romantic composers. He will be ignored by the fans of Berg and Stockhausen and Cage. Even as a youth, Hanson's idiom was never *avant-garde* or revolutionary. He has said:

> I am always classified as a neo-Romantic, and I suppose I really asked for it, naming my second symphony the 'Romantic'. I named it because at the particular time I had been back from

The Belmont home of Walter Piston in Massachusetts. Designed by Mrs. Piston, the house has one wing devoted to the composer's music room; on the other side is an artist's studio for Mrs. Piston.

The island retreat off the coast of Maine of Howard Hanson and his wife.

Europe not too long and I had been exposed to *avant-garde* experimentalism which is still going on; this was a sort of a reverse rebellion. I said, 'I am not only going to write a work which has a lot of tunes in it and some nice lush harmonies, but I am going to *call* it *Romantic Symphony,* so nobody can miss that I am doing this on purpose.[21]

Howard Hanson was born on October 28, 1896, in Wahoo, Nebraska, a small midwestern town of 2500 whose population consisted primarily of Swedes and Bohemians. The country-side was one of rolling hills and thickly wooded areas. There were few native Indians left during Hanson's youth; to see one in native dress was so rare that it was "a little startling to see one at your backdoor."

Hanson received his first music lessons from his mother; his first composition dates from age seven. By the time he was in high school he played cello with the school orchestra. Its director, a cornet player, was the school's math teacher. Before long he asked the youthful Hanson to conduct, his first experience at this activity.

By 1912, when Hanson graduated from Wahoo High School as valedictorian, he had played the piano and organ in all the churches in town, had sung Bach and works of many other composers in choir performances, had played cello in a quartet and in the school orchestra, and had been the conductor of the high school orchestra. But, at least in Wahoo in 1912, music was not considered a field for serious professional study. The Superintendent of Schools said to Hanson at the time of his graduation, "But why do you go into music? You have brains! "

Although Hanson spent a year at the state university at Lincoln, he was off at 16 for New York City, then as now the center for aspiring musicians. He enrolled at the Institute of Musical Art, the forerunner of the Juilliard School of Music, and studied composition with Percy Goetschius. "I was very fond of Goetschius," Hanson later remarked, "but he liked Mendelssohn, and lumped Wagner [chord] progressions together as 'wandering harmonies.' "

At the end of a year Hanson received a diploma from the Academy of Musical Arts. He was not yet 18 and, aspiring to be a college professor, decided to enroll at Northwestern University just outside Chicago. He completed his degree in two years. "In those days," Hanson recounts, "it was not necessary to take a course if you could already pass an examination in its subject matter. . . . All those music courses I had taken, not only at the Institute but at Luther Academy while I was still in high school, enabled me to gain credit by examination at Northwestern, so that I could graduate sooner. Incidentally, while I was at Northwestern, Frederick Stock and the Chicago Symphony played one of my pieces."

Upon graduation in 1916, the 19-year old youth took a position teaching theory and composition at the College of the Pacific in San Jose, California (now enlarged, it is known as the University of the Pacific and located at Stockton). By the age of 20 Hanson had realized two dreams: he was a composer with performances by Damrosch and Stock to prove it, and he was indeed a college professor. "A full professor too," he says smiling, "not an assistant or an associate."

Within three years Hanson was promoted to the Deanship of the Conservatory of Fine Arts. "It was a school of caliber," he says, "drawing from an area without much competition in music education; the student body in music alone numbered some two hundred."

That same year Hanson was invited by the Los Angeles Philharmonic Orchestra to conduct his own *Symphonic Rhapsody,* a thrill he .has never forgotten. Before his 25th birthday he was one of the three winners of the first American *Prix de Rome* competition. The prize consisted of three years' residence in Rome, as a fellow of the American Academy to study, to listen, to compose.

During his stay in Italy, Hanson completed his *Symphony No.1* which he subtitled "The Nordic" in memory of his Swedish forbears. He conducted the premiere performance of it with the Augusteo Orchestra of Rome in 1922.

During Hanson's third year in Italy he was invited back to the United States to conduct a performance of his symphonic poem *North and West* with the New York Symphony. The young Rochester (N.Y.) Symphony wished to perform his works as well, so invited him to follow his New York City visit with a trip to Rochester to conduct the *"Nordic" Symphony.* It was on that fateful occasion that Howard Hanson met George Eastman, inventor of the Kodak Camera and founder of The Eastman Kodak

Company. Eastman had decided to give the University of Rochester four million dollars with which to found an Eastman School of Music within the larger structure. He needed a Dean for his new school. After meeting Hanson, he knew he had found his man.

From that day in 1924 until his retirement 40 years later, in 1964, Dr. Hanson served the Eastman School of Music and the cause of American music eminently. He instituted the American Composers Concerts to give first performances of worthy new compositions. During his tenure at Eastman Hanson conducted over 1,500 premieres of compositions by more than 1,000 different composers! Among the gifted students who studied composition with him were David Diamond, Gail Kubik, John La Montaine, Robert Ward, Peter Mennin, William Bergsma and Ulysses Kay.

He was one of the founders and presidents of the National Association of Schools of Music, of the Music Teachers National Association, and of the National Music Council, and a member of the board of directors of the Music Educators National Conference. He was also elected to membership in the National Institute of Arts and Letters, and became a fellow of the Swedish Royal Academy of Music. He holds 30 honorary degrees.

Asked how, as a young man, he could teach, organize and administer the program for the new school, *and* compose, he replied: "It was exciting, but it was also hard work and very taxing. Working eight or nine hours a day at school, writing [my opera] *Merry Mount* until two in the morning, working weekends. Building courses and students, while George Eastman was building the school with money."

Merry Mount, along with his *Symphony No. 4,* are the composer's own favorites from among his works. The opera was produced at the Metropolitan Opera House in New York in 1934 and ran nine performances. Most critics agreed that the choruses were the strongest parts of the work. His fourth symphony, premiered in 1943, "is well made and imaginative," according to the composer. "It has substance -- and it communicates, though it is harder to listen to than some."

Hanson has written a number of good choral works. His first was *Lament for Beowulf* (1925) reviewed in the following section. It was followed by *Heroic Elegy* (1927) for wordless chorus and orchestra; *Drum Taps* (1935) on a text of Walt Whitman; *The*

Cherubic Hymn (1950), a setting of part of the Greek Orthodox Liturgy; *Song of Democracy* (1958) to a text of Walt Whitman; and *Psalm CL* (1968) for baritone, chorus and orchestra.

Hanson's *Symphony No. 6* was premiered in 1968 with the composer conducting the New York Philharmonic Orchestra at Lincoln Center. Conservative in style and neo-Romantic in flavor, "the audience liked the work, but the composer was more thrilled than the audience," wrote the New York music critic, Harold Schonberg. He then goes on to say, "this well-made, expert piece of music is a romantic work that looks back to such composers as Sibelius. It has dignity, strongly marked melodies, and a bit of rhetoric."

In retirement Hanson lives with his wife and two pet dogs (Peter Bolshoi and Tamara) on his own little island off the coast of Maine; the only electricity on this isle is provided by batteries for outgoing telephone calls by radio. He loves cards, poker and hearts in particular. He also enjoys swimming and is a boat enthusiast. He is a reader of occasional controversial nonfiction and in days gone by has served as a substitute preacher at the Presbyterian Church.

Hanson summed up his most recent views on music well when he said in a magazine article:

> In this age of mechanization we desperately need the creative arts. We need the love of music. We need its tremendous power of spiritual communication. . . . We need the great music of creators of the present as well as of the past. We need a spiritual rebirth. We need a new dedication, a new gospel of the arts, a gospel dedicated once again to the spiritual welfare of men and women and, yes — even in this sophisticated age — to the glory of God.
>
> Such a philosophy served Palestrina, Bach and Handel well indeed. May it again serve us.[22]

LAMENT FOR BEOWULF

Shortly after Howard Hanson arrived in Italy as one of the first winners of the Prix de Rome, he arranged to make a trip north. While he was in England he came across a translation of the eighth-century version of *Beowulf* by William Morris and A.J. Wyatt. The section dealing with the hero's death particularly

appealed to Hanson and seemed "to cry out for a musical setting."
He began to sketch it immediately thereafter in Scotland — "an
environment rugged, swept with mist, and wholly appropriate to
the scene of my story."

Back in Rome Hanson worked on it further and then put it
aside. He returned to it only after arriving back in the United
States, completing it shortly after his appointment to the staff of
the new Eastman School of Music. The composer conducted the
work's first performance at the Ann Arbor Festival of 1926.

Beowulf, an Anglo-Saxon epic of great importance, is one of
the earliest extant pieces of literature in the English language. The
original manuscript, now in the British Museum, dates from about
1000 A.D., but the composition of the poem "must be placed at
least three centuries earlier." The manuscript is carelessly written
by two different hands in the West-Saxon dialect, but the original
poem "must have been in the Northumbrian dialect." The name of
the poet is unknown.

The legend starts as the King of the Danes builds a great
mead hall for himself and his warriors. For 12 years the King is
plagued by an evil descendant of the Cain of Biblical renown. Then
Beowulf, nephew of the King of Geatas (now southern Sweden)
sails to Denmark with 14 warriors to kill the monster. After many
struggles he accomplishes his purpose; he returns to Geatas and
eventually ascends to its throne, reigning gloriously for 50 years.
But a dragon, angered by the plundering of his hoard, devastates
the country with fire. With assistance Beowulf kills the dragon, but
is himself mortally wounded in the fight. His body is burned on a
great funeral pyre, with solemn ceremonies.

"My intention," Hanson states, "has been to realize in the
music the austerity and stoicism and the heroic atmosphere of the
poem. This is true Anglo-Saxon poetry and may well serve as a
basis for music composed by an American."

In the music Hanson has tried to depict the tragic despair felt
by the Geatas over the loss of their king, setting the text in a
mood which is somber yet majestic. "There is a brief picture,"
Hanson tells us, "of the great burial mound by the sea on which
the funeral pyre of the hero is built. A great beacon mound is
constructed and on it are placed the trophies of the hero,
mementos of his famous battles and victories. The women lament
as the mound is built by the warriors. Then follows an episode in

which the wife of the hero and her hand-maids voice their grief. The young warriors in a group surround the bier of their dead king and tell of his prowess. The work ends with the eulogy of the great hero."

There is a long (54 measure) instrumental introduction characterized by an incessant rhythm (Example 1) which intimates the "austerity and stoicism . . . of the poem." From time to time horns and trumpets sound forth, suggesting the heroic atmosphere.

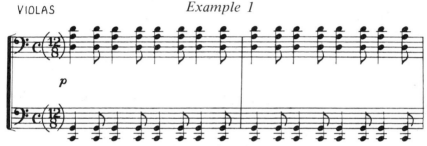

Example 1

VIOLAS

CELLOS + BASSES

The voices enter in a manner typical of this work: one voice at a time, building into blocks of modern chords of the 9th and 13th. The persistent rhythm of Example 1 continues as an accompaniment.

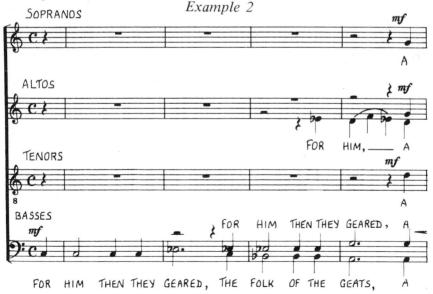

Example 2

The chorus next enters in descending order, starting with the sopranos:

With warhelms behung,
And with boards of the battle,
And bright byrnies,*
E'en after the boon** that he bade.

The men start the next quatrain, joined by the women's voices in the last half:

Laid down then amid
Most their King mighty famous
The warriors lamenting
The lief*** lord of them.

---

*   a byrnie is a piece of armor, a defensive shirt, usually of mail
**   a boon is a favor sought
*** lief=beloved

Then follows the climax of the poem and musical composition. The rhythm changes in this passage:

Example 3

The rhythm of the accompaniment established in Example 3 continues as the voices enter in a sustained passage in unison:

The wood reek went up
Swart over the smoky glow,
Sound of the flame
Bewound with the weeping,

The sounds of trumpets and horns are heard in the orchestral texture as the incessant rhythm which started in Example 3 ceases. Women's voices enter first, followed by tenors and then the basses. It is an extended passage treated polyphonically:

Sound of the flame
Bewound with the weeping,
The wind blending stilled,
Bewound with the weeping.

Until at last the bone house
Had broken, hot at the heart.
All unglad of mind with moodcare
They mourned their liege-lord's quelling.

The orchestral interlude is low in pitch, soft in dynamics, subdued in flavor. The text is now projected by one voice at a time (sopranos, then tenors and finally basses) against a countermelody, then a counterpoint of voices on a neutral syllable. In one of the most beautiful choral passages of the work, the voices bring this section to a close without words.

Likewise a sad
Lay the wife of a foretime
For Beowulf the king
With her hair unbounden
  Sang sorrow careful;

That harm days
For herself she dreaded,
Shaming and bondage,
The slaughter falls many,
  Much fear of the warrior.
  Heav'n swallowed the reek*

The rhythm and tempo established in Example 1 returns. In a passage that moves largely in triadic harmony, the voices twice reach a dynamic climax:

Wrought there and fashioned
The folk of the Weders.
A howe** on the lithe***
That high was and broad.

Unto the wavefarers
Wide to be seen:
Then it they betimber'd
In time of ten days.

*   reek = sweat, blood
**   howe = hole
*** lithe = stone

The battle strong's beacons,
The brands' very leavings
They bewrought with a wail
In the worthiest of ways,
    That men of all Wisdom
    Might find how to work.

The tempo changes to *Allegro con brio.* In a polyphonic passage, the basses enter first, imitated a sixth higher by the tenors. The women's voices enter in unison, the men's voices dropping out for two measures. When they re-enter, tenors double the sopranos and basses the altos. The music is then marked *Maestoso (molto meno mosso);* the dynamic level gradually drops from *fortissimo* to *piano.* The text for this extended passage:

Into burg then did they
The rings and bright sun-gems,
And all such adornments
As in the hoard there
    The war-minded men
    Had taken e'en now.

The earl's treasures
Let they the earth to be beholding,
Gold in the grit,
Wherein yet it liveth,
    As useless to men
    As e'er it erst was.

There is a soft orchestral interlude. A syncopated rhythm is heard. The tenors enter; the basses then take over the text.

*Then round the howe**
Rode the deer of the battle
*The bairns*** *of the athelings****
Twelve were they in all.

*   howe = also a dell
** bairns = sons (or daughters)
*** athelings = of royal blood; prince

Their care would they mourn,
And bemoan them their king.
The wordlay would they utter
And over the man speak:

The tempo accelerates slightly; the string accompaniment is quite syncopated. Tenors and sopranos are in unison octaves as are altos and basses when they enter a measure and a half later.

They accounted his earlship
And mighty deeds done,
And doughtily deemed them;
As due as it is
    That each one his friendlord
    With words should belaud.

There follows immediately a fortissimo, chordal passage:

And love in his heart,
Whenas forth shall he
Away from the body
Be fleeting at last.

The tenors carry a melodic line on a neutral syllable that moves down to the basses.

The rhythm and tempo of Example 1 returns. First sopranos and altos in unison are heard. They are joined by tenors and basses for a short section in four-part harmony.

In suchwise they grieved,
The folk of the Geats,
For the fall of their lord,
E'en they his hearth-fellows.

Arpeggios by woodwinds and harp are heard. Tenors and basses enter in unison:

Quoth they that
He was a world King
    forsooth

The women's voices respond:

The mildest of all men,
Unto men kindest,

In a beautiful choral passage the voices move from the text to a neutral syllable to bring the *Lament* to a quiet close:

To his folk the most gentlest,
Most yearning of fame.

VII

VIRGIL THOMSON (1896-   ) is a contemporary composer for whom a good melody is still one of the most important ingredients in a good composition. Aaron Copland says of his friend:

> Thomson is a man with a thesis. Whether or not his own compositions really come off, his theory about music has validity for all of us. For a long time now, ever since the middle '20s, Thomson has maintained that so-called modern music is much too involved and pretentious in every way. While most composers of the musical left are busily engaged in inventing all sorts of new rhythmic and harmonic devices, intent upon being as original and different as possible, Thomson goes to the opposite extreme and deliberately writes music as ordinary as possible.... This idea is derived from the conviction that modern music has forgotten its audience almost completely, that the purpose of music is not to impress and overwhelm the listener, but to entertain and charm him. Thomson seems determined to win adherents through music of an absolute simplicity and directness. [23]

Much of the simplicity, the basic honesty, the "solidness" of structure, the inventiveness of Thomson's music stems from his bringing-up in Kansas City, Missouri, where he was born. The sparkle, the wit, the charm of the music — its suavity — are the result of Thomson's long residence in Paris.

Virgil Thomson's father had been a farmer, but shortly before his son's birth he gave up the rural life, moved to Kansas City and became a grip man on a cable car line. The elder Thomson was tone deaf and had no interest in any form of music. After his son's birth it was the lad's mother who encouraged the boy in music. By the time he was two he was singing, and at five he was given piano lessons at his own request. As the boy's interest in music became apparent, he was given singing lessons by the tenor soloist at the Baptist Church and organ lessons by the organist at the Episcopal Church. At 12 Virgil was giving recitals both at church and in school; he also served as the substitute organist for the Baptist Church.

Of his youth in Kansas City Thomson has said:

These years [were] in the first decade of this century, when there were as yet no movies, radio or television. Our mass-produced entertainment consisted wholly of books and of the Sunday comics. We lived in a middle-class neighborhood in a middle-sized Middle Western city, our whole existence as permeated by rural residues as our residential blocks were checkered with vacant lots; and every car line ended in the country. Downtown there were theaters and big stores, ... but in our neighborhoods we lived a small-town life centered on school and church, with lots of play and reading thrown in.[24]

After graduation from Central High School in Kansas City, Thomson enrolled at the newly formed Junior College. He became a straight "A" student and was acknowledged as the brightest scholar in the school. It was at this time that he debated whether to follow a literary career or one in music, exceptional talent in both fields being in evidence.

The next 20 years of Thomson's life are succinctly stated by the composer himself:

I grew up [in Kansas City] and went to war from there. That was the other war. Then I was educated some more in Boston and Paris. In composition I was chiefly the pupil of Nadia Boulanger. While I was still young, I taught music at Harvard and played the organ at King's Chapel, Boston. Then I returned to Paris and lived there for many years, till the Germans came, in fact. [25]

"The other war" was, of course, World War I during which Thomson enlisted in the Army and served as a second lieutenant in the Aviation Corps. His education in Boston consisted chiefly of completing undergraduate work at Harvard University where he studied both piano and organ. On graduation he won both the Naumberg and Payne fellowships, the latter a traveling fellowship that enabled the composer to go to Paris and study with Nadia Boulanger.

In France Thomson was greatly affected by the eclectic style of Erik Satie, and it was probably Satie's influence that led Thomson to include a tango theme (played by clarinet and muted trumpet) in his "Church Sonata" *(Sonata da Chiesa)* of 1926. Old hymn tunes, remembered from his youthful days as a church organist, also kept appearing in his music. The *Symphony On a Hymn Tune* of 1928 used *How Firm a Foundation* as its Principal Subject, and *Yes, Jesus Loves Me* as its Second Subject.

In 1934 one of his major works was given a performance in Hartford under the auspices of the Society of Friends and Enemies of Modern Music of which Virgil Thomson served as a Director from 1934 to 1937. It was a production of his opera *Four Saints in Three Acts* to a text by his friend of Paris days, Gertrude Stein. The text actually made no sense, but was a series of sonorous sounding words; a deliberate confusion was perpetrated by the author, for there were actually four acts and more than a dozen saints, one of them in duplicate. The composer's almost solemn, hymn-like treatment (with tongue in cheek, of course) created a hilarious modern *opera buffa.* It was given more than 60 performances in one year, "at that time something of a record in the United States for a contemporary opera composed in English," stated the composer. The work was revived in 1941 for two concert performances in the Museum of Modern Art. Alfred Wallenstein broadcast it in 1942 under the auspices of the Treasury Department to sell war bonds, and in 1947 it was conducted by the composer for a broadcast over the Columbia network. In 1952 the opera was completely restaged for performances in New York and Paris. A production of it was mounted in Japan, and the West Coast premiere was given by a group of musically gifted high school students in Los Angeles in 1962. For the latter performance, the Music Critic of the Los Angeles *Times* said: "One can envision a more professional production than the one we saw . . .

but on the whole it came off nicely. Whatever the parents thought of such strange goings-on, one thing is sure: the boys and girls will never be the same again."

When Thomson returned from Paris at the start of World War II, he became the music critic for the *Herald Tribune* of New York. His reviews and articles were widely read; five series of them have been published in book form. He resigned as music critic in 1954 to devote more time to composition.

A second opera to a text by Gertrude Stein, *The Mother of Us All,* was premiered in 1947. This time, however, the text definitely made sense for it related the life story of Susan B. Anthony, the woman suffragette. The opera was restaged at the University of California at Los Angeles in 1965.

Virgil Thomson was invested as a Chevalier of the French Legion of Honor in 1947. He was at the time staying in Cap d'Antibes and it was arranged that the ribbon and medal should be presented in a full military ceremony by the resident First Moroccan Infantry. This, according to the composer, "consisted of a band, a headquarters platoon, and the regimental mascot, a bearded goat. And in their presence, in a public square in Nice, I was pinned and kissed while bagpipes and drums played *The Star-Spangled Banner* and *La Marseillaise,* both in florid Moroccan style."

Thomson has earned an outstanding reputation for the music scores he has provided for films. His first effort in this direction was the score for *The Plough That Broke the Plains* produced by the U. S. government in 1936. The following year he composed the score for *The River,* another documentary for the U.S. government. In 1948 he provided the score for Robert Flaherty's *Louisiana Story* from which two frequently performed orchestral suites have been made.

Since his retirement Thomson has continued to write prodigiously. The list of works includes choral and orchestral pieces, dozens of songs and *pièces diverses* for solo piano and assorted instruments. Truly, in the words of Aaron Copland, "The evidence is conclusive: Virgil Thomson is a unique personality in the recent history of our music."

Prologue to Act I of *Four Saints in Three Acts* by Virgil Thomson. The cast was all black, the scenery of cellophane. Commère and Compère sit to the extreme left and right of the stage as St. Ignatius kneels, center, surrounded by the other saints (of which there are more than four!)

FOUR SAINTS IN THREE ACTS

Act I

Virgil Thomson, in *About Four Saints,* has given the background of this most unusual opera. He says:

It was early in 1927 that Gertrude Stein and I conceived the idea of writing an opera together. Naturally the theme had to be one that interested us both. 'Something from the lives of the saints' was my proposal; that it should take place in Spain was hers. She then chose (and I agreed) two Spanish saints, Teresa of Avila and Ignatius Loyola. The fact that these two, historically, never knew each other did not seem to either of us an inconvenience.

Miss Stein loved these saints because they were Spanish. I liked them for being powerful and saints. She had traveled a great deal in Spain, loved its landscape and people; I had been brought up in Missouri among Southern Baptists and spent my youth as a church organist. The music of religious faith, from Gregorian chants to

Sunday School ditties, was my background, my nostalgia. So we made together, Gertrude Stein and I, an opera about the Spanish landscape and about the religious life. She gave me the libretto of *Four Saints in Three Acts* in June of 1927; and I completed the music in July of the following year. In 1934 it was produced in Hartford, Connecticut (and also New York and Chicago), by a group entitled The Friends and Enemies of Modern Music. . . .

For me the cooperation had been a happy one from the beginning, and its memory is still sweet. Miss Stein had said when she gave me the completed play, 'Do anything with this you like; cut, repeat, as composers have always done; make it work on a stage.' Actually I made no cuts or repeats in my first version. I put everything to music, even the stage directions, because they made such lovely lines for singing. Later I did make some cuts, with the advice of Maurice Grosser, who had added a scenario or plot, to facilitate the staging. That scenario pleased Miss Stein. She always said afterwards, 'Maurice understands my writing.'

Gertrude liked rhymes and jingles, and she had no fear of the commonplace. Her communion hymn for all the saints is 'When this you see remember me.' And when Saint Ignatius sees the Holy Ghost, she describes his vision as "Pigeons on the grass alas and a magpie in the sky." Also she loved to write vast finales like Beethoven's great codas, full of emphasis, insistence and repetition. She wrote poetry, in fact, very much as a composer works. She chose a theme and developed it; or rather, she let the words of it develop themselves through free expansion of sound and sense.

Putting to music poetry so musically conceived as Gertrude Stein's has long been a pleasure to me. The spontaneity of it, its easy flow, and its deep sincerity have always seemed to me just right for music. Whether my music is just right for it is not for me to say. But happiness was ours working together, and a great friendship grew up between us. This friendship lasted twenty years, till her death.[26]

The first production of *Four Saints in Three Acts* made theatrical history, as has already been mentioned. The scenery was made out of cellophane and the stage movements choreographed by Frederick Ashton (now *Sir* Frederick) and John Houseman. "It was also novel," states the composer, "that an all-Negro cast should be received so warmly in a work that had nothing whatever to do with Negro life. I had chosen them purely for beauty of voice, clarity of enunciation, and fine carriage. Their surprise gift to the production was their understanding of the work. They got the spirit of it, enjoyed its multiple meanings, even its obscurities, adopted it, moved in on it."

As Thomson has mentioned, the subject of *Four Saints in Three Acts* is religious life in Spain, particularly as it centers around the lives of Saint Teresa and Saint Ignatius. They are represented in imaginary scenes surrounded by younger saints who are their companions, pupils and apprentices. The *Compère* and *Commère* — the master and mistress of ceremonies — converse with each other, with the saints, and with the audience (commenting on the progress of the opera). Saint Settlement is Saint Teresa's confidante, and Saint Chavez is aid-de-camp to Saint Ignatius. These are the four saints of the title. Saint Settlement and Saint Chavez have no historical prototypes.

Thomson has cautioned the listener: "Please do not try to construe the words of this opera literally or to seek in it any abstruse symbolism. If, by means of the poet's liberties with logic and the composer's constant use of the simplest elements in our musical vernacular, something is here evoked of the childlike gaiety and mystical strength of lives devoted in common to a non-materialistic end, the authors will consider their message to have been communicated."

Maurice Grosser, who devised the scenario for Thomson, said in the preface to the opera's score:

> *Four Saints In Three Acts* is both an opera and a choreographic spectacle. Imaginary but characteristic incidents from the lives of the saints constitute its action. Its scene is laid in 16th-century Spain. . . . Saint Teresa, for reasons of musical convenience, is represented by two singers dressed exactly alike. This device of the composer has no hidden significance and is not anywhere indicated in the poet's text, though Miss Stein found it thoroughly acceptable. . . .

> One should not try to interpret too literally the words of this opera, nor should one fall into the opposite error of thinking that they mean nothing at all. On the contrary, they mean many things at once. The scenarist believes that any practicable interpretation of the text is legitimate and has allowed himself, in consequence, considerable liberty. . . . .

Act I takes place at Avila. It represents a pageant, or Sunday School entertainment, on the steps of the Cathedral. Saint Teresa enacts for the instruction of saints and visitors scenes from her own saintly life. ... The Compère and Commère, downstage at left and right, and Chorus I, grouped on the cathedral steps, sing a choral prologue.

Act I consists of the presentation of seven pictures, or tableaux: .... a garden in the spring, Saint Teresa II being photographed, Saint Ignatius serenading Saint Teresa II, Saint Ignatius offering flowers, Saint Teresa and Saint Ignatius admiring the model of a large house — the Heavenly Mansion, Saint Teresa II in an attitude of ecstasy, and in the seventh tableau, Saint Teresa II rocking in her arms an unseen child. After this the entertainment is over. The act ends with comments, congratulations and general sociability. [27]

The opening line of the opera gives an excellent idea of the nature and musical setting of the opera. After a snare drum roll, an unaccompanied accordian plays the simplest possible triadic harmony. Over this the chorus projects the text which cannot be taken too literally, yet does carry some meaning. As may be found throughout the opera, there are places in Example 1 where the harmony of the chorus is in direct conflict with the accompaniment until it is later resolved.

Example 1

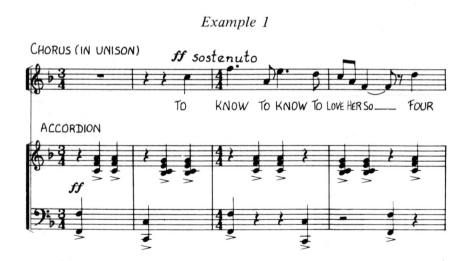

SAINTS PREPARE FOR SAINTS. IT MAKES IT WELL FISH. FOUR SAINTS IT MAKES IT WELL FISH.

The brief Prologue ends as Commère and Compère introduce, in a spoken voice, the saints, to which the chorus responds in a loud, downward phrase, "Any one to tease a saint seriously."

The music for the seven scenes of Act I is continuous, and, just as the harmony of the solo line changed at different points from the harmony of the accompaniment in Example 1 — the scenes on stage quite frequently change at different points (and with different numbers) than those announced by the saints on stage.

The first tableau is a garden at Avila in early spring. There is a wall, and under a nearby tree St. Teresa II is seated, painting flowers on very large eggs. Commère announces:

> *Saint Teresa in a storm at Avila*
> *There can be rain and warm snow and warm*
> *That is the water is warm*
> *The river is not warm*
> *The sun is not warm*
> *And if to stay to cry.*

The chorus of saints speak of Saint Teresa being half indoors and half outdoors, of Saint Ignatius not being there. After Compère commands, by singing *(fortissimo)* "Repeat first act," Commère responds with the spoken remark, "A pleasure, April Fool's day a pleasure. Saint Teresa seated."

There then follows a beautiful solo for Saint Teresa I; from time to time the chorus comments upon her words. The solo begins:

ST. TERESA I   *Example 2*

NOT APRIL FOOL'S DAY A PLEASURE.   NOT APRIL FOOL'S DAY A PLEASURE.

A- PRIL FOOL'S DAY A-PRIL FOOL'S DAY AS   NOT AS PLEASURE AS

A - PRIL FOOL'S DAY   NOT A PLEASURE.

As Compère repeats the line "Saint Teresa very nearly half inside and half outside, outside the house and not surrounded," Saint Teresa I makes her entrance. The two (in one) Saint Teresa's greet each other. After Saint Teresa I sings, "Nobody visits more than they do visits them, Saint Teresa," the chorus responds with a line typical of Gertrude Stein in its play upon words:

> As loud as that
> As allowed as that.

The second tableau is announced by the altos of the chorus who sing that "Saint Teresa could be photographed having been dressed like a lady." It is a relatively short scene.

Scene 3 is introduced by Compère: "Saint Teresa a young girl being widowed." In unison, the two Saint Teresa's respond with a Spanish folk melody:

Example 3

ST. TERESA I AND II

LEAVE LAT-ER GAI ____ LY THE TROU-BA-DOUR PLAYS HIS GUI- TAR.____

Scene four is introduced by the chorus's announcement, "Scene three." After Saint Ignatius presents Saint Teresa II with flowers (the chorus sings, "Does she want to be neglectful of hyacinths and violets") the choir launches into a robust, and syncopated chorus:

Example 4

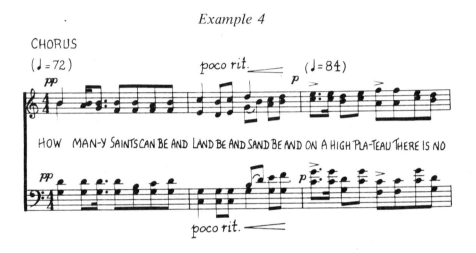

Scene 5 immediately follows. This is the view of the Heavenly Mansion. As Saint Ignatius shows Saint Teresa II the model of it, Saint Stephen sings:

*Saint Ignatius could be in porcelain actually
While he was young and standing.*

Saint Plan replies:

*Saint Teresa could not be young
And standing, she could be sitting.*

Saint Teresa II is seated, "in ecstasy, with an angel hovering" as Scene 6 opens. Tenderly Saint Ignatius sings of Saint Teresa. A bell tone introduces his solo which begins:

Example 5

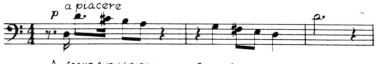

Saint Teresa responds with a beautiful aria. It begins:

Example 6

The seventh and final tableau shows Saint Teresa II rocking with a child cradled in her arms. The chorus sings the closing lines of Act I:

> *One, two, three, four, five, six, seven,*
> *All good children go to heaven.*
> *Some are good and some are bad.*
> *One, two, three, four, five, six, seven.*
>
> *Saint Teresa when she had been*
> *Left to come was left to come was left*
> *To right was right to left and there.*
> *There and not there by left and right.*
>
> *No one surrounded trees*
> *As there were none.*
> *This makes Saint Ignatius*
> *Act Two!*

VIII

HENRY COWELL (1897-1965) was one of the first composers of our time seriously concerned with the study of primitive music, folk music of all peoples, and non-Western elements in music. He was also intrigued by strange and exotic sounds. This led him to the discovery of several new ways of playing the piano and the thorough investigation of Oriental music. He also developed and formulated a theory concerning his use of *tone-clusters*.

In addition to having been a prolific composer — his catalogue lists more than 1,000 works — Henry Cowell participated in numerous activities concerned with the promotion of new music. In 1927 he founded the New Music Society in San Francisco and personally directed its activities which included lectures on modern

VIRGIL THOMSON   HENRY COWELL

music, the publication of articles and books, the production of recordings and the sponsorship of concerts. The most lasting contribution of the Society was the publication of the *New Music Quarterly*, a periodical which presented no comment, only the music itself of one or more new works, either American or foreign. Cowell served as editor for many years and was, in the *New Music Quarterly*, the first to publish a work by Charles Ives. As editor, Cowell would not publish any of his own compositions.

Cowell also became active in the Pan-American Association of Composers founded in 1928 by Edgar Varèse for the purpose of promoting music of the composers from the Western Hemisphere.

Perhaps the best portrait of Henry Cowell during these hurried, harried years is one written (in 1936) by Paul Rosenfeld:

> Wherever in his steady whirl he has set foot on earth, from Los Angeles in the west to Vladivostok in the east, concerts have sprung up, like flowers about the feet of Flora, and they have invariably included performances of the works of the leading American moderns. And he has got these revolutionary scores not only played, but printed and recorded as well. And he has been

writing about this music and getting his articles published in important organs and interesting colleges, forums and clubs in it, and making fruitful contacts with musical people in Russia, Germany, and for all one knows in Kamchatka and at home, and in the meanwhile composing. He has indeed become very influential, and if in person he is still as little and rapid and shiny as of yore, you will find him. . . . in his den . . . . amid an imposing litter of African war drums, ringing telephones, grand pianos, heaps of new music in printed and manuscript form, collaborators of all ages and sexes, adorers aged from 14 to 80, electrical musical appliances of his own invention, and philosophizing musicologists; and after speaking with you for a few minutes about 'creative music' and 'indigenous music,' two mysterious terms frequently on his lips, he will probably dash away − in so doing giving a few last touches to an acid Virginia reel for Theremin or an atonal sinfonietta for classic orchestra − probably to give a lesson.[28]

This active career started in California, in 1897, when Henry Cowell was born on March 11th in Menlo Park, a town on the southern tip of San Francisco Bay. His father was Irish and his mother was from an Irish-English family which had settled in the Middle West.

Cowell began violin lessons when he was five and made such progress that two years later he was able to appear in a recital in San Francisco. Apparently the violin didn't agree with him, for at nine he gave the instrument away and told people that he had decided to become a composer instead of a violinist.

The Cowells were too poor to be able to afford a piano, so Henry had to practice composing mentally. "While my friends were practicing the piano for an hour a day," Cowell later recalled, "I'd sit in my room and practice composing by listening to all kinds of sounds that came into my head."

The Cowells moved to San Francisco, living for a time on the edge of Chinatown, the largest such settlement in the United States. Henry attended school with a number of Chinese students, and from them learned many Oriental songs. He also became acquainted with Chinese opera during this period.

His youthful education in music, at best an informal one, included an introduction to Gregorian chant through the organist of the local Catholic church and a chance to hear vaudeville music by attending the Orpheum Theater with his father.

At 11 he began composing his first opera. Three years later the Cowells were able to afford an old, battered upright piano. Henry, without any guidance as to how a piano should be played "properly," began all kinds of experiments on it. He wrote several works for the instrument, pieces that included in their performance the use of fists and forearms on the keys. When Cowell gave his second recital in San Francisco, in 1912, devoted exclusively to his own compositions, he included many of these strange pieces.

The next years were spent in Kansas, where Cowell supported himself and his mother until her death when he was 18. One means of earning a livelihood during these difficult days was by finding, cultivating and selling rare wild plants.

Cowell returned to California to attend the University of California, studying composition with Charles Seeger (even though he had over 100 works to his credit by this time). He left at the end of three and a half years, unable to graduate because he lacked a high school diploma.

He served as an Army band director during World War I, and then resumed his studies for two years at the Institute of Applied Music in New York. Following this, from 1923 to 1933, Cowell made an annual concert tour of the United States, playing his own piano music. During this period he also made five European tours.

At first the public reacted violently to Cowell's bold innovations: passages played with the forearms or fists on the keyboard, tones produced by reaching *inside* the piano to pluck or strike a string, strange sounds produced by placing objects of wood or metal on the strings of a piano.* In Leipzig, in 1923, according to one music critic,

> the police were called in to quell the riot caused by one of his pieces; during the disturbance Cowell calmly continued at the piano, never halting his performance. During this initial period of making his music known Cowell was to have a rough time of it; a New York daily paper once sent out a sports writer to cover his recital, duly publishing the review on the sports page as an account of the bout between 'Battling Cowell' and 'Kid Knabe.'[29]

By the mid-1920's the large part of the public, those most interested in new music, were no longer shocked by Cowell's

*later called a *prepared piano*

unorthodox approach. Concerts were arranged for him in Europe by such leading figures as the pianist Artur Schnabel, Béla Bartók the composer, and the painter Kandinsky.

In 1931 Cowell was awarded a Guggenheim fellowship which he used to study the music of non-Western cultures at the University of Berlin. At the end of the year he returned to New York where he was placed in charge of the music program at The New School for Social Research. Later he taught, at one time or another, at many different schools across the country: Stanford University, Mills College, Peabody Conservatory, University of Southern California and Columbia University.

During World War II he was consultant on music and chief music editor for the Office of War Information. Following that assignment, he and his wife spent seven years collecting the material for their biography of friend and fellow-composer Charles Ives, a man whose music Cowell had championed for 30 years. *Charles Ives and His Music* was published in 1955, just four days after Ives' death.

As an innovator, Cowell is best known for his introduction of *tone clusters.* According to the composer,

> Tone-clusters . . . are chords built from major and minor seconds, which in turn may be derived from the upper reaches of the overtone series and have, therefore, a sound foundation. In building up clusters from seconds, it will be seen that since both major and minor seconds are used, just as major and minor thirds are used in the familiar system in thirds, there is an exact resemblance between the two systems, and the same amount of potential variety in each. [30]

Cowell first used tone clusters in an orchestral composition in 1916: *Some Music and Some More Music.* A more extensive use of them was made in the *Piano Concerto* of 1929 and in *Synchrony* of 1930. They are treated polyphonically in *Movement* for string quartet.

Cowell has employed other revolutionary ideas and devices. In *Ritournelle,* from the incidental music to Jean Cocteau's *Les Maries de le tour eiffel,* the composer used an "elastic form" — one that can be made into any desired length from three to 104 measures by the proper selection of bars according to a key furnished by the composer.

In 1931 Cowell devised and had built by Leon Theremin an electric instrument known as the rhythmicon which could play metrical combinations of virtually unlimited complexity. He composed a concerto for it, *Rhythmicana.*

Most of Cowell's music seems to fall within one of three "ethnic spheres." It was undoubtedly his Irish ancestry that led him to such works as *The Irish Girl, The Irishman Lilts, The Banshee, Lilt of the Reel, Fiddler's Jig, Gaelic Symphony, Irish Suite* and *Celtic Suite.* His proximity to things Oriental when he lived in San Francisco probably first interested him in non-Western music. "Nothing in my early musical experience had prepared me for the professional musical world's fanatical belief that the conventions of the European tradition of that time were the only possible ones," the composer wrote. "I do not see why a composer's choice should be limited to the musical materials used in Europe for the past 350 years alone. What interests me in music itself is organized sound, its forms, and all the possibilities of a musical idea; to write as beautifully and as interestingly as I can."

"If you understand the classical ingredients of Oriental music," Cowell said at another time, "you can use them as your own." This he did in his orchestral work, *The Snows of Fujiyama.* His *Ongaku for Orchestra* was written after a trip to Japan in 1957. Not all of Cowell's "oriental" music, however, is as easily discovered from titles as are the Irish ones. Many of the movements of chamber and orchestral works in the larger forms show Cowell's Far East influence. The Middle East is represented by the *Persian Set* of 1957 and his *Homage to Iran* written in 1959.

The third influence found in Cowell's music probably stemmed from his youthful days spent in Kansas. It was perhaps the congregational singing in church and the revival songs heard at tent meetings which inspired him to write a series of works for orchestra and for various chamber combinations called *Hymns and Fuguing Tunes.* One movement of his *Symphony No. 4* is based on a similar approach, and in his *Symphony No. 10* the first movement is a hymn, the second a Fuguing Tune.

By 1962, when Cowell got to his 16th symphony (he composed 20 altogether) he was interested in Icelandic music. The work bears the name of that country as its subtitle.

Cowell was still actively composing when he passed away quite suddenly in December of 1965. His last completed work was a *Trio* for violin, cello and piano, a piece "full of happiness, light, wit, and delight in making music," according to a review in The Musical Quarterly. It goes on to say that "The *Trio* is a fitting, final work, and a major one."

During his 68 years, Cowell made an immeasurable contribution to the music of the United States, as composer, critic, and champion of the works of other American composers.

THE BANSHEE

The Banshee is a short, ethereal piece of music which, when heard for the first time, truly suggests its prototype. A banshee, in Irish mythology, is a mysterious woman who hovers over the house of someone about to die and makes strange wailing or shrieking sounds. Non-believers in mythology claim the sound they hear is but the whistle and howl of the wind outside.

The "method" or manner of playing this short work for piano solo is described in a Preface written by the composer and printed in the sheet music:

> *The Banshee* is played on the open strings of the piano, the player standing at the crook. Another person must sit at the keyboard and hold down the damper pedal throughout the composition. The whole work should be played an octave lower than written.[31]

He then goes on to list 12 different methods of producing the sounds and tones of this work, each identified by a letter of the alphabet in the score. In Example 1 below, these letters represent the following, according to the composer:

A   indicates a sweep with the flesh of the finger from the lowest string up to the note given

B   sweep lengthwise along the string of the note given with flesh of finger

C   sweep up and back from lowest A to highest B-flat given in this composition

D   pluck string with flesh of finger, where written, instead
      of octave lower

E   sweep along three notes together in the same manner as
      B

The opening measures are notated as follows:

Example 1

The music becomes harsher as the back of the finger nail is used to brush across the strings. The dynamic level subsides as both hands are used to sweep lightly across the strings simultaneously in opposite directions.

The music accelerates as sweeps are made along the strings of chords built out of four and five seconds *(tone clusters).*

Example 2

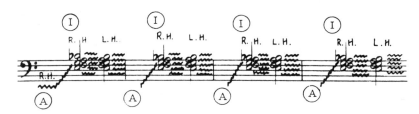

The dynamic level subsides; the tempo slows down. Sweeps along simple triadic chords are made. A final tone cluster — E-sharp, F, and G-sharp — resolves to sweeps on E and F-sharp, resolving *ppp* to a sweep on only the E string.

Was it a wail, a shriek or the howl of the wind?

Cowell rubs the strings of a piano with his right hand while the left hand gently presses down the keys of an E-minor chord to release the dampers so that the proper strings will vibrate when rubbed.

This 1940 oil portrait of Roy Harris by Franz Rederer was inspired by the fugue subject in the composer's Third Symphony.

ROY HARRIS in 1965.

IX

ROY HARRIS (1898-   ) was born in a log cabin in Lincoln County, Oklahoma, on Lincoln's birthday. This indirect association with Lincoln seems to have had a lasting effect on Harris, pervading his thinking, his composing and even his home-spun, eclectic philosophy. He has, in his compositions, tried to be *the* American composer, the poet who speaks musically for the United States. As Virgil Thomson has said, "One would think to read his prefaces that he had been awarded by God, or at least by popular vote, a monopolistic privilege of expressing our nations' deepest ideals and highest aspirations."

One need only look at his catalogue of works to see this preoccupation with things American: in 1927, the *Whitman Triptych* for women's voices on poems of Walt Whitman; in 1934, *When Johnny Comes Marching Home* scored for orchestra, and reset in 1935 for unaccompanied voices; in 1941, *Songs of Democracy* for voices, followed a year later by *Sons of Uncle Sam* also for voices; *March in Time of War* in 1943; *Kentucky Spring* for orchestra in 1949 and a *Red Cross Hymn* in 1951. In 1965 Harris again showed his interest in Lincoln and composed his *Symphony No. 10*, subtitled "The Lincoln." "I expect this symphony to be one of my outstanding works," the composer said just previous to the first performance of it. "I have wanted to write this work for a long, long time." It was premiered on April 14, 1965, the anniversary 100 years to the day, of the assassination of Abraham Lincoln.

His *Symphony No. 11*, first performed by the New York Philharmonic under the composer's baton in 1968, was intended to "get brighter, and end with optimism for the Great Society which we hope we get." Instead, *Time* magazine reported, "it all seemed pumped up, and the amplified piano vibrations that ended the work were like the rasps of escaping air as the climax, the theme of hope, and the listener's expectations all deflated at once."

Unfortunately Harris never surpassed his *Symphony No. 3* written in 1937, a completely abstract work without any programatic suggestions at all.

Much of Harris' attempt at Americanism stems from his rural, agrarian background as a youth. He grew up on a farm that had been homesteaded by his father. Because of a siege of malaria near their farm, his family moved to the San Gabriel Valley in California when he was five. At Covina High School, Harris played football so vigorously that while on the team he broke both his nose and an arm.

The family purchased an old upright piano shortly after moving to California, and it was on this instrument that Harris received his first lessons in piano from his mother. As he grew older he also experimented with the clarinet and the pipe organ. All his musical activities took place in spare moments when he could get away from his chores on the family farm where he helped his father till and harvest the fields. By the time he was 20 he owned a farm of his own.

World War I interrupted both Harris's farming chores and his studies. He served as a private in the army but did not see action in Europe. When he was discharged he returned to southern California and started work at the University. During these days at the University of California, Southern Branch (as the University of California at Los Angeles was then called) he paid his way by driving a dairy truck in the daytime and attending classes at night. Actually this was to be his first serious study of music, for although he had dabbled in piano, clarinet, and organ, he played none of them well. One of his youthful compositions from University days was his *Suite for String Orchestra.* After graduation Harris served for a time as the music critic for the Los Angeles Daily News and at the same time taught at a music school in Hollywood. In 1926 Howard Hanson played one of Harris's compositions, *Andante* for orchestra, at a concert in Rochester. Harris borrowed enough funds to travel east and hear the performance.

In this same year the *Andante* appeared on the program of the New York Stadium Concerts. From this date, Harris's compositions were to take their place on orchestral concerts. Later that year Harris journeyed to Paris to study with Nadia Boulanger at the American Academy. While he was there he won the Guggenheim Fellowship two consecutive years, 1927-1928. At the end of the two years an injury to his spine caused him to be hospitalized and he eventually had to return to the United States for a successful operation. During the time he spend immobilized in bed, he discovered he could compose away from the piano. This immobilization caused him to turn from writing in pianistic style to writing works conceived directly in the orchestral idiom.

He returned to the United States in 1929 and won the Creative Fellowship from the Pasadena Music and Arts Association the following year. Four years later he was appointed head of the composition department at the Westminster Choir School in Princeton, New Jersey, where he served from 1934 to 1938. It was during his tenure at the Westminster school that he wrote his *Third Symphony.* Serge Koussevitsky, then director of the Boston Symphony and an authority on contemporary music, said that it was the greatest American work written so far in the 20th century. It has since been recorded and performed more than any other American symphony of this century. Eugene Ormandy featured the work on his international tour with the Philadelphia Orchestra in 1957-58 and performed it at the World's Fair in Belguim and in Moscow.

After 1933 Harris taught at the Juilliard School of Music in the summer months when away from the Westminster school. In 1941 he was appointed composer in residence at Cornell University to be followed by positions at Colorado College, Utah State Agricultural College, Peabody College for Teachers, Pennsylvania College for Women, and Indiana University at Bloomington. During World War II he obtained a leave from Cornell University and served in the Overseas Branch of the Office of War Information as head of the music section. Since 1964 Harris has taught composition at the University of California at Los Angeles.

Although Harris has written for the motion pictures and for ballet, he has not yet attempted opera. His compositions include 11 symphonies, five string quartets, a quantity of chamber music, and numerous choral works.

SYMPHONY NO. 3

The *Symphony No. 3* of Roy Harris is cast in one movement, although the composer has outlined five sections in this work. The sections include: *Section I* – Tragic, low string sonorities; *Section II* – Lyric, - strings, horns, woodwinds; *Section III* – Pastoral, - woodwinds with a polytonal string background; *Section IV* – Fugue, - dramatic; and *Section V* – Dramatic, tragic.

Section I – Tragic, - low string sonorities (2/2)

The symphony opens with the cellos playing a recitative-like melody unaccompanied, a melody which eventually uses all the tones of the chromatic scale:

Example 1

The cellos are joined by the violas (divided). As they continue, the violas play intervals of fourths and fifths (organum) against the divided cellos. In this they are later joined by bassoon, string bass, and bass clarinet. Eventually a third is added to the harmonic structure.

The melody then receives a contrapuntal treatment which leads to the introduction of a second theme.

The violins enter for the first time with a sonorous melody:

Example 2

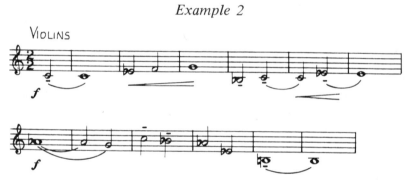

This is a long melody, 29 measures in length. Example 2 like the first theme, uses all the tones of the chromatic scale.

The woodwinds repeat this theme and develop it while the strings accompany it with a counter-melody that becomes increasingly strong.

A unison passage for violins brings this section to a close with a final descending figure for solo flute.

Section II — Lyric, - strings, horns, woodwinds.

The *lyric section* opens with a lyrical melody in A major in the upper strings.

Example 3

VIOLINS

f

The strings and woodwinds then answer each other and alternate with this theme, punctuated first by the French horns and then by the trumpets.

A descending counter-melody is played strongly by the strings. It is based on the same melody the solo flute played when introducing this section.

An eighth-note figure appears in the clarinets and flutes and prepares the transition to the next section.

Section III — Pastoral, - woodwinds with a polytonal string background.

This section opens with an undulating figure for strings, eighth-note arpeggios in contrasting motion (in a polytonal pattern).

The theme is introduced by the English horn:

Example 4

ENGLISH HORN

mf

Fragments of this theme and extensions of it appear in the clarinet, then the oboe, next the flute, followed by the English horn which plays a variation of it.

This theme (Example 4) is repeated in identical or in altered form by the following instruments in succession:

   solo clarinet
   bassoon
   flutes in octaves
   clarinet and bass clarinet in octaves
   all woodwinds - (chords in vibraphone and trumpets)

The music accelerates and against an accompaniment of strings, variations of the theme (Example 4) are played by:

> French horn
> solo trombone
> trumpet
> French horn
> trumpet
> trumpets and trombones in octaves
> horns, then trumpets, then trombones play fragments of the theme contrapuntally (during this extended passage strings gradually remove mutes)

The accompaniment figures move from strings to woodwinds.

The strings play bold pizzicato chords that bring this section to a close.

Section IV — Fugue, - dramatic

The subject of the fugue appears first in the strings:

Example 5

This is answered by a rhythmic figure in the timpani. The subject of this fugue moves as follows:

> trombones
> French horns
> trumpets
> (short episode)
> trombones followed by trumpets in canon
> percussion (with rhythmic pattern of subject)
> French horns and trumpets in canonical repetition
> trombones and trumpets in canon

A legato passage in contrary motion for the woodwinds is derived from the theme of the Pastoral section (Example 4) accompanied by the horns and later the strings playing derivations of Example 5.

The fugue subject (Example 5) then appears in the trumpet and trombones, then in full brass.

A predominately rhythmic transition of 16 measures leads to Section V.

Section V — Dramatic, tragic

From Section I, Example 2 (augmented) is played by strings, followed three measures later in canon at the fifth in the woodwinds, while the brass state the rhythmical figure of the fugal section.

A repeated D on the timpani (pedal point) appears and is heard up to the closing 16 measures.

Over the pedal point the strings play Example 2 while the horns and woodwinds suggest Example 3 from the Lyric Section.

Repeated rolls on the timpani lead to a final cadence ending on a g minor chord.

X

GEORGE GERSHWIN (1898-1937), at the age of 19, announced to his parents that he was quitting school to go into the music business. Before he could say another word, his parents — immigrants from Russia who had no use for music — exploded. Quit school? Impossible! Nobody got ahead without an education. Musicians were always out of work.

But, George protested, he *had* a job. One that would pay $15 a week! The following day, George Gershwin began his professional career in music as a Tin Pan Alley song plugger. He worked

George Gershwin completes an oil portrait of Arnold Schoenberg. A talented artist who both painted in oils and sketched in charcoal, Gershwin admired the music of Schoenberg and Ravel.

for Remick's, a music publisher, in a cubicle about the size of a self-service elevator, pounding out songs on the piano for entertainers who came looking for new material.

After work he studied "classical" music with one of the outstanding pianists of his day, Edward Kilenyi. Gershwin also wrote his own tunes, and soon got a chance to play one for Sophie Tucker, a rising young singer who was to become the famous "Red Hot Mamma." She liked it, recommended it to a music publisher, and at 18, Gershwin was a published composer. The song neither made him rich nor famous (he earned a grand total of $5 in royalties from it), but the time was not far distant when the boy from the Lower East Side of New York would be represented on Broadway by such hit tunes as *Swanee, Fascinating Rhythm, The Man I Love* and *Embraceable You.* (And in the process, earn enough money to afford a penthouse on the upper east side.)

Striving for something beyond the style of Tin Pan Alley, George Gershwin sought a truly American idiom. With *Rhapsody in Blue*, he found that idiom and brought jazz to the concert stage in the country of its origin. And in the powerful rhythms of a black prayer meeting, he found inspiration for *Porgy and Bess,* one of the few masterpieces of native American opera.

For George Gershwin, in spite of all the fame and money he eventually enjoyed, life was not easy. His father, a mild-mannered, humorous man, was always busy trying to provide for his family — three boys and a girl. He was forever buying and selling businesses: for a restaurant he would swap a stationery store; the restaurant, in turn, was traded for a bakery. The bakery for a rooming house, the rooming house for a Turkish bath. This meant the family was continually changing residences so he could be near his place of business. George's older brother, Ira, recalled in later years that the family lived in 28 different apartments between 1900 and 1917.

The elder Gershwin's only interest in and talent for music was his ability to play a few tunes on a pocket comb wrapped with a piece of tissue paper. He could see no reason for wasting money on the purchase of a piano. He was a man who had fled Czarist Russia to escape the Jewish pogroms; more often than not he conversed with his wife in Russian. Theirs was a frugal life; there was no room in it for music.

At school George met a classmate named Max Rosenzweig (later shortened to Rosen) who, at eight, was already proficient on the violin. George was fascinated as he listened to the boy play; the music entranced him. The two became the best of friends. "We chummed about arm in arm," Gershwin later recalled. "Max opened the world of music to me. When we'd play hooky together, we'd talk eternally about music — that is, when we weren't wrestling. I used to throw him every time, by the way, though he was one of those chubby, stocky kids."

All of this made George think about making music himself. He started visiting a friend whose folks owned a piano and started picking out the tunes he had heard at school, *Annie Laurie* and *Old Black Joe.* He did the best he could improvising harmony with the left hand. For two years George kept this up; his family knew nothing about it. It wasn't that he was trying to hide the facts from them, it was that they just didn't care, one way or the other.

However, after a neighbor acquired a piano, George's mother, wanting to "keep up" with the neighbors, decided they too should have one. Even then it wasn't George who received the 50-cent lessons from a professional teacher at first. Ira was the older, so he should receive the paid lessons. Not until Ira and his teacher gave up in despair did George finally have a chance at the Gershwin piano, the "professional" teacher and the 50-cent lessons in piano and harmony.

One day late in the winter of 1914 Ira came home from college and announced that he had been placed in charge of the entertainment for the literary club to which he belonged. He asked George to be an accompanist for the show and to play a solo for it. When he later asked George what he was going to perform so that it could be listed on the program, George told him to simply print "Piano solo" on the program.

Robert Rushmore describes the sequence of events from that point:

> The night of the entertainment arrived and George's solo turned out to be a lively and catchy tango which oddly enough no one seemed to have heard before. Had it just been published? he was asked later. Who was the composer? No, the tango had never been published, George replied and confessed that he was the composer. That night, for the first time in public, George Gershwin had played George Gershwin.[32]

George then quit school and obtained the job already mentioned with Remick plugging songs. By day he sat and played the latest popular pieces for the entertainers who came shopping for new musical materials for their acts and skits. By night Gershwin studied piano, harmony and orchestration of the classics with Edward Kilenyi.

Gershwin then became a rehearsal pianist, working with such talented composers as Irving Berlin. He composed songs to his brother Ira's lyrics. Eventually he was writing Broadway shows, starting with *La, La Lucille* in 1919. He wrote songs for the legitimate acts at silent movie theaters. One of these, *Swanee,* sky-rocketed Gershwin to fame when a singer by the name of Al Jolson picked it up and sang it in black face.

With the coming of the 1920s the United States became involved in a jazz craze. At the same time Broadway was aglitter with the latest stage spectacles of Ziegfield. For five years Gershwin provided all the music for Ziegfield's chief competitor, the annual "George White Scandals." Although no outstanding music came out of this association, it did provide a steady income for the composer.

In the spring of 1923 Gershwin went to London to write a musical comedy for the English stage. It was not a success. Shortly after his return to the United States the famous soprano Eva Gauthier decided to include three songs by Gershwin on her Aeolian Hall recital in New York, November 1, 1923. She was going to call her program "Recital of Ancient and Modern Music for the Voice." The "ancients" included Bellini and Purcell; the "moderns" included (in the order of the program) Béla Bartók, Paul Hindemith (two songs), Jerome Kern, Irving Berlin, George Gershwin (three songs), Arnold Schoenberg, Arthur Bliss (cycle of songs). She asked Gershwin to accompany her at the piano in the songs from the United States.

The music critic turned novelist, Carl van Vechten, wrote:

I consider this one of the very most important events in American musical history and it will lure me back to the concert hall, from which I have held aloof for two years. It is a pleasure to do everything one can for an artist who is perspicacious enough to realize the importance of the only really alive music that is being composed anywhere today. . . .

I suggest that we get up a torchlight procession headed by Paul
Whiteman and his orchestra to honor Miss Gauthier, the pioneer.
Mind you, I prophesy that the Philharmonic will be doing it in two
years. [33]

How right he was! Within a year Paul Whiteman was
performing George Gershwin's *Rhapsody in Blue* at Aeolian Hall,
and before the two years were up, the New York Symphony (not
the Philharmonic) was playing George Gershwin's *Concerto in F*
for piano and orchestra which its conductor, Walter Damrosch, had
commissioned.

The public was divided in its reaction to Gershwin's "concert
hall" music. It was as though some were afraid to sit back and
enjoy it because the composer was suspect of coming from the
wrong side of the tracks, from the field of popular music. Apropos
of his use of jazz, George Gershwin said:

Jazz I regard as an American folk-music; not the only one, but a
very powerful one which is probably in the blood and feeling of
the American people more than any other style of folk music. I
believe it can be made the basis of serious symphonic works of
lasting value, in the hands of a composer with talent for both jazz
and symphonic music. [34]

At another time Gershwin wrote:

It is difficult to determine what enduring values, aesthetically, jazz
has contributed, because 'jazz' is a word which has been used for
at least five or six different types of music. It is really a
conglomeration of many things. It has a little bit of ragtime, the
blues, classicism and spirituals. Basically, it is a matter of rhythm.
After rhythm in importance comes intervals, music intervals which
are peculiar to the rhythm. After all, there is nothing new in
music. I maintained years ago that there is very little difference in
the music of different nations. There is just that little individual
touch. One country may prefer a peculiar rhythm or a note like
the seventh. This it stresses, and it becomes identified with that
nation. In America, this preferred rhythm is called jazz. Jazz is
music; it uses the same notes Bach used. When jazz is played in
another nation, it is called American. When it is played in another
country, it sounds false. Jazz is the result of the energy stored up
in America. It is a very energetic kind of music, noisy, boisterous,
and even vulgar. One thing is certain. Jazz has contributed an

enduring value to America in the sense that it has expressed ourselves. It is an original American achievement which will endure, not as jazz perhaps, but which will leave its mark on future music in one form or another. [35]

Gershwin went on to write an interesting set of piano *Preludes* which incorporated some of his reflections on jazz in music. A trip to Paris to supervise some concerts of his music at the Opéra led to another fine work for orchestra, the tone poem, *An American in Paris.* While in Europe, Gershwin became acquainted with Ravel, Stravinsky and Prokofiev in Paris, and Alban Berg in Vienna.

Days were now crowded with work for the composer, but he found time to take up painting, demonstrating far more than average talent.

Although Gershwin complained from time to time about stomach pains, his health seemed excellent otherwise. He composed one of his best Broadway shows, *Girl Crazy* in 1930. (Playing in the pit orchestra for it were Benny Goodman, Gene Krupa, Glenn Miller, Jack Teagarden and Red Nichols. On stage, a new singer was making her debut, Ethel Merman, in a secondary role.)

Now that sound had been added to movies, it was only natural that Hollywood would want to make use of Gershwin's talents, so after *Girl Crazy* George and Ira Gershwin moved to Beverly Hills. Together they wrote music for movies.

In the meantime Gershwin had been working on an opera inspired by a story he had read by DuBose Heyward, *Porgy.* The author lived in South Carolina, scene of the action of the story, so as soon as Gershwin could get away from a radio contract in New York, he moved south for the summer for two reasons: first, to be near the librettist, and, more importantly, to absorb the atmosphere of the setting of this tale about the South's poor blacks. Gershwin moved from his New York penthouse to Folly Island and a primitive shack with an old iron bedstead and a few pieces of crumbling furniture. Drinking water had to be brought in five-gallon jugs to the little island on which the cabin stood. An old, upright piano was moved in for composing. Here, unshaven and mostly clad in a bathing suit, Gershwin lived by the sea and sand under the hot summer sun and worked with an excitement bounding on ecstasy which he had never known before.

In September he returned to New York with the music for

the opera more or less sketched out. He could write a Broadway show tune in half an hour and make a fortune from it, but to complete complex choral passages, contrapuntal writing and the orchestration of *Porgy and Bess* took another whole year. It was on September 2, 1935 that Gershwin marked the 600-page score of his opera "finished."

The opera was put into six weeks of rehearsal, and on September 30, 1935, four days after Gershwin's 37th birthday, it opened at the Colonial Theater in Boston. In a newspaper interview the composer outlined what he had tried to do in *Porgy and Bess:*

> [Gershwin] has called it a folk opera, and by that he meant that he had based his score on Negro folk music — spirituals, 'shouts,' working songs, street cries, scat singing — though in fact all the music in the opera was entirely his own invention. He believed that opera should be entertaining, should have humor and contain songs, and he pointed to past examples such as *The Marriage of Figaro* and *Carmen* and *La Boheme.* Finally, because it was a folk opera, he had sought to tell more than just the story of crippled Porgy and Bess. They are its leading characters, but the true protagonist of the opera was meant to be the Negro himself, in all his moods, his sorrows, his ecstasies. [36]

After ten days the production moved to the Alvin Theatre in New York; the Metropolitan Opera House couldn't even consider the work as it had, at that time, not a single black singer in its company. *Porgy and Bess* was a commercial failure; it ran only 124 performances in New York, and failed to earn its running expenses and its initial cost of $70,000. Gershwin and DuBose Heyward each lost the money they had invested in it. The 16 weeks in New York were followed by a three-month road tour. But, as Robert Payne later reported, the opera was not headed for oblivion:

> The play possessed, even in its musical form, a raw, naked strength; the music included the best songs Gershwin had written. When Cheryl Crawford revived it in 1941. . . . it played for 8 months in New York and went on tour through 26 cities. . . .

> The triumph of *Porgy and Bess* was only beginning. It played in the Danish Royal Opera in Copenhagen during the German occupation with an all-Danish cast; and the Danish underground took savage

delight in broadcasting, "It Ain't Necessarily So" after each announcement of a Nazi victory. It was played in Moscow in May, 1945 by the Stanislavsky Players, and a month later at the Zurich Festival of music. Thereafter it was seen and heard in nearly every country of Europe. It was seen in Stockholm, Gothenburg, Berlin, Venice, Belgrade, Athens, Naples, Milan, Rome, Turin, Marseilles, Paris, Antwerp. It was shown all over South America, and behind the Iron Curtain. In 1956 it reached Moscow, and went on to play at the Warsaw Opera House. In four years it played in 29 countries, and its journeys have only begun. In 1959 it became a wide-screen technicolor film with Sidney Poitier playing the rôle of Porgy and Dorothy Dandridge playing Bess. . . .

Gershwin never knew his greatest triumph. Worn out, he left for Hollywood to recoup his fortune. . . . When he spoke of Hollywood, he laughed nervously and said, 'I'll take their money, and put it back into writing good opera.'[37]

Gershwin planned another opera with DuBose Heyward, one that would deal with the people of the Virgin Islands. He got no further than the planning stage, for after completing the music for a Ginger Rogers — Fred Astaire picture ("Shall We Dance? ") and one for Astaire and Joan Fontaine, while he was writing music for Samuel Goldwyn's movie musical extravaganza, *The Goldwyn Follies*, it was discovered he had a tumor on the brain. A delicate operation revealed to the doctors that it was in a part of the brain from which it could not be removed. He never regained consciousness and passed away on July 11, 1937, aged 38.

RHAPSODY IN BLUE

George Gershwin was not the first composer to adapt jazz to concert music (Stravinsky and Milhaud among others had preceded him), but he was one of the early pioneers in the field. Posterity may also record that of them all, he was the most successful. His initial effort in this new hybrid form was the *Rhapsody in Blue.*

The idea that Gershwin compose something of larger scope than Broadway musical comedy scores came from Paul Whiteman (1890-1968). The bandleader was planning an "educational" jazz concert at Aeolian Hall in New York, and he wanted Gershwin to write something for it.

Gershwin didn't take Whiteman very seriously. It was therefore with quite a shock that Gershwin read in the *New York
Tribune* of January 4, 1924, that Whiteman had scheduled his
concert for February 12, and that "George Gershwin is at work on
a jazz concerto." Here is the composer's own story of what
happened after that:

> Suddenly an idea occured to me. There had been so much talk
> about the limitations of jazz, not to speak of the manifest
> misunderstanding of its function. Jazz, they said, had to be in
> strict time. It had to cling to dance rhythms. I resolved, if possible,
> to kill that misconception with one sturdy blow. Inspired by this
> aim, I set to work composing.

> I had no set plan, no structure to which my music could conform.
> The *Rhapsody,* you see, began as a purpose, not a plan. I worked
> out a few themes, but just at this time I had to appear in Boston
> for the premiere of *Sweet Little Devil.* It was on the train, with its
> steely rhythms, its rattlety-bang that is so often stimulating to a
> composer (I frequently hear music in the very heart of noise), that
> I suddenly heard — even saw on paper — the complete construc-
> tion of the *Rhapsody* from beginning to end. No new themes came
> to me, but I worked on the thematic material already in my mind,
> and tried to conceive the composition as a whole. I heard it as a
> sort of musical kaleidoscope of America — of our vast melting-pot,
> of our incomparable national pep, our blues, our metropolitan
> madness. By the time I reached Boston, I had the definite plot of
> the piece, as distinguished from its actual substance.

> The middle theme came upon me suddenly as my music often
> does. It was at the home of a friend, just after I got back to New
> York. I must do a great deal of what you might call subconscious
> composing, and this is an example. Playing at parties is one of my
> notorious weaknesses. As I was playing, without a thought of the
> *Rhapsody*, all at once I heard myself playing a theme that must
> have been haunting me inside, seeking outlet. No sooner had it
> oozed out of my fingers than I realized I had found it. Within a
> week of my return from Boston I had completed the structure, in
> the rough, of the *Rhapsody in Blue.* [38]

In the ensuing weeks before the concert, Gershwin worked on
revisions in the *Rhapsody.* The composition was written for two

pianos, with a few suggestions of instrumentation jotted down in the music. Because of the pressure of time, and because Gershwin had had little experience in orchestration, Whiteman's arranger, Ferde Grofé, made the setting for an enlarged dance band, and later for symphony orchestra. The final version of the solo part wasn't even ready at concert time, and there were whole blank pages of piano music which Gershwin improvised on the spot. Whiteman must have had his hands full conducting a score that in one long blank space bore the notation, "wait for nod."

For the Aeolian Hall concert at which the *Rhapsody* was premiered, Whiteman had invited as guests the violinists Fritz Kreisler and Jascha Heifetz, conductors Walter Damrosch and Leopold Stokowski, and composers Serge Rachmaninoff and Igor Stravinsky. Suddenly, at the last minute, panic overtook Whiteman. What had he done, inviting all the biggest names in music to hear an "educational" experiment of his. "Black fear simply possessed me," he later recalled. "I paced the floor, gnawed my thumbs and vowed I'd give $5,000 if we could stop right then and there."

But the concert went on. The program was a very long one with more than 20 selections on it. *Rhapsody in Blue* was to be the next to last item. The audience received the earlier works on the program with mild applause and no enthusiasm. (A jazz selection written by Victor Herbert was quite bad. He could compose the world's best operettas, but not jazz.)

Finally it came time for the *Rhapsody*. Ross Gorman, the band's brilliant clarinetist lifted his instrument and let out that famous, slowly ascending wail which opens the *Rhapsody* (the *glissando* that other clarinetists said was impossible to play). The conductor could feel the attention the audience was giving this new work. "Somewhere in the middle of the score I began crying," Whiteman later recalled. "When I came to myself I was 11 pages along and to this day I cannot tell you how I conducted that far." The final bold, brash notes died away and the audience rose to its feet and gave the *Rhapsody* a wild ovation. Thus its career was successfully launched.

By definition, the *Rhapsody* is in a free, rhapsodic form, ideally suited to Gershwin's purposes. Melodically there are five ideas involved, three of which occur at the very beginning and are variants of the old jazz trick of turning the final chord of a piece into the dominant seventh of the key a fourth higher.

The first is heard immediately: the long, slowly ascending 17-note glissando of the clarinet and the theme which follows it.

Example 1

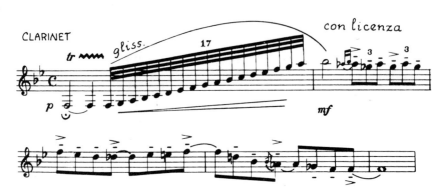

This is followed almost immediately by the second idea, punctuated first by bassoons and horns with a sustained B-flat. then played by the bass clarinet and a single horn:

Example 2

Introduced by a clarinet glissando, a trumpet, with a *wha-wha* mute, plays the melodic idea of Example 1; the full orchestra repeats it.

The piano introduces the third thematic idea, Example 3, in an extended solo passage of some 48 measures which also involves the idea of Example 1.

Example 3

PIANO

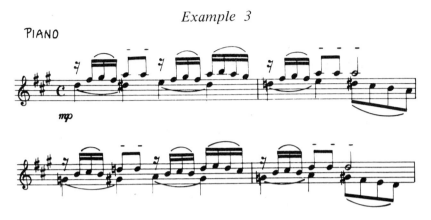

mp

The full orchestra plays the melody of Example 1 *fortissimo* and elaborates on it.

Trumpets in octaves announce the *Rhapsody*'s fourth melodic idea:

Example 4

TRUMPETS   FLUTTER

mf

The clarinet, followed by full orchestra, returns to the melodic idea of Example 2. The orchestra, *marcato,* moves on to the melodic material which follows Example 3 in an extended and lengthy development.

A lengthy passage for solo piano, suggestive of a cadenza, is based on all the thematic material so far introduced.

The tempo changes to *Andantino moderato con espressione*; the strings and reeds introduce the *Rhapsody*'s most famous theme:

Example 5

VIOLINS

p

After an extended passage in which the theme of Example 5 builds to one dynamic climax after another, the solo piano is heard again. It is a cadenza built on Example 5.

In the closing section of the *Rhapsody,* the order of the thematic ideas is reversed. Example 5 is heard first, played by the brass. Example 3 follows in the piano, *Agitato,* building to a climax. Example 2 appears in the solo piano; it is accompanied by woodwinds and strings. A final, bold and brief statement of Example 1 brings the *Rhapsody* to a swift conclusion.

XI

AARON COPLAND (1900-   ) has been a champion of American music in the 20th century, and throughout the world is probably this country's best-known contemporary composer. His works *El Salón México, Rodeo,* and *Billy the Kid* have become standard orchestral fare. In several books, including *What to Listen for In Music, The New Music,* and *Music and Imagination*, Copland has tried to explain how to become an appreciative listener, how to know what the contemporary composer is trying to say in his music.

Copland was born in an old house in Brooklyn, New York and spent the first 20 years of his life there. Around ten years of age, he first became interested in music. At 13, he decided to become a musician. Because the family had spent good money giving music lessons to four older children, only to have them lose all interest in music, Aaron had to plead with his parents many times before they would consent to lessons for him. When his parents finally relented, he had to go on his own to find a piano instructor and arrange for the lessons. Two years after he started work on the piano, he decided to become a composer. His compositions of this period include mostly two-page songs and works for the piano. One was entitled *The Cat and the Mouse* and

GEORGE GERSHWIN

AARON COPLAND

GEORGE ANTHEIL

SAMUEL BARBER

was so modern in its structure that his teacher frankly admitted he was unable to judge it because he had been schooled in traditional harmony.

It had become a tradition for incipient composers to travel to Europe for the study of music and Copland looked forward to making such a pilgrimage. As World War I had just ended, Germany was no longer the place to go. A new school for Americans was opening in Fontainebleau, just outside Paris, and in 1921 Copland left for a year's study at the new school. He faced training in traditional harmony which he felt he already knew; he wanted something to guide him into more modern music. It was suggested that he look in on a class by Nadia Boulanger, who was teaching there. He was so impressed with her work that he enrolled and extended his visit from one to three years. During his days in Fontainebleau, Copland wrote several motets, a *Passacaglia* for piano, and a one-act ballet called *Grohg.*

Before his return to the United States in 1924 he was asked by Nadia Boulanger to compose a work for organ and orchestra since she was soon to appear as a soloist with the New York Symphony. Copland had never tried writing a composition of such length before. He started working on his *First Symphony for Orchestra and Organ* on his return to America, and completed it while playing in a hotel trio providing "dinner music," in Lilford, Pennsylvania. Nadia Boulanger performed the symphony with the New York Philharmonic and later repeated it with the Boston Symphony Orchestra.

This same year the League of Composers wished to perform two of Copland's works. They selected *The Cat and the Mouse,* and the *Passacaglia* that had been written in Paris. Following the Boston orchestra's performance of his *Symphony for Orchestra and Organ,* the director, Serge Koussevitsky, requested a new chamber selection. To make his work more American, Copland turned to the jazz idiom. He called this new piece *Music for the Theater*, and it was performed by Koussevitzky and the Boston orchestra.

After the Guggenheim Memorial Foundation had been established in 1925, Copland was the first recipient of a grant. Copland's next work was a *Concerto for Piano and Orchestra*, his last attempt to use the jazz idiom. This work also was premiered by the Boston Symphony Orchestra. They then commissioned him to write a work for performance at their Fiftieth Anniversary

Concert. For this occasion Copland wrote his *Symphonic Ode.*

It was at this point in his career that Copland decided that the works of his contemporaries as well as his own were not appealing to the public. He decided that music must be simpler in style, "spare in sonority, lean in texture." His *El Salón México* was the first composition in his "new" style, a work based on Mexican folk tunes. Two ballets followed written for Agnes de Mille, the dancer, *Billy the Kid* and *Rodeo,* both using cowboy tunes.

For several years Copland had hoped to complete a ballet for his friend Martha Graham, another dancer of the modern school, and had talked to her about it, but it remained for a commission from the Coolidge Foundation to bring him actually to work on such a score. His *Appalachian Spring,* written for Miss Graham, was first presented in Washington, D. C., in 1944. The following year the work won the Pulitzer Prize.

Copland's *Third Symphony* was performed by the Boston Symphony Orchestra in 1946. Four years later the League of Composers honored his 50th birthday by a concert devoted to his works. The program included such diverse works as the *Piano Quartet* of 1950 and *As It Fell Upon a Day* of 1929.

The New York City Center presented Copland's opera, *The Tender Land,* in 1954, a two-act work which was fairly simple in style. It received a "curiously tentative reception" despite an excellent review by critics. The following year Copland's *Canticle of Freedom* for chorus and orchestra was presented by the Symphony of the Air with Leonard Bernstein conducting. This was a semi-religious work, mystical in quality, and somewhat modal in style.

Copland's investigation of and experimentation with composition in the 12-tone method is best explained by the composer himself, who writes:

I first consciously tried my hand at 12-tone composition in my *Piano Quartet* of 1950.

As it turned out, the Schoenberg method (not the aesthetic) continued to intrigue me in subsequent works, such as the *Piano Fantasy* (1957) and the *Connotations for Orchestra* (1962). I found 12-tone writing to be especially liberating in two respects: it forces the tonal composer to unconventualize his thinking with respect to chordal structure, and it tends to freshen his melodic and figurational imagination. The *Connotations* was my first 12-tone orchestral work; it was composed on commission from the New York Philharmonic for the opening program in its new hall at Lincoln Center [1962]. The acidulous harmonies of my score, sharpened by the shrill acoustics of the new auditorium, upset a good many people, especially those who were expecting another *Appalachian Spring.* It brought to the fore once again a continuing discussion concerning the apparent dichotomy between my 'serious' and my 'popular' works. I can only say that those commentators who would like to split me down the middle into two opposing personalities will get no encouragement from me. I prefer to think that I write my music from a single vision; when the results differ it is because I take into account with each new piece the purpose for which it is intended and the nature of the musical materials with which I begin to work. Musical ideas engender pieces, and the ideas by their character dictate the nature of the composition to be written. It bothers me not at all to realize that my range as composer includes both accessible and problematical works. To have confined myself to a single compositional approach would have enhanced my reputation for consistency, no doubt, but would have afforded me less pleasure as a creator. The English critic Wilfred Mellers puts it this way: 'There is no fundamental disparity between the two styles; the same sensibility adapts the technique to the purpose in hand.' I like to believe that what he says is true. [39]

SONATA FOR VIOLIN AND PIANO

I. Andante semplice

The *Sonata for Violin and Piano,* a completely abstract work, dates from 1942 and 1943, the so-called "popular" period in which Copland was involved in writing ballet music based on folk idioms: *El Salón México* (1936), *Billy the Kid* (1938), *Rodeo* (1942) and *Appalachian Spring* (1944). The *Sonata* was one of three works composed simultaneously. The more humorous aspects of this situation are explained by the composer, who says:

Most of *Appalachian Spring* and a good part of my *Violin Sonata* were composed at night at the Samuel Goldwyn Studios in Hollywood. An air of mystery hovers over a film studio after dark. Its silent and empty streets give off something of the atmosphere of a walled medieval town; no one gets in or out without passing muster with the guards at the gates. This seclusion provided the required calm for evoking the peaceful, open countryside of rural Pennsylvania depicted in *Appalachian Spring.* [Copland was at work in the daytime on the music score for Goldwyn's movie North Star.]

During this time Groucho Marx was employed by Mr. Goldwyn, and I used to see him occasionally in the studio lunch room, where we exchanged pleasantries. One night I was genuinely surprised to come upon him at a concert of modern music in downtown Los Angeles where my Piano Sonato was being given a local premiere. 'Whatever you do,' I said with a smile, 'don't tell Mr. Goldwyn about this advanced stuff I write, or you might frighten him. After all,' I added jokingly, 'I have a split personality.'

Groucho came right back with, 'Well, it's O.K., as long as you split it with Mr. Goldwyn.' [40]

The *Sonata for Violin and Piano* was given its first performance in New York City on January 17, 1944. The dedication reads: to Lt. Harry H. Dunham (1910-1943), "a friend of mine," the composer has said, "who lost his life while on duty in the South Pacific."

"There are three movements — moderate tempo, slow and fast. . . . . . The first movement alternates in mood between a tender lyricism and a more rapidly paced section."

The *Sonata* opens with a soft, sustained and moderately slow introduction. Chords typical of Copland's harmonic idiom are heard in the piano; the violin enters with a motive which later will expand into the Principal Theme. The opening measures:

Example 1

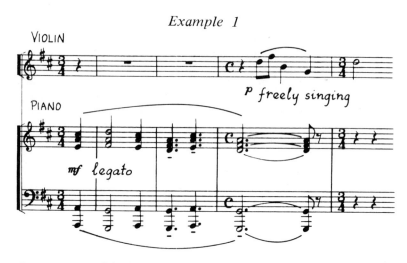

At measure 24 the tempo starts to accelerate and the violin motive of the introduction is expanded into a full melody, the Principal Theme of the movement. (Arthur Berger, in his book on Copland says this "method of constructing longer melodic lines out of short, nuclear elements by interpolation or extension has remained Copland's characteristic way).

Example 2 **(Principal Theme)**

After a repetition of a variant of Example 2 is played by the violin, the piano takes it up with a sustained counter-melody in the violin.

The tempo accelerates slightly as the violin introduces the "more rapidly paced scherzo." Example 3 is heard in counterpoint to some busy figurations in the piano derived from motives in it.

Example 3 **(Second Theme)**

The dynamic level subsides, the violin drops out, the tempo slackens. The Principal Theme, Example 2, returns in the violin to sustained A's and the G's in the piano accompaniment. A very lyrical section follows based on a derivative of the Principal Theme, answered by the chord motive of Example 1:

Example 4

Eventually the Principal Theme, Example 2, breaks out and is played by the piano it its lower octave. The Recapitulation has begun. On its repetition, the violin takes up a sustained counter-melody.

The tempo accelerates and the Second Theme, Example 3, is heard again in a passage of busy counterpoint.

The rather long Coda is based on the more energetic Second Theme, Example 3, treated contrapuntally (usually in stretto). It builds to a strong and vigorous closing.

XII

GEORGE ANTHEIL (1900-1959) was dubbed by a critic "the bad boy of music" because of the wild, almost unbelievable piano compositions he was writing and playing early in his career. Although Antheil* later turned to more conventional methods of composition, he never could shake this epithet.

Actually George Antheil's life lends proof to the old adage that truth is sometimes stranger than fiction. He got his introduction to music in plebeian Trenton when two innocent-looking old ladies covered up a jailbreak by thundering on the piano. After that, nothing about his life was plebeian. Practising the piano 16 hours a day, he toured Europe, played French compositions in Germany, married a Hungarian in Paris, and there became a leader of Left Bank iconoclasts.

In 1929 he returned to the United States for the performance of his *Ballet mécanique* (scored for machines and airplane propeller). It caused a sensation among critics and sent him back to Europe penniless. In 1933 he returned to this country again and led an even more bizarre life. He wrote several books, including (in 1940) *The Shape of the War to Come* which predicted the bombing of Pearl Harbor by the Japanese in January of 1942 (off by one month). He wrote magazine articles, including one for *Esquire* titled "Chopin in Two Lessons." "It taught you how to play piano music immediately," the composer said, "but not by ear." He became an expert in criminology and published a book called, "Every Man His Own Detective." He also wrote some mystery novels and provided advice to police departments in his area of specialization, criminal endocrinology. He went to Hollywood and composed the score for movies including *The Scoundrel* and *The Pride and the Passion.* He wrote an advice-to-the-love-lorn column called "Boy Advises Girl" for *The Chicago-Sun* newspaper syndicate. With movie star Hedy Lamarr he invented and patented a radio torpedo.

*pronounced An´- tile

His close friends in Paris, New York and Hollywood included Igor Stravinsky, James Joyce, Gertrude Stein, Leopold Stokowski, Salvador Dali, Ernest Hemingway and the aforementioned Hedy Lamarr. Even his autobiography was a bit eccentric. "It doesn't pretend to know anything about Antheil," Antheil says in it, "whether or not he's ever destined to be anything of a permanent addition to musical literature; but it does propose to let you in on the inside of Antheil, happenings that 'triggered,' so to speak, his compositions." He then proceeds to describe his childhood:

I had been born in Trenton, New Jersey, across the street from a very noisy machine shop; thus, in all probability, giving (but without any scientific justifications) ammunition into the hands of those who claim there is such a thing as prenatal influence. A year later my parents moved several blocks away to across the street from an infinitely more silent but also infinitely more ominous structure, the Trenton State Penitentiary.

One of my first memories in life is of looking out of our front window to a brown wall and guard tower right across the street.

My first memory of music is also connected with this view.

One day, right next door, there moved in two old maids and their piano. To the intense indignation of my parents, these old maids then proceeded to play this piano day and night.

They played the *Midnight Fire Alarm* by E. T. Paul, *The Maiden's Prayer, Star of the Sea* (over two million copies sold, the frontispiece said), and practically every other piece in an album which I was afterwards able to identify as "Five Hundred Favorite Salon Melodies." They also played in shifts and, if my parents had been concerned less with the noise in the house than in the cellar, they might have been able to detect a faint grating, crunching sound and so prevented one of the most sensational prisonbreaks in the history of Trenton Penitentiary.

For suddenly one night the two old maids stopped playing. The next morning both of them had disappeared. So had sixteen desperate men in the prison across the street. The incessant piano playing, of course, had been a cover for the noise of digging an underground tunnel from the cellar of the house next door to the prison yard.

> In any case, and by whatever means, my love for music — and especially for piano playing — had been gained, and it has never departed. [41]

When George was five the Antheil's moved away from the prison neighborhood to a newly developed district of Trenton where, even though every house was like every other house in the block, they were all brand new.

> When I was eight years old a lot of the kids in our neighborhood formed a club which had its headquarters in an unused garage in the back yard of one of the kids. We continued this club under many names until I was thirteen: Easy Going Club, The Seneca Detective Agency, 101 Ranch. On the outside, so to speak, I commenced the study of the violin, then the piano. None of the kids thought any the worse of me for it. Most of them had to learn how to play one instrument or another too. The only difference between them and me was that I enjoyed practicing. They didn't know this until, one day, I invited them all into our front parlor and played for them a new piano "sonata" which I had written.

> It was called *The Sinking of the Titanic.*

> It was a very stormy piece, with great rolling chords in the bass and a touching version of *Nearer My God to Thee* as a grand finale. It was also an unqualified success, being greeted with cheers and whoops.

> I became the club's official composer. Thereafter, in quick succession, I turned out three other "sonatas," one dedicated to Buffalo Bill, one on the subject of Ayesha (heroine of a Rider Haggard novel), and one on "The Dying Gladiator."

> All these, in my own private circle, were huge successes.

> Outside of this one musical variation, my early youth did not differ an iota from that of the average kid in our neighborhood, which means most of the neighborhoods in America. [42]

George Antheil began the study of harmony when he was 12. His first music teacher of importance was Constantine von Sternberg, a former pupil of Liszt. "He was an old man, but devoted to my talent," the composer later remarked. "He insisted upon a strict contrapuntal basis. Many persons believe . . . that I have had little theoretical training, but this is not so. I studied very intensively during those early adolescent years, and was able to write passable, and even musical fugues when I was 18. Also sonata-allegro movements."

After Antheil heard Stravinsky's *Petrushka* for the first time at a Philadelphia Orchestra concert, he studied every piece of new music he could get his hands on. He then left Sternberg in 1919 and went to New York to study composition with Ernest Bloch. "It was while I was with Bloch that I composed my *First Symphony.* I wanted the Symphony to express that part of America which I saw all around me: Trenton, the Delaware River, the people I knew, the sounds and emotions I felt."

His old teacher, Sternberg, introduced the youth to Mrs. Bok (later Mrs. Efrem Zimbalist) who awarded Antheil a scholarship to the Settlement School, the forerunner of the Curtis Institute of Music.

In 1922 Antheil went on a tour of Europe as a concert pianist, making his debut in London on June 22. It was about this time that he earned the reputation of being the "Bad Boy of Music." For a while he settled in Berlin where his *Symphony No. 1* was premiered by the Berlin Philharmonic. He then moved on to France.

On October 4, 1923, I played Paris for the first time..... My little group of piano pieces, the *Mechanisms,* the *Airplane Sonata* and the *Sonata Sauvage* were to go on as a prelude to the opening of the brilliant Ballets Suédois (Swedish Ballet) which Rolf de Mare was bringing to Paris this season for the first time. The theater, the famous Champs Elysées, was crowded with famous personages of the day, among others Picasso, Stravinsky, Auric, Milhaud, James Joyce, Erik Satie, Man Ray, Diaghileff, Miro, Artur Rubinstein, Ford Maddox Ford, and unnumbered others. They had not come to hear me, but to see the ballets.

My piano was wheeled out on the front of the stage, before the huge Leger cubist curtain, and I commenced playing. Rioting broke out almost immediately. I remember May Ray [an artist photographer] punching somebody in the nose in the front row. Marcel Duchamps [the painter of the controversial "Nude Descending a Staircase"] was arguing loudly with someone else in the second row. In a box near by Erik Satie was shouting, 'What precision! What precision! ' and applauding. The spotlight was turned on the audience by some wag upstairs. It struck James Joyce full in the face, hurting his sensitive eyes. A big burly poet got up in one of the boxes and yelled, 'You are all pigs! ' In the gallery the police came in and arrested the surrealists who, liking the music, were punching everybody who objected.

It was a full twenty minutes later, when I had finished playing, that order was finally restored, and the curtain raised on the first of the ballets. But from October 4, 1923, everybody in Paris knew who I was. I represented the anti-expressive, anti-romantic, coldly mechanistic aesthetic of the early twenties. Shortly thereafter I wrote some music to a film by Fernand Leger called *Ballet mécanique,* a film that had been inspired by my *Mechanisms* . . . .

Without knowing it I had, unconsciously, changed the entire future course of my life. I lost interest in the concert field, year by year becoming more and more a composer until composing alone would no longer support me. [43]

His fame soared rapidly, especially in the more fashionable Paris salons. His concerts were sell-outs. Jean Cocteau sang his praises; Ezra Pound spoke of him as a genius in a book entitled *Antheil and the Theory of Harmony.*

Unfortunately a performance of the *Ballet mécanique* went very badly in New York. Henry Cowell recalls:

The first concert performance of George Antheil's *Ballet mécanique* was a front-page sensation: the propellers of the Liberty motors required by the score not only made the loudest noise ever heard in Carnegie Hall, but they literally blew front row auditors out of their seats. Eight pianos played by well-known musical figures (I recall Aaron Copland, Colin McPhee and Erno Balogh among others), crowded the stage, together with a large number of noisemaking performers, not all of them musicians. At least one of them had to be skillful with an alarm clock. The work is always recalled as *the* sensational classic of percussion music. [44]

The airplane propellers were too much for the audience; New Yorkers considered the *Ballet mécanique* more a hoax than music. That fact, coupled with the failure of Antheil's *Piano Concerto*

"The City" by Fernand Léger (1881-1955), the artist who furnished the backdrop for the Carnegie Hall premiere of Antheil's *Ballet mècanique.*

(premiered in Budapest and repeated in Paris) led to several very discouraging years for the composer.

In 1930 Antheil's fortune took a turn for the better. His opera *Transatlantic* was a big success at the Frankfurt opera, receiving 20 curtain calls on opening night. Built around a presidential candidate and his hunt for Helena, a beautiful woman, it was, according to David Ewen, "a saga of America, racy with jazz effects and idioms. It was novel; it was modern; it was American to the core. It spoke of modern hotels, Childs restaurants, department stores. One of the arias was sung in a bathtub. The German audiences loved its feverish tempo and jazzy atmosphere."

Two years later Antheil won a Guggenheim Fellowship which enabled him to write another opera, *Helen Retires* (about Helen of Troy) with a libretto by John Erskine. It was first presented at the Juilliard School of Music in 1934; it was a failure.

In 1933 Antheil moved to Hollywood where he started writing music for the movies and also worked on his *Symphony No. 3.* Ten years later his *Symphony No. 4* was introduced by the NBC Symphony under the direction of Leopold Stokowski. "I put everything I knew into this symphony [written during World War II].... Mostly into it had gone El Alamein, Stalingrad and the new America I saw awakening. The feeling of it. You can put these big abstractions into music."

This symphony proved to be one of Antheil's most popular works with symphony orchestras in spite of its strange mixture of styles. It incorporates military music, waltzes, a fugue, music for eccentric dancing, Red Army choruses, etc.

Although Antheil went on to write a *Symphony No. 6,* it was his opera *Volpone,* first performed in New York in 1953, which was the crowning achievement of his last years. He passed away on February 12th, 1959.

BALLET MECANIQUE

During the winter of 1923-4 George Antheil worked on a large composition for orchestra. In its own way it was to be a sequel to the *Sonata Sauvage,* the *Airplane Sonata* and the *Mechanisms.* "But it was a work of greater length and orchestration; it also said more exactly what I wanted to say in that medium."

The music was originally intended to accompany a film, but in those days of silent movies there was no known way of synchronizing the two, so Antheil simply completed the work as an independent concert piece. The score called for ten player pianos and all sorts of mechanical noisemakers, including door bells and the sound of airplane propellers. After assigning the work its title the composer feared the public misunderstood the composition because of it. He said in his biography:

> Its title ... seems to imply that it is a "mechanical dance," a ballet of mechanism, machinery, possibly to illustrate the interior of a factory. But it must be remembered that 1924 was the beginning of the day of titles without connection. If one wrote a book then, for instance, one usually gave it a name as far removed from the contents as possible; as, for example, the titles of Hemingway's or

Ford Maddox Ford's novels were hardly connected with their contents. (This has even continued to be the style!) I called my musical piece *Ballet mécanique,* but I really do not remember why. Actually I called it *Ballet mécanique* against the better advice of Sylvia Beach, who was certain that the title would be misinterpreted by the French as "Mechanical Broom"; the words for "ballet" and "broom" sound exactly alike in French.

My original title for the work (given on the manuscript started in Germany) was "Message to Mars." Considered from the purely euphonistic point of view, it is, of course, a much worse one than *Ballet mécanique*; moreover it implies all kinds of moralistic and mystic things which would certainly be allergic to the ice blocks of its music. The words 'Ballet mécanique' were brutal, contemporary, hard-boiled, symbolic of the spiritual exhaustion, the superathletic, non-sentimental period commencing The Long Armistice.[45]

Since the basic timbre of the work is supplied by the many pianos, it is interesting to note the composer's purpose in using them. He has said:

My original idea in writing the work was to both synthesize and expand the piano sonatas. Also to eliminate whatever effect *Les Noces* [by Stravinsky] might have made upon me through the first movement of the First Violin Sonata — all this in a work of sufficient size that the public could, so to speak, see it better. The *Ballet mécanique* strictly followed 'the dream'; it had nothing whatsoever to do with the actual description of factories, machinery — and if this has been misunderstood by others, Honegger, Mossolov included, it is not my fault; had they considered it purely as music (as, being musicians, they should have), they might have found it rather a 'mechanistic' dance of life or even a signal of these troubled and war-potential 1924 times placed in a rocket and shot to Mars.

But certainly not a mundane piece of machinery!

It is true that at the time I did consider machines very beautiful, and I had even advised aesthetes to have a good look at them; still, I repeat again and again, even frantically, I had no idea (as did Honegger and Mossolov, for example) of *copying* a machine directly down into music, so to speak. My idea, rather, was to warn the age in which I was living of the simultaneous beauty and danger of its own unconscious mechanistic philosophy, aesthetic.

> As I saw it, my *Ballet mécanique* (*properly* played!) was stream-
> lined, glistening, cold, often as 'musically silent' as interplanetary
> space, and also often as hot as an electric furnace, but always
> *attempting* at least to operate on new principles of construction
> beyond the normal fixed (since Beethoven's Ninth and Bruckner)
> boundaries.
>
> I was not successful *en toto,* but it *was* a 'try' towards a new
> form, new musical conception, extending, I think, into the
> future. [46]

If the Paris premiere had caused consternation among the
patrons of the first night audience, it was nothing compared to the
miserable experience the composer was to undergo in New York.
The American impresario who was arranging the details decided
that the *sound* of an airplane propeller required near the end of
the work would become a focal point if he used an actual one in
center stage. That, plus a "huge, sensational visual curtain, hung
against the back wall of Carnegie Hall [was] an element I particularly regret. . . . This gigantic, tasteless curtain (representing a 1927
jazz-mad America!) single-handedly accomplished two things: it
sent me back to Europe broke – and gave an air of complete
charlatanism to the whole proceedings."

The work was received much differently when it·was repeated
in a revised version in a concert of the Composers Forum in 1954.
Both Antheil and the conductor Carlos Surinach received a
standing ovation afterwards.

For the revised version the composer wrote a preface in the
score that describes the work quite well. He says:

> This *Ballet mécanique* was originally written as a score to the first
> abstract motion picture of that name. However, since it was soon
> discovered that one could not synchronize a motion picture score
> that closely, (during 1924-25), it was written as an independent
> piece.
>
> I have confined this editing mostly to cutting. Repetitious
> measures, intended to synchronize only with the film, have been
> cut out abundantly, reducing the playing time from the original of
> more than a half hour to less than 18 minutes. The player piano
> has been deleted entirely, its role given to the pianos. The eight
> original pianos have been cut down to four; the four original

xylophones to two, etc. But its basic character has, I hope, remained. It has merely been made more concise.

Interpretively speaking, *Ballet mécanique* was never intended to demonstrate (as has been erroneously said) 'the beauty and precision of machines'. Rather it was to experiment with and thus, to demonstrate a new principle in music construction, that of 'Time-Space', or in which the time principle, rather than the tonal principle, is held to be of main importance.

To demonstrate. Up until Stravinsky and Schoenberg, most contemporary music had been constructed, architecturally speaking, on the tonal principle. A sonata allegro movement, for example, spread out a tonality, departed from it in the development, returned again in the recapitulation — usually with a vengeance. It is still an excellent principle. But it neglects 'Time-Space'.

Stravinsky attempted to move away from its iron grip by making his music 'super-tonal' so to speak. Schoenberg, going to the opposite pole, destroyed tonality entirely by removing all tonal centers in the 12 tone system.

Ballet mécanique, while utilizing (subconsciously, for at the time this work was written, 12 tone-ism was unknown as such) both systems, concentrated on what I then called 'the time canvas'. Rather than to consider musical form as a series of tonalities, atonalities with a tonal center, or a tonal center at all, it supposed that music actually takes place in time; and that, therefore, time is the real construction principle, 'stuff of music', as it unreels. It is the musician's 'canvas.' The tones which he uses, therefore, are merely his crayons, his colors. The 'Time-Space' principle, therefore, is an aesthetic of 'looking,' so to speak, at a piece of music 'all at once.' One might propose, therefore, that it is a sort of 'Fourth Dimension' — a way of looking at music; its constructive principles may, or may not have been touched in this work, but they have been attempted.

I always hesitate to give any 'program' to any piece of music, preferring to have it speak for itself. However, and if this piece had any program beyond that outlined above, it would be towards the barbaric and mystic splendor of modern civilization; mathematics of the universe in which the abstraction of 'the human soul' lives. More locally, the first 'theme' may be considered that of mechanical scientific civilization; the second and third barbaric ones, not

unrelated to the American continent, Indian, Negro. These plus the
mathematical 2,3,4,5,6,7,8,7,6,5,4,3,2 principle, and 'Time-Space'
make up the musical body and spiritual outline of this work. [47]

The work is scored for bells, small and large "Airplane
propeller sound," gong, cymbal, woodblock, triangle, military
drum, tambourine, small and large electric door bells, tenor and
bass drums, 2 xylophones and 4 pianos. It has been divided by the
composer into 3 parts.

After a brief, three-measure introduction in which the timpani
is prominent, the xylophones introduce a melody characterized by
its rhythmic qualities:

Example 1

Five variants for xylophones of Figure B follow immediately;
the xylophones then drop out.

The music is marked *Misterioso*. Two pianos and one xylophone introduce a melody whose chief characteristic is its arch
design:

Example 2

Melodic figures from Example 2 rise higher and higher in the
register of the pianos and xylophone; the sound of airplane
propellers is heard. After two short xylophone figures in 16th-
notes, *fff*, the pianos announce a melody in full chords of
sevenths.

Example 3

PIANOS I AND II

A *marcato* passage soon follows; the four pianos, in unison, are unaccompanied except for the bells which "punctuate" the melody from time to time. The melody is in the left hand.

The dynamic level drops to *piano;* gong, cymbals and triangle softly accent a legato passage, one also marked *Misterioso,* for the piano.

Over strong beats of the timpani, the wood block is heard with an insistent little rhythm figure. Xylophone and military drum quickly respond.

There follows a section which the composer advises should be played "almost impressionistically." Over tone-clusters in the four pianos, the xylophone plays a saucy, rhythmic figure:

Example 4

XYLOPHONE

This extended section based on variants of Figure C, reaches its dynamic climax with insistent, repeated 16th-notes for the xylophone followed by ascending and descending chromatic runs.

The military drum becomes prominent; the bells and xylophone (*piano,* "with soft sticks") answer each other. Others respond and answer back and forth. Eventually the xylophone plays a loud series of C-major scales in 16th-notes; this is answered by the pianos with chordal runs in contrary motion.

A very soft timpani figure is heard; trills for the xylophone answer. The piano and bells enter with staccato figures in thirds. The xylophone again answers with trills.

After the thunderous sound of an airplane propeller, the piano takes up Example 5 accompanied by "the sound of a small airplane propeller."

Example 5

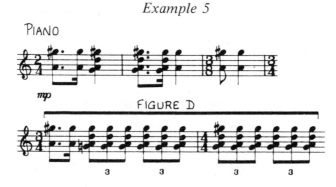

Repetitions of Figure D follow. A bridge passage succeeds this.

Piano II announces a Subject, Example 6, which is treated fugally. Piano I answers at the interval of a fifth. Xylophone II and the bells repeat the Subject, Example 6, a second higher in pitch.

Example 6

Variants of the Subject, Example 6, are heard in the pianos, xylophones and bells. Finally, in a passage marked *marcato,* Pianos I and II make a final statement of the Subject.

The original tempo returns and one piano and the bells boldly repeat variants of Figure A from Example 1. The xylophone responds with Figure C from Example 4. In an extended passage, the music builds to a dynamic climax. Figure C returns in the xylophone; the airplane propeller is heard again. Another dynamic climax follows built on Figure C in the pianos.

Pianos and xylophones drop out. The military drum, triangle and cymbals become prominent. Variants of Figure C played by the piano are accompanied by what the composer chooses to call "a new pattern of *time-space;* ... the mathematical 2,3,4,5,6,7,8,7,6,5,4,3,2 principle."

Example 7

The tenor drum repeats this cumulative *time-space* figure.

This is followed by a very long section in which the pianos are prominent; it was originally scored for *pianola* or "player piano." In this lengthy section, patterns of four long whole notes regroup, double up, compress themselves and then spread out.

The Coda is marked by *glissando*s for the pianos accompanied by the sounds of both large and small airplane propellers, small and large electric bells, and xylophone.

Once more the composer repeats his *time-space* idea; all instruments drop out except the wood block and drums. Repeated eighth-notes are punctuated at time intervals of 8, then 7, then 6,5,4,3,2 and 1. Once again the dynamic level increases; piano *glissando*s alternate with rhythmic figures for the xylophone, leading to the culmination of the composition.

XIII

SAMUEL BARBER (1910-   ) is perhaps the best known composer working in the "mainstream." He has consistently produced works in a traditional idiom, highly lyric, definitely tonal, and only occasionally unsettling in their dissonances. His music, unlike that of Harris and early Copland, is not consciously concerned with Americana, but is allied rather, to the traditions of European Romanticism.

Samuel Barber was born in a century old home in the quiet Pennsylvania community of West Chester. His father was a successful doctor with little interest in music and anxious for his son also to become a doctor. Barber's mother was a pianist and her sister, Louise Homer, was a leading singer at the Metropolitan Opera. Young Barber started piano lessons at the age of six and tried his hand at composition a year later. He later recalled this experience:

> I began composing at seven and have never stopped. At nine I wrote my first opera, still in manuscript. I called it *The Rose Tree*. The libretto was by our cook, Annie Sullivan Brosius Noble. She had been imported from Ireland by my grandmother and was older than my mother, for whom she then worked. .... Quick to pounce on literary talent — and miraculously close to home, at that — I asked her to write a text for me. She complied according to her moods, evasive or enthusiastic, like all librettists.

Samuel Barber (far right) in Italy during the summer of 1929 at the Castle of Montestrutto. To the left of Barber is his teacher, Rosario Scalero, and behind Scalero is Gian-Carlo Menotti.

Thank heaven, this opera had an American setting. It took place no more than a mile from my own home, which was in Chester County, Pennsylvania. It concerned itself with, of all things, a band of wandering gypsies, apparently very prevalent along the Main Line at the time. The opening chorus, which seems to me now a good example of 'opera-ese' . . . is as follows:

> A wandering gypsy we!
> The whole wide world is ours;
> We dance and sing with gladsome glee
> Through the sunny hours. . . . .

The hero was a tenor on vacation from the Metropolitan Opera Company who fell in love with a soprano by the good old Chester County name of Juanita Alverado.

This opera did not progress beyond Act I, not because the cook left, for they didn't leave in those days. Annie died. [48]

In high school Barber organized a small orchestra which he conducted in performances for local social organizations for a small fee. His hobbies included reading and taking long walks in the country, two hobbies he has never lost. The Curtis Institute of Philadelphia was just beginning during Barber's early high school days and he arranged to take lessons at the Institute on Friday mornings. By special action of the school board in West Chester (his father was chairman and had served on the board for 25 years) he was permitted to attend the concerts of the Philadelphia Orchestra under Leopold Stokowski on Friday afternoons.

At the Curtis Institute Barber became the first student to major in three fields: piano, composition, and voice. One day at the Institute Barber saw a notice posted on the bulletin board offering a $1200 prize (The Bearns Prize) for composition. He submitted his *Sonata for Violin* and won the prize.

With the money Barber went to Salzburg to study. This was the first of many trips to Europe. Money from his family allowed him to spend the summers of 1929 and 1930 in Italy with the family of his friend, Gian-Carlo Menotti.

Before World War II Barber spent a great deal of time in Italy, first on a Pulitzer Traveling Scholarship of $1500 and then on a $2500 award of the Prix de Rome for study at the American Academy there. It was in Italy that Barber completed his overture to *The School for Scandal* and later his *Symphony No. 1.*

In 1936 Barber met the Italian conductor Bernardino Molinari who conducted the first performance of his *First Symphony* which later won the Pulitzer Prize. Barber journeyed to the United States to hear the first American performance of this work in Cleveland and then to Salzburg to hear it performed as the first American work at the Salzburg Festival. Arturo Toscanini was so impressed by this work at the Salzburg Festival that he approached Barber about a composition for presentation by the new NBC Symphony that was being organized for him to conduct. For this occasion Barber submitted to Toscanini his *Adagio for Strings* and his *Essay for Orchestra,* both of which Toscanini presented.

Because of the gathering war clouds in Europe, Barber returned to the United States where he assumed a position at the Curtis Institute of Music teaching orchestration and conducting a chorus. He was inducted into the Army in 1943 and soon transferred to the Air Force for which he was asked to write some band music, producing his *Commando March.* The Army Air Force then asked him to write a symphony. When it was completed as his *Symphony No. 2* it was dedicated to the Air Force. Its first performance was conducted by Serge Koussevitsky in 1944.

After Barber was discharged from the service he moved to the mountain retreat he and Menotti had purchased in 1943. One of his first works written there was the ballet *Medea* for Martha Graham who entitled it *Cave of the Heart.* On an invitation from the London Gramophone Corporation Barber traveled to Denmark and then to England in 1950 to conduct performances of some of his works for recording purposes. At that time he felt the American composer was being ignored by the American recording companies.

Returning from the recording session in London to his "Capricorn," he completed his work for soprano, chorus and orchestra, *Prayers of Kierkegaard,* in 1954. Then, in collaboration with Menotti as his librettist, he produced the opera *Vanessa* in 1956 at the Metropolitan Opera House. Barber was granted an honorary Doctor of Music degree in June of 1959 by Harvard University.

In 1966 he was commissioned to write a work for the opening of the new Metropolitan Opera House in the Lincoln Center complex of New York. For his text the composer turned to Shakespeare's story of Antony and Cleopatra; the libretto was adapted for him by the brilliant Italian stage director Franco Zeffirelli. The starring roles were sung by Leontyne Price and Justino Diaz on opening night, a brilliant performance televised nationally; the wife of the President of the United States was guest of honor for the occasion.

The public's reaction to *Antony and Cleopatra* was mixed. Many felt the opera and its musical idiom to be too conservative, too much an adaptation of the style and format of late 19th-century Italian opera. Little interest has been shown in this opera other than at the Metropolitan.

Barber's *Mutations for Brass and Timpani* of 1968 "preserved the status quo" according to one New York critic. The work "is a straightforward orchestration of Bach's settings of *Christe, O Lamm Gottes.*"

ADAGIO FOR STRINGS

In the summer of 1935 Samuel Barber was awarded the Prix

de Rome. Only two of his major compositions had at that time been publicly performed. At 25, he was essentially an unknown composer.

The Prix de Rome allowed the recipient to study at the American Academy in Rome, and offered $2500 for expenses plus free living quarters. Towards the end of August, Barber sailed for Italy. He was pleased with the studio provided for him at the Academy — the old Villa Auerelia — but disliked his room in an apartment building. He wrote to a friend:

> Do you know that I have not unpacked my trunk . . . because I do not wish to feel at home in this room. My half-full trunk stands open, in complete disorder, the scandal of the Academy. And I *shall not* unpack it. I will never call this room mine! Not so for my studio which is full of charm, and I love the garden, the pines by moonlight, Rome in the distance, the yellow stone stairs. [49]

During the two years that Barber was at the Academy, he spent as much time away from Rome as he could. In the spring of 1936 he took off with his friend, fellow-composer Gian-Carlo Menotti, for a trip northward to Lugano and Salzburg. They rented a little lodge in the woods at St. Wolfgang, a few miles from Salzburg. It was a game warden's cottage which the two rented for $100 for the whole summer. This fee included the services of the warden's wife who did all the cooking and housekeeping.

The lodge was located at the foot of a mountain; a stream ran past the cottage. Amidst such rustic beauty Barber was inspired! He quickly composed one of his finest choral works, *Let Down the Bars, O Death*, and his *String Quartet in B minor.*

Later in the summer, the Italian-American conductor, Arturo Toscanini, asked Barber to show him some of his shorter compositions with the idea in mind that perhaps he could find something for use on his broadcasts with the NBC Symphony the following season. Barber thereupon set to work scoring the slow movement, *Molto adagio*, from his *String Quartet* for a string orchestra. Toscanini liked this new *Adagio for Strings* and broadcast it nationwide with his orchestra on November 5th, 1938. He later scheduled it for his South America concerts when he toured with his orchestra, the only work he performed by an American composer. Since then, the work has enjoyed a wide popularity.

Molto adagio espressivo cantando — "Very slow, with a

song-like expression"— is the marking at the beginning of the score. In B-flat minor, the original meter signature is 4/2, but there are measures marked 5/2, 6/2 and 3/2. Although the tempo is slow and the melody flowing, the basic rhythm and pulse are never lost.

The *Adagio for Strings*, some seven and half minutes in length, is based entirely on one melodic idea which is then treated in a somewhat contrapuntal manner.

This melodic idea, Example 1, consists of three phrases, the first and third being identical except for their closing. Example 1 is heard immediately over sustained chords played by divided second violins (two parts), violas, divided cellos (two parts) and double basses.

Example 1

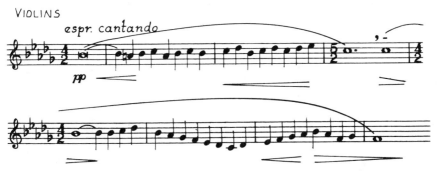

The violas enter under the final note of Example 1 in imitation. They play Example 1 with a few minor variants, on a different pitch level.

A brief dialogue between violins and violas, in contrapuntal style, follows.

The cellos, now in unison, take up the theme, Example 1. The music increases in intensity during the cello statement.

In counterpoint to the cellos, the first violins play the first phrase of the theme; the second violins, now in unison, repeat the first phrase to a countermelody in the first violins. The first phrase is heard a third time, the first violins playing it an octave higher in pitch than the second violins. This leads to a forceful and dramatic climax on an F-flat major chord.

A pause follows. There are some soft, sustained chords.

The first violins and violas, now in unison, make a final statement of the theme, Example 1, in altered form. The music dies away at the end in soft, sustained chords, coming to rest on a final chord of F major.

XIV

VLADIMIR USSACHEVSKY (1911-   ) and
OTTO LUENING (1900-   ) first joined forces to create a musical composition when a commission from the Louisville Symphony Orchestra was given them in 1953. Since that time their names have appeared more frequently together on programs than separately.

Speaking of this collaborative effort, Howard Shanet, in program notes from the New York Philharmonic Orchestra, has said: "The nature and degree of their collaboration vary from one composition to another. . . . . In general they work quite independently, the collaboration usually taking the form of criticism and suggestions offered to each other at frequent stages along the road."

Together Ussachevsky and Luening have explored new avenues of electronic music in the United States. Earlier they had each been independent composers in their own right.

Otto Luening, the older of the two, was born in Milwaukee, Wisconsin in 1900. As a precocious lad of 15 he went to Europe to study flute and composition. After taking courses at the Royal Academy of Music in Munich and the Zurich Conservatory in Switzerland, he studied privately with Ferruccio Busoni. From 1915 to 1920 Luening toured the continent, the United States and Canada, sometimes appearing as a flutist, sometimes as a piano accompanist, sometimes as a conductor. He returned to the United States in 1920 to become one of the co-founders of the American

OTTO LUENING   VLADIMIR USSACHEVSKY

The Electronic Music Center used by Luening and Ussachevksy and known as the Columbia-Princeton Electronic Music Center.

Grand Opera Company in Chicago. From 1925-28 he was head of the opera department at the Eastman School of Music. In 1930-31 he won a Guggenheim Fellowship, and in 1933 was awarded the David Bispham Medal for American opera with his *Evangeline.* He later taught at the University of Arizona, Bennington College, Barnard College, and is now at Columbia University.

Vladimir Ussachevsky, the younger of the two, was born in Hailar, Manchuria, of Russian parents on November 3, 1911. He came to the United States in 1930 and enrolled at Pomona College in California, graduating in 1935. He then attended the Eastman School of Music in Rochester, New York, to study composition with Howard Hanson and Bernard Rogers, receiving his Ph.D. in 1939. His early works include a *Theme and Variations* for orchestra written in 1935, and a *Jubilee Cantata* for chorus and orchestra completed in 1938. He served in the United States Army during World War II. After his discharge he was appointed to the faculty at Columbia University. His post-war compositions include *Miniatures for a Curious Child* (1950) for orchestra, a *Piano Concerto* in 1951 and a *Piano Sonata* in 1952.

Ussachevsky's growing interest in electronic music was outlined in an interesting article titled, "Unfinished History of Electronic Music" written by his friend and future collaborator Otto Luening. In it Luening said:

> The story of electronic music in the United States takes quite a different turn from the paths followed in Europe. The first public demonstration of the new medium was given by Vladimir Ussachevsky at his Composers Forum on May 9, 1952, in McMillin Theatre, Columbia University, shortly before Meyer-Eppler's lectures at the Summer School in Darmstadt. Ussachevsky, whose training has been traditional (Ph.D. in composition from the Eastman School of Music), is a brilliant contrapuntist and a superior vocal composer. Long before his Forum, he had had a predeliction for electroacoustical speculations. His experiments were quite independent of any in Europe. The equipment at his disposal consisted of an Ampex tape recorder (7½ and 15 ips) presented by the Ditson Fund to the music department at Columbia University for the purpose of recording student concerts and a simple box-like device designed by the brilliant young engineer, Peter Mauzey, to create feedback, a form of mechanical reverberation. Other equipment was borrowed or purchased with personal funds. The Forum attracted a great deal of attention and Henry

Cowell in *The Musical Quarterly* (Vol. 38, October, 1952) wrote a positive review of Ussachevsky's demonstration that ended: 'Ussachevsky is now in the process of incorporating some of these sounds into a composition. The pitfalls are many; we wish him well!' [50]

Luening as Chairman then invited Ussachevsky to present his experiments at the Bennington composers conference in 1952. Concerning these he has said:

At Bennington, Ussachevsky, at the controls of the Ampex, conducted a series of experiments involving violin, clarinet, piano and vocal sounds. Equipped with earphones and a flute, I began developing my first tape recorder composition. Both of us were fluent improvisors and the medium fired our imaginations. We played several tiny pieces informally at a party. After our demonstration a number of composers almost solemnly congratulated us saying, 'This is it' ('it' meaning the music of the future). [51]

Word was soon passed around about this experiment and the two men were invited to produce a group of short pieces for a program at the Museum of Modern Art under the direction of Leopold Stokowski. For the purpose of creating this music, Henry Cowell placed his studio at their disposal. With borrowed equipment in the back of Ussachevsky's car, the two composers left Bennington for Cowell's Woodstock home and stayed two weeks. Later Luening said of the adventure:

Using the flute as a sound source I developed an impressionistic virtuoso piece, *Fantasy in Space* and *Low Speed,* an exotic composition that took the flute far below its normal range. *Invention in Twelve Tones,* with complex contrapuntal combinations, was also sketched. Ussachevsky began work on an eight-minute composition with piano as the main sound source, transformed by simple devices into sounds like deep-toned gongs and bells, tone clusters on an organ, and a gamelan orchestra with metallic crescendos organized in an expressive whole. [52]

From Henry Cowell's studio, Ussachevsky and Luening moved their equipment back to New York after school started in September. A place in which to set up their equipment was always a problem; they now moved it into Ussachevsky's living room so that they could complete their commission for Stokowski. "David

Sarser, Arturo Toscanini's sound engineer, invited us to use the studio in the basement of Toscanini's Riverdale home to put the finishing touches on our compositions," Luening later recalled. "These visits generally occurred between midnight and 3 a.m., but apparently never bothered the maestro."

The concert took place at the Museum of Modern Art on October 28, 1952. It was the first public concert of tape recorder music in the United States. The program included Ussachevsky's *Ionic Contours* and Luening's *Low Speed, Invention* and *Fantasy in Space.* The public seemed to enjoy the concert, and Jay Harrison wrote in the New York *Herald-Tribune* the next day:

> It has been a long time in coming, but music and the machine are now wed. . . . . The result is as nothing encountered before. It is the music of fevered dreams, of sensations called back from a dim past. It is the sound of echo. . . . . It is vaporous, tantalizing, cushioned. It is in the room and yet not part of it. It is something entirely new. And genesis cannot be described. [53]

In April of 1953 Ussachevsky went to Europe to represent the United States and "tape music" (as it was called in America) at a festival sponsored by *Radiodiffusion Française.* Later that year Stokowski commissioned Ussachevsky and Luening to do a 2½ minute piece for his CBS program, "Twentieth-Century Concert Hall." *"Incantation* was the piece produced in the Ussachevsky living room by the two of us," Luening writes. "We used wood-wind instruments, voice, bell sonorities, piano sounds, and anything else available as sound sources."

It was performed in October and a request followed a month later for background tape music for the CBS Studio One's production of "Crime At Blossom" under the musical direction of Alfredo Antonini. In late 1953, Leuning writes:

> I received a commission from the Louisville Orchestra. I also received a small faculty grant from Barnard College. Ussachevsky consented to share these with me and to produce a joint composition to test the feasibility of combining the new medium with a symphony orchestra, even though we knew that we would have to purchase some materials and equipment from personal funds, a repeated necessity for a number of years. [54]

The result of that collaboration, *Rhapsodic Variations,* was first performed on March 20, 1954, by the Louisville Symphony, the first performance of tape recorder music with symphony orchestra anywhere.

The *Rhapsodic Variations* was followed by a joint effort in creating the ballet, *Of Identity*, commissioned by the American Mime Theatre. Soon afterwards the conductor Alfred Wallenstein, then director of the Los Angeles Philharmonic Orchestra, became interested in the work of these two men. He encouraged them to write *A Poem of Cycles and Bells* for tape recorder and symphony orchestra. When the composition was later recorded, it proved to be the most popular of the LPs of electronic music.

Barnard College, in 1955, received a grant of $10,000 from the Rockefeller Foundation to enable Ussachevsky and Luening to devote some time to creative research in electronic music. They started out by visiting Europe for six weeks to learn first hand what was going on there. They went first to Paris to visit the studios of *Radiodiffusion Française* where Pierre Schaeffer among others, was a host. They traveled to Bonn University, visiting the eminent physicist Meyer-Eppler and his Phonetic Institute. They also met in nearby Cologne Karlheinz Stockhausen who introduced them to Herbert Eimert, director of the Cologne Studio. In Baden-Baden they saw the studio of the Southwest German Radio where an interesting *Klangumwandler* (sound transformer) had been developed and was being perfected. Ussachevsky was invited back at a later date to spend a month working with it and testing it.

In Switzerland the men found the unique electro-acoustical studio founded by the conductor Hermann Scherchen to be of great interest. They also attended an International Congress on Music while they were there. In Milan the two saw Luciano Berio again, a man who was inspired to co-found (with Bruno Maderna) the electronic studio at RAI (Italian State Radio) after hearing an early program of music by Ussachevsky and Luening.

Once back in the United States Ussachevsky and Luening toured this country to observe the state of electronic music. With the exception of some work at the Bell Telephone laboratories and at Ampex, they found no one interested in basic research and experimentation. Not one radio station in the United States was interested in developing a studio similar to their counterparts in Europe. Most universities in the country were not yet interested in electronic music. The exceptions were Hiller and Isaacson at Illinois and Hugh LeCaire at the Canadian Research Council. "So," writes Luening, "Ussachevsky and I decided that university auspices would best help electronic music to develop in the United States. Douglas Moore, executive officer of the Columbia University music department, gave us permission to deal directly with Grayson Kirk, president, and Jacques Barzun, provost. In turn, they helped us with space and with some outside contracts, which we were permitted to develop on our own."

The next major assignment came from Orson Welles who wanted an abstract sound score for his production of Shakespeare's *King Lear* at the New York City Center. He was so impressed with the results that he said, "This is the greatest thing to have happened in the theater since the invention of incandescent lights."

In 1955, RCA demonstrated the Olson-Belan Sound Synthesizer. It was eventually arranged for this extremely expensive piece of equipment to be housed at Columbia University, its use administered by a joint committee of Ussachevsky (chairman) and Luening from Columbia, and Milton Babbitt and Roger Sessions of Princeton. Composers from all over the world arrived to use the synthesizer and to work at the center: Michiko Toyama from Japan, Bülenr Arel from Turkey, Mario Davidovsky from Argentina, Halim El-Dabh from Egypt, and Charles Wuorinen of the United States.

A commission was given to Ussachevsky and Luening in 1960 by Leonard Bernstein who wanted a work for tape recorder and orchestra. The result, *Concerted Piece,* was first performed at a Youth Concert televised nationwide on March 20, 1960, and later repeated on four subscription concerts at Carnegie Hall, one of which was broadcast on the CBS network.

The "team" of Luening and Ussachevsky has contributed much to the field of electronic music in the United States. They started out as lone pioneers; within 15 years more than 50 electronic studios had been developed in the United States, most on college and university campuses.

> For future guidance [Luening writes], one can only paraphrase Busoni's statements of 1907: 'Only further ear training and careful experimentation will continue to make this material plastic, artis-

tically useful, and humanly satisfying.' Novelty and tradition, methodology and complete freedom, systems and automation are by themselves not enough to bring music to new heights.

Only if we develop a sense of responsibility and a deep desire to bring human satisfaction to large numbers of individuals can our vision become penetrating enough to draw on the greatness of the past, add to it our new findings, and move forward into a future that even now promises beautiful new experiences as yet un-dreamed of. [55]

A POEM IN CYCLES AND BELLS

A *Poem in Cycles and Bells* was commissioned in 1954 by Alfred Wallenstein, at that time the conductor of the Los Angeles Philharmonic Orchestra.

Wallenstein started out by asking for a private audition of all the "tape recorder" music that had been written both jointly and separately by Messrs. Luening and Ussachevsky. He then suggested that two solo tape compositions, Luening's *Fantasy In Space* and Ussachevsky's *Sonic Contours*, could be adapted and expanded into a single composition for tape recorder and orchestra.

The conductor felt that the possibilities for sound were unlimited through the use of the tape recorder. Lester Trimble, the American composer, puts it well when he says:

Among all the musical innovations that have taken place in the 20th-century, none has been more dramatic in its reassortment of traditional values than the composition of music for tape recorder, with the recorder acting both as a creative medium and as a performer. This development has, in one action, exploded the element of sound much as the cyclotron has shattered the atom, reducing the component parts to a state of such non-connotative simplicity that they can be reassembled, combined, and spun out in time as an utterly new kind of music. Electronic developments have made it possible to separate fundamentals from their over-tones; to pick and choose among these overtones the ones that satisfy the needs of the tape-composer at a given moment; to superimpose abstracted sounds one upon another. A single timpani stroke can be manipulated by electronic instruments and by the tape recorder until it has produced a whole bevy of non-associative sounds ranging from almost inaudible depth to inaudible height. The intonation of a human voice, a drip of water, an auto horn, or a pure, electronically produced tone — all or any can be used. Rather than an impoverishment of materials, the composer is presented with a universe of aural substance so vast that severe disciplines must be self-imposed in its examination.[56]

A *Poem in Cycles and Bells* is sectional in nature, sections by the tape recorder responding to ones by the orchestra.

After an introduction by woodwinds, horns and strings, the theme of the first section is presented by the orchestra unaccompanied. The harp, bells and clarinet introduce a short passage based on a combination of C-sharp minor, E minor and A minor chords.

Example 1

A bridge leads to trills in the woodwinds. Then a solo for horn and chimes introduces a ballad-like theme, Example 2, played by the violins. They are joined alternately in this by woodwinds, trombones, trumpets and bells.

Example 2

In the second section, the material already presented is played by the tape recorder. With the flute as the sound source, many involved variations and transformations are heard. There is a soft, delicate background provided by muted strings and occasional solo winds with triangle.

The tape recorder plays the ballad-like theme, Example 2, unaccompanied; the background is elaborately varied and developed. Celesta, harp, English horn, bells and cellos enter very softly, restating Example 2, while the tape recorder brings its variations to a high point and then fades away. There is a brief transition by the tape recorder into the next section.

An orchestral transition follows with a firm statement of a harmonic progression, Example 3, from which much of the material in the following section is derived.

Example 3

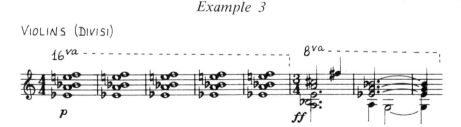

The tape recorder enters, serving as a low, pedal bass underneath an expanded variant of Example 3.

A series of low, bell-like tones, and new thematic material is introduced by the tape recorder. A long, slightly metallic melodic line occurs against a background of low chords, which increases in volume and frequency to burst in organ-like harmonic clusters.

As the melodic line disappears in a final low, metallic *crescendo*, new material enters. A modal theme for tape recorder — noted in the conductor's score as in Example 4 — is presented in canonic imitation by sounds resembling a Balinese gamelan orchestra.

Example 4

TAPE RECORDER

As this section draws to a close, other faint, tinkling bells are heard, followed by strangely distorted voices (is it a blues tune or a radio or what?).

The orchestra enters very quietly; the tape recorder introduces an insistent rhythm which continues to the end, having the effect of a maze of echoes, always receding into the distance and intertwining with a dance-like tune. The orchestra is subdued until the Coda, when it emerges over the pulsating mass of sound and marches on to a forceful, polytonal ending. The work concludes with unaccompanied, deep gong tones for the tape recorder.

XV

JOHN CAGE (1912-   ) is undoubtedly the most controversial composer of our time. Frequently he is dismissed as an incompetent and a fraud. The first charge can be countered by a glance at his academic background which includes study with both Arnold Schoenberg and Henry Cowell among others. The second accusation, that of fraud, should be considered in terms of the composer's stated objectives, goals and achievements. Early in his career John Cage began experimenting, seeking new ways of looking at and listening to music. When it takes him, as Cage himself has stated, a solid year of work to write a composition such as *HPSCHD,* one can scarcely dismiss so much endeavor as "fraud" whether one likes the resulting piece of music or not.

Cage has also been considered by some as a "philosopher" rather than a composer, but the distinction is one that he would probably consider irrelevant. His writing, both of music and books, is deeply influenced by Far Eastern philosophy, most notably by Zen Bhuddism, which leads to a mistrust of the rational mind and a seeking out of ways to circumvent its power over one. Elliott Schwartz says in his book on contemporary composers, "Music is, for [Cage], not the restricted art form that our civilization has always assumed, but a vastly enlarged area of speculation that emerges as both a branch of theater and a branch of philosophy. His experiments in this area are often moving, amusing, at times frightening, occasionally enlightening, always entertaining, and undeniably related to the use of sounds."

John Cage was born in Los Angeles on September 15, 1912, and led a youthful life not much different from the other children in his neighborhood. "My first experience with music," Cage later recalled, "was through neighborhood piano teachers, and particularly my Aunt Phoebe. She said of the work of Bach and Beethoven that it couldn't possibly interest me, she herself being devoted to music of the 19th century. She introduced me to Moszkowski and what you might call the piano music the whole world loves to play. In that volume, it seemed to me that the works of Grieg were more interesting than the others."

Cage has always had a sense of humor, and it is evident in a story he tells of boyhood days at the beach near Los Angeles:

> When I was growing up in California there were two things that everyone assumed were good for you. There were, of course, others — spinach and oatmeal, for instance — but right now I'm thinking of sunshine and orange juice. When we lived at Ocean Park, I was sent out every morning to the beach where I spent the day building roller-coasters in the sand, complicated down-hill tracks with tunnels and inclines upon which I rolled a small hard rubber ball. Every day toward noon I fainted because the sun was too much for me. When I fainted I didn't fall down, but I couldn't see; there were flocks of black spots wherever I looked. I soon learned to find my way in that blindness to a hamburger store where I'd ask for something to eat. Sitting in the shade, I'd come to. It took me much longer, about 35 years in fact, to learn that orange juice was not good for me either. [57]

For a time Cage flirted with literature, painting and architecture before deciding on a career in music. After he had studied piano for a while with Fannie Charles Dillon in Los Angeles, his work came to the attention of Henry Cowell who encouraged him in 1933 to go to New York to study composition with Adolf Weiss, a former pupil of Arnold Schoenberg. The following year he returned to Los Angeles to study with Schoenberg himself. However, even at this early date Cage was experiencing difficulty with the rules of harmony. "Several times," he has said, "I tried to explain to Schoenberg that I had no feeling for harmony. He told me that without a feeling for harmony I would always encounter an obstacle, a wall through which I wouldn't be able to pass. My reply was that in that case I would devote my life to beating my head against that wall — and maybe this is what I've been doing ever since."

Cage moved about, living in Seattle, Chicago and elsewhere, studying piano with Lazare-Lévy in Paris, composition and non-Western music with Cowell in California. He taught at the Cornish

Lejaren Hiller at the keyboard of the computer programming *HPSCHD* as John Cage checks the operating circuits.

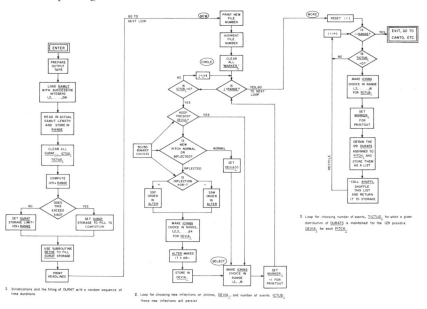

The computer "Flow Chart" for John Cage's *HPSCHD*.

School, Seattle; Mills College, California; The School of Design in
Chicago and Black Mountain College, North Carolina.

By writing works for percussion ensembles in the 1930's Cage
avoided problems with harmony. Soon he was experimenting with
what he called a "prepared piano," one that had all kinds of bolts,
plastic and metal objects placed strategically on the strings. It all
started in 1938 when a dancer named Syvilla Fort asked him to
write the music for her new dance, *Bacchanale*. He described the
results as "a percussion orchestra under the control of a single
player."

The effects of a "prepared piano" are described in a review
Virgil Thomson wrote for a concert Cage gave at the New School
for Social Research in New York:

> The effect in general is slightly reminiscent, on first hearing, of
> Indonesian gamelan orchestras, though the interior structure of Mr.
> Cage's music is not Oriental at all. His work attaches itself, in fact,
> to two different traditions of Western modernism. One is the
> percussive experiments begun by Marinetti's Futurist Noisemakers
> and continued in the music of Edgar Varèse, Henry Cowell, and
> George Antheil, all of which, though made in full awareness of
> Oriental methods, is thoroughly Western in its expression. The
> other is, curiously enough, the atonal music of Arnold Schoenberg.
>
> Mr. Cage has carried Schoenberg's harmonic maneuvers to their
> logical conclusion. He has produced atonal music not by causing
> the twelve tones of the chromatic scale to contradict one another
> consistently, but by eliminating, to start with, all sounds of precise
> pitch. He substitutes for the chromatic scale a gamut of pings,
> plucks, and delicate thuds that is both varied and expressive and
> that is different in each piece. By thus getting rid, at the
> beginning, of the constricting element in atonal writing — which is
> the necessity of taking constant care to avoid making classical
> harmony with a standardized palette of instrumental sounds and
> pitches that exists primarily for the purpose of producing such
> harmony — Mr. Cage has been free to develop the rhythmic
> element of composition, which is the weakest element in the
> Schoenbergian style, to a point of sophistication unmatched in the
> technique of any other living composer.
>
> His continuity devices are chiefly those of the Schoenberg school.
> There are themes and sometimes melodies, even, though these are
> limited, when they have real pitch, to the range of a fourth, thus

avoiding the tonal effect of dominant and tonic. All these appear in augmentation, diminution, inversion, fragmentation, and the various kinds of canon. That these procedures do not take over a piece and become its subject, or game, is due to Cage's genius as a musician. He writes music for expressive purposes; and the novelty of his timbres, the logic of his discourse, are used to intensify communication, not as ends in themselves. His work represents, in consequence, not only the most advanced methods now in use anywhere but original expression of the very highest poetic quality. And this has been proved now through all the classical occasions — theater, ballet, song, orchestral composition, and chamber music.[58]

Around the time of Cage's divorce from his wife, he suffered serious anxieties, both personal and creative. Help came early in the 1940s when a young music student of his, Gita Sarabhai — a young Indian woman, reciprocated by teaching him about Indian music. "One day," Cage relates, "I asked her what her teacher in India had thought was the purpose of music. She replied that he had said the function of music was 'to sober and quiet the mind, thus rendering it susceptible to divine influences.' I was tremendously struck by this. And then something really extraordinary happened. Lou Harrison, who had been doing research on early English music, came across a statement by the 17th-century English composer Thomas Mace expressing the same idea in almost exactly the same words. I decided then and there that this *was* the proper purpose of music. In time, I also came to see that all art before the Renaissance, both Oriental and Western, had shared the same basis, that Oriental art had continued to do so right along, and that the Renaissance idea of self-expressive art was therefore heretical."

From his first experience with non-Western music, Cage was led to further investigation. He developed a system in composition which had much in common with the system of *tāls*, or rhythmic cycles, of Indian music. He also became interested in *I Ching*, a Chinese "Book of Changes" which helped him create a "music of chance" by tables of basic trigrams as well as by the throw of dice.

By 1950, Cage had decided to eliminate preconceived "ideas of order" in his music. To achieve this, he used chance operations in composing *The Music of Changes* for piano in 1951; the structure of the work became indeterminate. Although the public was slow to accept this idea of a performer jumping about on the music page to play a bit here and a bit there at his own choosing, Cage explained the idea well in a simile:

> Have you ever noticed how you read a newspaper? Jumping around, leaving articles unread, or partially read, turning here and there. Not at all the way one reads Bach in public, but precisely the way one reads in public *Duo II for Pianists* by Christian Wolff. [59]

Cage shocked the music world in 1952 with his composition (if that is the proper word) *4'33"* — a piece four minutes and 33 seconds long and divided into three movements of specified length, but containing not a single note. Silence. Cage has a logical explanation for this. He says:

> In this new music nothing takes places but sounds: those that are notated and those that are not. Those that are not notated appear in the written music as silences, opening the doors of the music to the sounds that happen to be in the environment. This openness exists in the fields of modern sculpture and architecture. The glass houses of Mies van der Rohe reflect their environment presenting to the eye images of clouds, trees, or grass, according to the situation. And while looking at the constructions in wire of the sculptor, Richard Lippold, it is inevitable that one will see other things, and people, too, if they happen to be there at the same time, through the network of wires. There is no such thing as an empty space or an empty time. There is always something to see, something to hear. In fact, try as we may to make a silence, we cannot. For certain engineering purposes, it is desirable to have as silent a situation as possible. Such a room is called an anechoic chamber, its six walls made of special material, a room without echoes. I entered one at Harvard University several years ago and heard two sounds, one high and one low. On describing them to the engineer in charge, he informed me that the high one was my nervous system in operation, the low one my blood in circulation. Until I die there will be sounds. And they will continue following my death. One need not fear about the future of music. [60]

John Cage feels that new music still has a long way to go, and that its next step is to involve the listener more. "Most people mistakenly think that when they hear a piece of music, that they're not *doing* anything, but that something is being done to them. Now this is not true, and we must arrange our music, we must arrange our Art, we must arrange everything, I believe, so that people realize they themselves are doing it, and not that something is being done to them."

Down in Greensboro, North Carolina, Cage and his friend, the pianist David Tudor, gave a two-piano concert of contemporary works. Cage explained to the audience in this instance how he felt they should realize they "were doing something." Referring to the program of works they had selected he said:

> All of these pieces are composed in various ways that have in common indeterminacy of performance. Each performance is unique, as interesting to the composers and performers as to the audience. Everyone in fact, that is, becomes a listener. I explained all this to the audience before the musical program began. I pointed out that one is accustomed to thinking of a piece of music as an object suitable for understanding and subsequent evaluation, but that here the situation was quite other. These pieces, I said, are not objects but processes essentially purposeless. Naturally then I had to explain the purpose of having something be purposeless. I said the sounds were just sounds and that if they weren't just sounds that we would (I was of course using the editorial we) do something about it in the next composition. I said that since the sounds were sounds this gave people hearing them the chance to be people, centered within themselves where they actually are, not off artificially in the distance as they are accustomed to be, trying to figure out what is being said by some artist by means of sounds. Finally I said that the purpose of this purposeless music would be achieved if people learned to listen: that when they listened they might discover that they preferred the sounds of everyday life to the ones they would presently hear in the musical program; that that was all right as far as I was concerned. [61]

In 1969 Cage completed a work called *Knobs* through the use of a programmed computer. The composition involved the listener as performer. Included with the phonograph recording are directions "suggesting to the listener when and what dials of the stereo set to turn. There are 20 different ways of listening to the record, which ought to suggest that one could listen also in other ways. We have the solo, which is the 12-tone computer output, equally on both channels; ... each channel will have 25 of the computer tape outputs, probably even numbers on one channel and odd numbers on the other. Then, if you shift the volume and tone controls. . . ."

Be he charlatan or genius, Cage continues to investigate new areas of sound and silence, he continues to compose, he continues to be heard.

HPSCHD

Having worked with all the new materials, devices and methods discovered in the 20th century — the 12-tone method, the prepared piano, music of indetermanency and chance, and electronic music — it was only logical that John Cage would accept the challenge of trying to compose a piece of computer music.

Invited to make use of the computer at the University of Illinois, Cage decided to combine such a work with an earlier request by the harpsichordist Sylvia Marlowe for a composition for her instrument. ("I must admit," Cage writes, "I've never particularly liked the instrument. It sounded to me like a sewing machine.")

The finished composition makes use of up to 51 tapes and seven harpsichords. ("Up to . . ." because chance is again involved). "In effect," states Cage, "there will be a maximum of 58 channels [if the seven "live" harpsichords are amplified]. The piece could be expressed by a performance of one to seven live harpsichords and one to 51 tapes, according to how large a performance one wished to give. The solos are obviously all for the 12-tone scale, one of them being the computer output for the 12-tone scale made into notation for live performance."

Each tape is 20 minutes in length, as is each piece of music for harpsichord. This means the resulting composition could be made extremely lengthy by playing each of the 58 in sequence, or the music could be refined to a 20-minute performance of infinitely complex sound by the simultaneous use of all 58.

Because Cage was unfamiliar with computers, he had decided when accepting this project at the University to work with Lejaren Hiller who would program the machine. When asked how a computer translates information into sound, Hiller gave a very technical answer (that some might wish to skip):

> By a process known as 'digital-to-analog conversion' . . . a usable
> system for converting mathematical representations of musical

parameters into actual sound. . . . [We] solve mathematical equations for sine waves, sawtooth waves, and the rest of it, storing the successive points along the curve of a waveform as numbers in the computer. These numbers, after they are all computed, are read out and converted into a continuously fluctuating voltage which is impressed on the audio tape. There are no standard signal generators of any sort. [62]

Cage's basic plan for *HPSCHD* seemed an ideal one for computer:

The original idea came from a notion I had about Mozart's music and how it differed from Bach's music. In the case of Bach, if one looked at a few measures and at the different voices, they would all be observing more or less the same scalar movement, . . . whereas, in the case of Mozart, if one looked at just a small amount of his music, one could see the chromatic scale, the diatonic scale, and a use of chords melodically, like a scale, but made up of larger steps. I thought to extend this 'moving-away-from-unity' and 'moving-toward-multiplicity' and, taking advantage of the computer facility, to multiply the detail of the tones and durations of a piece of music. So this piece divides the five octaves into all divisions: from five tones per octave to 56 tones per octave. Then, having observed large chordal/melodic steps, the diatonic and chromatic, even smaller steps were made, which would be microtonal with respect to each one of the tones in any one of these octaves. This arose from the *I Ching** which uses the number "64" and from the binary function which is so implicit in the computer – zero or one. Multiplying 64 by two, you would get, for each one of these tones, 129 possible pitches. We have very small steps – microtonal, small steps – chromatic, larger steps – diatonic, then, the very large steps consisting of leaps, in all the divisions from five to 56. [63]

In the end, what the computer produced was 581 pages of manuscript for live performance and the 51 tapes.

Each of the 20 minute pieces for "live" performance is varied in nature. Hiller says:

The simplest –'Version 1'– is Mozart's *Musical Dice Game*, K. 294d, realized 20 times with computer. Each realization is

---

**I Ching,* an ancient Chinese book of divination, in which 64 pairs of eight symbols are shown with various interpretations; also called "Book of Changes"

64 bars long and lasts one minute; hence the total realization comes out to be 20 minutes. John likes to refer to this as our "Satie-like" realization of Mozart. By the way, we know that some people think this music is not Mozart's, but I don't think that's too important; if not, it could well have been. Then there are four versions in which a number of bars of the music were replaced each time before a new realization — a new "pass" — was generated. In other words, after the first realization was finished, we entered another loop and called subroutine "I Ching" 20 times in order to obtain 20 chance values between one and 64. Since the *Musical Dice Game* is 64 bars long — a neat coincidence — we used the I Ching values to designate those bars of the dice game which were to be replaced by other music. For this we selected two sets of compositions. One set provides replacement of Mozart by Mozart. These are passages from sections of his piano sonatas. John went through one of the regular editions of the Mozart piano sonatas and used the I Ching to choose which sonata and which movement. The passages so chosen — each of one-minute duration — were labelled "Replacement Music 1," "Replacement Music 2," and so forth. For example, on pass two of the program — to get back to the process — if subroutine I Ching supplied the integer 38, bar 38 of the *Musical Dice Game* was replaced by "Replacement Music 1." If I Ching happened to supply, by chance, integer 49 twice in the set of 20 values, then "Replacement Music 1" was by-passed and "Replacement Music 2" was used instead. On pass three this process was repeated and continued until pass 20 was reached. We set a limit of seven replacement musics so that we would end up with a fairly complete version of the terminal piece. Notice how this process provided a gradual but statistically controlled series of substitutions of one composition by another, and then by another, and so on. The original composition is eventually "erased," and others take its place. However, the substitution process never approaches completion until the end, because the rate of formation of measures of intermediate compositions is the same, on the average, as their rate of removal. This is reminiscent to me of chain reactions in chemistry.[64]

The involved use of the computer is organized according to a flow chart (see the illustration). It is a graphic description of the logic of a computer program. It charts what is done, the decisions that are made, indicates the paths that must be travelled and the consequences of decisions and calculations.

A good over-all view of the intended effect of *HPSCHD* was

given by Richard Kostelanetz in his review after the first performance in Urbana, Illinois, on May 16th, 1969. He wrote:

Flashing on the outside under-walls of the huge, double-saucer Assembly Hall at the University of Illinois' Urbana campus, were an endless number of slides from 52 projectors; and inside, between 7 pm and just after midnight on Friday, May 16, was a John Cage—Lejaren Hiller collaboration, "HPSCHD," one of the great artistic environments of the decade. In the middle of the circular sports arena were suspended several parallel sheets of semi-transparent material, each 100 by 40 feet; and from both sides were projected numerous films and slides whose collaged imagery passed through several sheets. Running around a circular ceiling rim was a continuous 340-foot screen, and from a hidden point inside were projected slides with imagery as various as outer-space scenes, pages of Mozart music, computer instructions and nonrepresentational blotches. Beams of light were aimed across the undulated interior roof. In several upper locations mirrored balls were spinning, reflecting dots of light in all directions — a device reminiscent of a discotheque or a planetarium. There was such an incredible abundance to see that the eye could scarcely focus on anything in particular; and no reporter could possibly write everything down.

The scene was bathed in a sea of various sounds with no distinct relation to each other — an atonal and astructural chaos so continually in flux that one could pick out nothing more specific than a few seconds of repetition. Fading in and out through the mix were snatches of harpsichord music that sounded more like Mozart than anything else; these came from the seven instrumentalists visible on platforms in the center of the Assembly Hall. Around these bases of stability were flowing several thousand people, most of them students at the University, but some who came from far away — museum directors from Chicago and Minneapolis, writers, artists and film crew (doing a profile of Cage) from New York, students who hitchhiked from all over the midwest, and the lady harpsichordist who first commissioned "HPSCHD," all the way from Switzerland.

Most of the audience milled about the floor while hundreds took seats in the bleachers. But all over the place, some of those present were supine, their eyes closed, grooving on the multiple stereophony. No one hissed or booed; no one stripped off his clothes (á la New York) although one mother conspicuously breast-fed her new-born child. A few people at times broke into dance, creating a show within a show that simply added more to the mix. Some young people painted their faces with Dayglo colors.

The aural content of "HPSCHD" — what one should hear — is literally 59 channels of sound, even though most of us can scarcely separate more than one or two from the others at any time. "You don't have to choose, really but, so to speak, experience it," Cage added between puffs of his filtered and mentholated cigarette. "As you go from one point of the hall to another, the experience changes; and here, too, each man determines what he hears. The situation relates to individuals differently, because attention isn't focused in one direction. Freedom of movement, you see, is basic to both this art and this society. With all those parts and no conductor, you can see that even this populous a society can function without a conductor."

XVI

MILTON BABBITT (1916-   ) displayed equal aptitude for mathematics and music in high school, and when he matriculated at New York University in 1931, his interests were mathematics and logic. His discovery of music by Schoenberg and Webern during University days—especially compositions in the 12-tone method—reawakened his interest in music. Then he changed his academic major, returning to mathematics only once: during World War II he taught the subject at Princeton.

It was undoubtedly this duality of interest that led Babbitt to investigate the numerical complexities of Schoenberg's method with its many permutations and transpositions of a basic row. "The 12-tone system, as system, is indeed 'simple,' " Babbit has said. "It is simple in its principles of formation and transformation, but enormously complex and deep in its ramification, in the necessary inferences that can be drawn from these principles."

JOHN CAGE

MILTON BABBITT

Babbitt at the RCA Electronic Sound Source Synthesizer at Columbia.

During the 1940s, Babbitt wrote a number of 12-tone works which were completely serialized, works which are believed to contain the earliest application of serial techniques to all the parameters of a musical composition: rhythm, timbre, dynamics, instrumentation, and, of course, pitch. In other words, a rigid control, a strict numerical discipline all based on permutations and transpositions of the basic row with reference to every element. It is his conviction that "the 12-tone set must absolutely determine *every* aspect of a piece of music." Two examples of such works are his *Three Compositions for Piano* (1947) and the *Composition for Four Instruments* (1948).

All of this makes Babbitt a very intellectual composer, evident even in his academic titles for compositions. "I believe in cerebral music," he has stated, "and I never choose a note unless I know why I want it there." His mind, trained in mathematical logic, follows a similar course in music. He explains the genesis of a composition by saying that "the structural idea is the idea from which I begin."

Babbitt feels that it is no more logical to expect a layman to understand advanced present day music than it would be to expect him to understand advanced mathematics or physics. To this point he titled an article he wrote for *High Fidelity* magazine in 1958, "Who Cares If You Listen?" In it he says ·(the italics are the authors'):

> [The] composer expends an enormous amount of time and energy—and usually, considerable money—on the creation of a commodity which has little, no, or negative commodity value. He is, in essence, a 'vanity' composer. The general public is largely unaware of and uninterested in his music. The majority of performers shun it and resent it. Consequently, the music is little performed, and then primarily at poorly attended concerts before an audience consisting in the main of fellow professionals. At best, the music would appear to be for, of, and by specialists.
>
> Toward this condition of musical and societal 'isolation' a variety of attitudes has been expressed, usually with the purpose of assigning blame, often to the music itself, occasionally to critics or performers, and very occasionally to the public. But to assign blame is to imply that this isolation is unnecessary and undesirable. *It is my contention that, on the contrary, this condition is not only inevitable, but potentially advantageous for the composer and*

his music. From my point of view, the composer would do well to consider means of realizing, consolidating, and extending the advantage.[65]

Milton Babbitt, the son and brother of professional mathematicians, was born in Philadelphia on May 10, 1916, but was reared in Jackson, Mississippi, where his father worked as an insurance actuary. From there he went to New York University at 15 to take up the study of mathematics. As a young man, he won a national popular-song contest, and through his 20s he wrote "gobs of popular songs to see if I could make a living at it. I couldn't."

While at New York University, Babbitt first discovered the works of Schoenberg and Webern. He then enrolled for classes in composition with Marion Bauer and Philip James. Upon graduation he enrolled at Princeton for graduate studies in composition with Roger Sessions, serving as an instructor himself on the staff. He received his M.A. degree in 1942.

Since that time Babbitt has held a series of teaching posts: from 1943 to 1945 he was a member of the mathematics faculty at Princeton; in 1952 he taught at the Seminary for American Studies at Salzburg; in 1954 he was appointed Philip Freneau Preceptor in Music at Princeton University; and, in 1961, he was appointed to be one of the four directors of the Columbia-Princeton Center for Electronic Music (the other directors were Roger Sessions, Otto Luening and Vladimir Ussachevsky).

Babbitt first became interested in electronic music about 1959. His *Composition for Synthesizer* (1961) was "the first extended musical composition produced entirely on the RCA Electronic Source Sound Synthesizer" at Columbia University. His *Vision and Prayer* (1961), with texts by Dylan Thomas, was written for soprano and synthesized accompaniment.

In the synthesizer Babbitt found a foil to human frailty. Since he had first completely serialized music, he found that many performers lacked the precision of execution necessitated by such compositions. With electronic means, the utmost precision could be expected as the norm.

The RCA Synthesizer, a sophisticated instrument specifically constructed for the production of synthesized electronic sound, was installed at the Columbia-Princeton Electronic Music Center in the late 1950s. Every aspect of both pitched and non-pitched sound—including duration, quality of attack and decay (dying away), intensity, tone color, etc.—can be set out with precise definition, and any sound can be tested immediately and, if necessary, re-adjusted down to the finest possible gradations. The synthesizer is simply a complex machine for creating sound; it cannot "compose" music any more than can the computer used by John Cage. The advantage of the synthesizer over the computer is that any tone programmed can be tested by listening immediately, whereas in computer music an additional step to realize the computations in sound must be done after the computer is all finished with its share of the work.

Milton Babbitt has stated all this another way. He has written:

> There is a great deal of misunderstanding when we talk about the computer production of sound. We should not confuse the idea of the computer with that of the synthesizer. Both are total media. With complete accuracy and definition, they both can produce anything the composer knows how to specify. Computer production of sound is based upon the fact that the composer can specify values of frequency, duration, intensity, spectrum, envelope—all the separable components of the musical event—in his usual notational terms. The musical specifications are communicated to the computer and then the computer literally computes these so that what results is a digital tape. This digital tape is then converted by a filtering process into a magnetic tape that can be directly played on a tape recorder.
>
> The synthesizer is in no sense a computer. With it, you're working in direct relation to the sound. For example, I try everything at first by hand. If I want a certain kind of sound or a certain kind of continuity, I test it before I ever punch it into the tape. When you punch it, you can listen to it *as* it passes through the machine. Knowing as little as we do about the relationship between specification and what the ear hears, particularly where it has been impossible to create such a sound or tempo relation before, there is a tremendous advantage in being able to test beforehand. This is the main advantage of the synthesizer.
>
> The difficulty with the computer is that you have to wait until the analog tape is made before you hear sound for the first time. The synthesizer, in this respect, is more efficient. For me, it is more comfortable because I'm working in direct relationship to

my ear at all times. If I've musically miscalculated what the result would be, I can change it immediately. At the present time, the computer demands a great deal more knowledge than we possess, so it is less convenient.[66]

The synthesizer has a tremendous advantage over a regular "tape studio," for in the latter, to connect one specified musical event with another requires the splicing of tape. "With the synthesizer," Babbitt says, "the composer punches in his specifications, and therefore makes musical continuity and musical specification of all these events a very simple manual operation. It's not nearly so time consuming, and above all, it makes anything possible. This is not quite true in a tape lab."

During an interview, Babbitt was asked how it was that he chose the synthesizer over the tape studio. He replied:

The tape studio was never for me. It did not reflect my musical needs. As a composer, I still feel that pitch is the single most important aspect of musical structure. I was not particularly interested in a medium that, in a sense, is least susceptible to pitch organization. I was waiting for the development of an electronic instrument that would make pitch succession, and therefore, rhythmic control of pitch succession, more suitable and feasible. In the early fifties, the engineers at RCA wanted to make it clear to the world that control of pitch, pitch succession, and tempo succession in music could be easily accomplished by punching it on a paper roll. As a result, they built the first synthesizer, which is now, I believe, being used only for linguistic purposes. It was never totally adequate for our purposes.

When RCA discovered that composers felt that this instrument had a real capacity for musical extension, they very quietly built a second, and much larger, synthesizer. This is the so-called Mark II. If you know how to specify it, any sound that can be passed by a loudspeaker can be created by this machine. If it can't do it, it is because we lack the empirical information. I could synthesize the equivalent of a recorded violin sound if I knew exactly what the relevant dimensions of such violin sound are. Here again, the machine is totally dumb. It does only what I can precisely and accurately specify.

Remember, when you work with the synthesizer, you never splice tape. You never, in any sense of the word, alter the signal after it's recorded. You don't modify it or mutate it. Everything you do is specified on the synthesizer's punched tape. You use magnetic tape here for recording exactly as you would in a normal recording studio. It's simply a storage medium. I have to punch my musical specifications on the paper tape in the synthesizer. The synthesizer provides the total frequency continuum, the total temporal continuum, and the total spectral continuum. Everything. In other words, there are no choices made by the machine. The choices are made entirely by the operator, who, so far, has always been the composer. When I finish punching the tape in the synthesizer, I run it through and record the result on a four-track tape recorder. The entire section of a piece is recorded at one time. This is a great advantage.[67]

Because of the complexity of the synthesizer as an instrument, many composers have been discouraged in attempts to use it. Charles Wuorinen has used it in parts of pieces combined with instruments, and a few young composers have used it for sources of sound, but actually the synthesizer has been used seriously by perhaps eight or ten composers at the most. By contrast, tape laboratories have been used by hundreds of composers. As for the computer, there are probably 50 composers working seriously with this medium in various parts of the country.

Milton Babbitt has twice combined live performance with tape in a pair of works for soprano and synthesizer. *Vision and Prayer* is a setting of poems by Dylan Thomas with a purely "synthesized" accompaniment, and *Philomel* (1964), a setting of a text by John Hollander, uses live voice, recorded vocal material and purely electronic sound. His best known work and the one most frequently released on records is *Ensembles for Synthesizer* completed in 1964. His *Correspondences for Strings and Tape* was premiered by the Buffalo Philharmonic in 1968, and a year later, in 1969, the New York Philharmonic gave the first performance of his *Relata II* which the orchestra had commissioned.

Babbitt's *Ensembles for Synthesizer* was the music used for a Composer's Showcase production at the Whitney Museum of American Art in New York City in 1969 of a blend of music, plastic movements of dancers and continuous light patterns — a sort of modern "happening". One reviewer wrote that it "created a fascinating entity even though it did not quite coalesce."

To those critics who claim Babbitt's compositions are the

work of a mathematician rather than an inspired artist, the composer replies:

> I have often been attacked as a mathematical composer, which I am not in any reasonable sense. I have had enough mathematical training not to misuse mathematics. But children rush to me now because they think that I possess mathematical prescriptions for writing music. They're much more informed mathematically and technologically than they are musically. The issue here is still a musical one. I'm not suddenly proclaiming my position as an "artist." I'm simply saying that the misapplication of mathematics to music is a very serious naivete. Mrs. Schoenberg once said to me, "You know, my husband used to be attacked as a mathematical composer and he didn't know anything about mathematics. Presently, young composers are proclaiming themselves as mathematical composers and people are deeply impressed and intimidated." I feel very much in the same position, from a slightly different point of view. The misunderstanding of the application of so-called mathematics to so-called music is so deep that there are always children who rush up with mathematical knowledge, which they've attained by the fifth year, yet still can't differentiate one interval from another. Regardless of the sophistication of present-day electronic music, pitch organization is still highly dependent upon intervalic relationship. [68]

ENSEMBLES FOR SYNTHESIZER

Part I

Ensembles for Synthesizer was composed on the huge Mark II Synthesizer, a one-of-a-kind instrument built at a cost of $250,000 by RCA and housed at the Columbia-Princeton Electronic Music Center in New York City. The synthesizer contains various sound generating devices—tuning fork oscillators, frequency multipliers, sine wave generators— in all, about 1,700 tubes, making it capable of producing any sound that can come out of a loudspeaker, limited only by the shortcomings of its composer-operator.

The instrument is 20 feet long and 7 feet high. On the face of the synthesizer are two keyboards that "program" the individual "tones," creating its sound-frequency, volume, timbre and envelope (degree of attack and decay). When the composer adjusts each one of these elements of a tone, the synthesizer immediately produces a sound. If the result is what the composer wants, he pushes a button and the tone is fixed onto the permanent tape. If the sound he hears is not quite what he wants, he can readjust his setting to alter it. The synthesizer also allows sound to be placed on top of sound, to transform live sounds in various ways, and to program wholly original scales.

Part I of *Ensembles for Synthesizer* was completed in December of 1962 and first performed (that is, the tape was played) publicly the same month. The total work, approximately twice the length of the first part, was not completed until November, 1964. The complete work received its premiere at Lincoln Center's Philharmonic Hall.

Although Babbitt states that Part I can be played as an independent composition, it is difficult for the untrained ear (and even most highly trained ears) to recognize the split-second break between the two parts. At precisely 4′49½″ there is a *tenuto* by the principal sound generating device (although other percussive sounds punctuate it). This is the first tone of Part II.

In a descriptive note prepared for the Lincoln Center performance of *Ensembles for Synthesizer*, the composer has written:

> The title *Ensembles* refers to the multiple characteristics of the work. In both its customary meaning and its more general one signifying 'collections,' the term refers most immediately to the different pitch, rhythmic, registral, texture and timbral 'ensembles' associated with each of the many so delineated sections of the composition, no two of which are identical, and no one of which is of more than a few seconds duration in this ten minute work. . . .
>
> Also, in its meaning of 'set,' the word 'ensemble' relevantly suggests the, I trust, familiar principles of tonal and temporal organization which are employed in this as in other of my compositions. . . .
>
> The version presented on phonograph records is a two-track reduction of the original four-track version.[69]

The composition exemplifies the most distinguishing characteristics of Babbitt's compositional technique: his adherence to the 12 pitches of the tempered scale, and the slight use of sound material from outside that domain. *Ensembles for Synthesizer* clearly demonstrates the kind of high-speed work of which the synthesizer is capable. Actually, in some cases, the speed is so great that pitch successions frequently move at rates approaching or surpassing thresholds of human perception.

XVII

NED ROREM (1923-   ) is "probably the world's best composer of art songs now living" writes *Time* magazine. Having composed over 300 songs in his youth, Rorem has said that "in a single day, I would sometimes spill out four or five songs, indiscriminately, some terrific, some terrible." By the time Rorem was 40, over 50 songs, six song cycles, and 12 songs for voice and orchestra had been published; innumerable ones had been recorded by more than a score of artists. Of these songs, William Flanagan, a friend and fellow-composer, has said, "the merger of words and music is almost invariably immediate and clear, and above all, right. The musical language is direct, uncomplicated."

In compositional style and idiom Rorem is what he chooses to call (and rightly) "a hard core conservative." He has never become involved in serial technique, electronic music or other 20th-century phenomena. To quote William Flanagan again: "Ned Rorem is one of those composers with regard to whom the usual stylistic labels mean nothing whatever, never have, and very likely never will. Take him or leave him—on his own terms."

In Rorem's pieces one never loses the melody; it reigns supreme throughout. (This quality makes him a grateful writer for singers.) His harmony is contemporary without being shockingly discordant. His compositions, be they short works for voice or piano, or large scale works for symphony orchestras or opera houses, are always structured on a well-designed and logical frame, a form dictated by inspiration, not by chance or mathematical formulae.

NED ROREM   GUNTHER SCHULLER

Although Ned Rorem was born in Richmond, Indiana, the family moved to Chicago when he was six months of age. His father, a medical economist, was a professor at the University of Chicago and had been a co-founder of Blue Cross. Neither Ned's mother nor father exhibited more than a nodding acquaintance with music, but they encouraged their son in his early pursuits of all the arts "which appealed equally and immediately."

Rorem started piano lessons when he was six; within three years he had composed his first song. By the time he was 12 he had made up his mind to become a professional musician. When asked why, he replied, "because I *had* to. There was never a doubt in my mind."

After graduation from high school Rorem enrolled at Northwestern University. By the end of his second year he had won a scholarship to the Curtis Institute of Music in Philadelphia, studying during the summer months at the Berkshire Music Center. In 1944 he studied orchestration with Virgil Thomson and later studied composition with Aaron Copland. Rorem completed his Master of Music degree at Juilliard School of Music in New York City in 1948.

The first of many awards was bestowed on the composer in 1948 when *The Lordly Hudson* was judged the "best published song of the year" by the Music Library Association. The following year he won the Gershwin Award for his *Overture in C* which was performed by the New York Philharmonic Orchestra.

That same summer (1949), he went abroad for a three month visit and stayed eight years, dividing his time between Paris, and Fez and Marrakech in Morocco. In Paris he lived in the elegant 18th-century mansion of his patroness, la Vicomtesse de Noailles, the "most wealthy, powerful, colonial, intelligent, talented, influential, and cultured woman in Europe" according to the composer.

In Fez and Marrakech he wrote his first extended works. Rorem remarked that he was "very young and liked the removal from New York. I never worked as well. The surroundings (i.e., native music) had no effect whatsoever on my work." During these years he wrote his *Symphony No. 1* which was premiered in Vienna (1951), and a ballet *Dorian Gray*, first performed in Barcelona (1952).

Following Rorem's return to the United States many major works were composed and widely performed: *Symphony No. 2* (1953), *Symphony No. 3* (1959) first performed by Leonard Bernstein and the New York Philharmonic Orchestra, *Design for Orchestra, Eagles* (played at many concerts of the Philadelphia Orchestra under Eugene Ormandy on a transcontinental tour), and his *Piano Concerto No. 2*.

In addition to many choral and chamber works, Rorem has continued in his favorite field of the art song. *Poems of Love and the Rain* (1962-63) is unique in that it is a cycle of 17 songs in "pyramidal" or "mirror" sequence, each text (except for the pivotal central one) set twice. The first text is also the last; the second text is the pentultimate, etc. "The technical problem I set for myself," the composer wrote, "is, so far as I know, unprecedented, going on the principle that if a poem is 'good' there is more than one way of musicalizing it."

After several chamber operas, Rorem turned to the composition of a major opera. He was at first attracted to DuBose Heyward's novel, *Mamba's Daughter,* and was deep into it when copyright problems stopped him. He then tried a libretto by a friend, a work called *Cave,* of which Rorem said, "after I finished the whole thing, nobody knew what it was all about, including me." He then turned to Colette's *Chéri*, but again ran into copyright problems. He hit upon Strindberg's story *Miss Julie* which, according to the composer, "fitted me. I am fascinated by death." The opera was presented for the first time on November 4, 1965, by the New York City Center Opera Company. *Musical America* said of the opera that "it is impossible not to like Rorem's melodic and rhythmic invention," while *Time* said that it was "a singable and at times memorable score."

Rorem's interest in poetry and the human voice has led to additional song cycles. In 1964 he completed *Two Poems of Plato* set in the original Greek, followed by *Hearing* in 1966—seven poems by Kenneth Koch. His cycle, *Some Trees,* dating from 1968, is a setting for three singers of poems by John Ashbury. His *Sun* of 1966 is a work for soprano and large orchestra.

The composer has written four books. Two are candid personal reminiscences (sometimes undoubtedly embarrassing to the personages involved)—*The Paris Diary* (1966) and *The New York Diary* (1967). The other two books deal with Rorem's personal outlook on subjects musical. *Music from Inside Out* (1967) gives an overview of the contemporary musical scene and Rorem's opinion of it; *Music and People* (1968) seems to be more hastily put together and deals with such subjects as the Beatles, Francis Poulenc, Lukas Foss and Ezra Pound.

Through all of Rorem's writing it is evident that a troubled and disturbed voice is speaking, a pessimistic one at best. Typical is the closing paragraph of *The New York Diary* as he looks to the future in the light of the past. He writes:

> Ignorance of the future is all that can save us. We need less the time to think than the time to think about what we think. Before finding the solution we must find the problem. Love, profession, society. Now I feel less than a flop in the first two. Assuming European doors will open as before, are love or acclaim also lurking? In my glib quick wit with smiles lighting, when others say: What! You sad? that's a laugh! Yet who ever shows his "real" side—assuming there is a real side? O God, when a whole life's spent wishing we could or had, then finding ourselves *in the fact* (as though suddenly) and wondering: well, this is it, and is this all? There must be something more! People keep wondering: where does the man leave off and the artist begin? This is where. [70]

EARLY IN THE MORNING

During the academic year 1959/60 Ned Rorem delivered the Slee Foundation lectures at Buffalo University. In his talk on "Writing Songs" he rather carefully outlined the procedure as he understood it. He said on that occasion:

> The composer's initial job is to find an appropriate poem. The test of this is a poem's final enhancement by music; it is contrariwise inappropriate when both words and music add up to an issue of mutual confusion. One poem may be so intrinsically musical that a vocal setting would be superfluous. Another may be so complex that an addition of music would mystify rather than clarify its meaning.

> All words of a song from lyric poetry are ideally understood in a continuing stream; making them comprehensible is the composer's (and ultimately the singer's) chief task. Some songwriters are free in reiterating words and phrases stated only once by the poet. It is uncertain whether such song-writers do this to illuminate the sense, or because they are carried away by their own music and haven't enough words to see them through. A poem *read* aloud with these gratuitous redundancies would not only sound wrong, but lose all of the author's metrical flavor.

> A song is not a poem read aloud but something else entirely; music inclines to alter a poet's rhythmic sublety, no matter the composer's will to prevent it. The sin of duplicating words at discretion is that it retards and cripples the motion intended in verse.

> Sung words will almost always be slower than spoken ones, even without repetition; songs last longer than their poems. If the poet is alive he can be consulted about alterations. If he is not, it would seem the more interesting problem is that of making a poem comprehensible without resorting to facile verbal repetition. However, specialized verse forms (such as certain folk songs, nursery rhymes, and jazz improvisation) can lend themselves to arbitrary inner repeating.

> A sung poem should be comprehensible without amending the text if declamation and prosody are correct, the tessitura plausible, melodic rise-and-fall natural, and tempo indication comfortable.[71]

Robert Hillyer's poem, *Early in the Morning*, is a poem that is enhanced by its musical setting. The poem itself is a "nostalgic evocation of an American's Paris," of a young man of 20 and "a lover in Paradise to stay."

Rorem's setting is both tender and romantic, both economic in its means and haunting in its melodiousness. The frame is simple: a ternary structure.

After a languid, four-bar piano introduction (strongly suggesting a lazy summer day), the first phrase is heard:

Example 1

EAR-LY IN THE MORNING OF A LOVELY SUM-MER DAY,—

The second line of the poem is set to a similar melodic line, the ending being more dramatic this time:

> *As they lowered the bright awning*
> *At the outdoor cafe.*

A new melody (but with a rhythm similar to Example 1) is heard:

Example 2

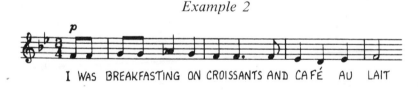

I WAS BREAKFASTING ON CROISSANTS AND CAFÉ AU LAIT

The melody of Example 2 is heard in a variant:

> *Under the greenery like scenery,*
> *Rue François Premier.*

A two-measure piano interlude sets off the first line of the middle section:

Example 3

THEY WERE HOSING THE HOT PAVEMENT WITH A DASH OF FLASHING SPRAY,

A variant of Example 3 is heard as the text continues:

And a smell of summer showers
When the dust is drenched away.

Four measures reminiscent of Example 2 are heard:

Under the greenery like scenery,
Rue François Premier.

Following a piano interlude, Example 1 and then Example 2 return:

I was twenty and a lover
And in Paradise to stay,
Very early in the morning
Of a lovely summer day.

XVIII

GUNTHER SCHULLER (1925-   ) has coined the expression, "third stream music," to designate those compositions in which modern jazz is combined with the more traditional or conventional style of symphonic writing. Schuller himself has composed a number of "third stream" works that include, among others, his *Symphonic Tribute to Duke Ellington* (1955), *Concertino for Jazz*

Quartet and Orchestra (1959), and *Variants On a Theme of Thelonius Monk* (1960) for chamber ensemble.

Actually Schuller's tastes in music are broad and all-encompassing, yet his own style of composition is usually the strictest kind of serial or dodecaphonic writing. His interests range from all manner of folk musics to jazz, from the *ars nova* of the 14th century to the most recent *avant-garde* music of the 20th century. Reared in a musical environment, he began playing French horn professionally in a symphony orchestra at 16, yet worked with John Lewis and the Modern Jazz Quartet, founding with Lewis the Society for Jazz and Classical Music.

Schuller feels that the jazz-inspired works of the 1920s—pieces by Stravinsky, Milhaud, Copland and Gershwin— quite missed the point: in his opinion, jazz is synonymous with improvisation. Or, to put it another way, without improvisation there is no jazz. Aaron Copland has replied to this charge by saying that, "during the '20s it would have been out of the question to expect a symphony player to be able to improvise in a jazz manner. Even today, when Schuller wishes to integrate jazz into a symphonic context he must bring into the concert hall or opera house a 'jazz combo' to improvise while the orchestra itself plays from the written notes provided by the composer."

In an article written for *Saturday Review,* Schuller, in a discussion concerned with jazz artist vs. the symphonic musician, speaks of improvisation, saying:

> Improvisation is the heart of jazz. . . . . .

> As for the purists who feel that . . . . all those works that seem to be gravitating toward classical or composed music do not qualify as jazz, one can only say that a music as vital and far-reaching as jazz will develop and deepen in an ever-widening circle of alternating penetration and absorption, of giving and taking.

> Actually it matters little what music is called; the important thing is that it is created and that it represents the thoughts and the ways of life of its times. Let the academicians worry about what to label it. Seen in this light, the future of this music—jazz or not—is an exciting one. And a fascinating one, because exactly what shape this future will take will not become entirely clear until the next Charlie Parker arrives on the scene.[72]

In spite of severe serial techniques employed in other than his "third stream" compositions, Schuller's music seems to have a broad, general appeal. Writing in the *Musical Quarterly,* Irving Lowens says: "Unlike the great majority of advanced composers, who tend to converse only among themselves in a private language comprehensible only to initiates, and who believe that their music 'speaks for itself' and requires no verbal explanation, Schuller insists on trying to make contact with the average concertgoer. It is his belief that the mystification of the contemporary audience when confronted with a 12-tone piece will tend to evaporate if the listener has some comprehension of the basic ground rules under which the composer operates, and furthermore, he feels that at least part of the responsibility for the listener's education belongs to the composer."

Gunther Schuller's life has been literally steeped in music since the time of his birth in 1925, in New York. His father was a violinist in the New York Philharmonic Orchestra, so as a youngster there was music all around him. He did not become actively interested in it himself, however, until he joined the St. Thomas Choir School at the age of 12 as a boy soprano. There his interest was aroused in both vocal and instrumental music, and in composition.

Schuller first learned to play the flute, then at 14 he switched to the French horn. He became so proficient on the latter that two years later he left high school and the Manhattan School of Music, where he had been studying theory and counterpoint, and joined the orchestra of the Ballet Theatre as a horn player. In 1945, he became the first horn player of the Cincinnati Symphony, and at 19 joined the Metropolitan Opera Orchestra as first horn, remaining with that company for the next 15 years.

Self-taught as a composer, Schuller resigned from the Metropolitan Opera Orchestra in 1959 to devote more time to composing. In 1960, he was the recipient of both the National Institute of Arts and Letters Award, and the Brandeis University's Creative Arts Award. In addition to composing, Schuller became involved with the Modern Jazz Quartet, taught privately and at the Manhattan School of Music, and in 1962 published his book titled *Horn Technique.* Later his book on the beginnings of jazz, *Early Jazz: Its Roots and Musical Development,* was published (1968), and he was appointed President of the New England Conservatory of Music (1968) and Head of the Composition Department at the

Berkshire Music Center at Tanglewood.

Commenting on Schuller's work and manifold activities, Eric Salzman said in an article appearing in the *New York Times:*

> Schuller's various musical activities are not unconnected with his creative work. In his music one can hear the instrumental know-how of the wind player; the idiomatic and finely calculated sensibility of the conductor; the technical mastery and brilliant eclecticism of the modern music expert, and the controlled freedom and invention of a creative personality that knows and understands jazz.
>
> What gives Schuller's music its impact, even on audiences quite unprepared for dissonance and up-to-date asymmetry, is its contact with the reality of the performance and of the player and of his instrument. It is this aspect of Schuller's music, as much as any literal references, that is allied to and informed by the jazz idea.[73]

Schuller has received favorable comment from public and press alike on a wide variety of his works. On May 16, 1960, following an all-Schuller concert, John S. Wilson said in the *New York Times:* "As evidence of the validity and potential of his 'third stream' of music, Mr. Schuller's concert was a rousing success." Speaking of a concert of chamber music, Eric Salzman said in a review: "Even though the harmonic, melodic and rhythmic techniques are theoretically forbidding, dissonant and fragmented . . . this music has a direct interest and excitement that stems from the composer's skill at writing for the instruments. And, by tieing this in with a real sense of phrase and motion (which operates even through broken up and sustained phrases), he is able to achieve shape, proportion and −yes − expression."

Schuller's orchestral work, *Seven Studies on Themes of Paul Klee* was completed in 1959. Paul Hume, in the *Washington Post,* said after its first local performance, "The work roused last night's National Symphony Orchestra audience to unusual and prolonged applause." Following the playing of Schuller's *Music for Brass Quintet* (1961) two weeks later, in Washington, the same critic said that it was "fascinating . . . superb . . . one of the high points of the concert."

Commissioned by the Donaueschingen Festival of Contemporary Music in 1961, Schuller's *Contrasts* also drew praise in reviews. Everett Helm reported that it "contained not only some arresting effects (as always in the music of this master orchestrator) but also some sound musical ideas, well-organized and carried out in this very substantial work." Following the world premiere of his opera *The Visitation* by the Hamburg State Opera in Germany in 1966, the *New York Times* stated, *"The Visitation* is believed to be the first solid success that a modern American opera has had in a European opera house since *Porgy and Bess* was brought abroad by an American Company."

SEVEN STUDIES ON THEMES OF PAUL KLEE

3. Little Blue Devil
4. The Twittering Machine

"Ever since I learned many years ago that Paul Klee was a fine amateur violinist and in his thousands of pictures frequently used musical forms and terms," writes Gunther Schuller, "I resolved to write a composition one day that would be based in some way on his work. The opportunity presented itself in 1959 when I received a commission from the Ford Foundation and the Minneapolis (now Minnesota) Symphony Orchestra in conjunction with the American Music Center, to write an orchestral composition. Unofficially it was suggested that, since as part of this commissioning project the works were to be played by at least nine other symphony orchestras, it would be in the best interests of all concerned if I could write a piece which might become a real contemporary repertory piece. This is, of course, every composer's dream when he writes a new work. And it seemed to me that a retranslation into musical terms of the 'musical' elements in certain Klee pictures might provide precisely the proper ingredients in fulfilling this commission.

"I therefore selected seven pictures which either permitted a direct translation of their visual-structural elements into musical terms (*Antique Harmonies, Abstract Trio* and *Pastorale*), or provided at least a natural inspiration for a freely invented parallel musical conception. . . . .

"The comic-seriousness of Klee's famous cubist demon, *Little Blue Devil (Kleiner blauer Teufel),* evolved into a jazz "third

stream" piece with a perky, fragmented tune and 'blue' instrumental colorings."[74]

After a loud opening chord, the percussion—snare drum and a
pair of suspended cymbals—establishes the jazz rhythm. Short,
rising figures for the strings break in a couple of times. The
trumpet enters three times with variants of Figure A.

A single double bass, slapped (*pizzicato*) plays a rhythmic bass
line. Four horns respond the second and third time to the
trumpets, Figure A's with syncopated chords in close position,
fulfilling the role of the saxophones in a true jazz combo.

Finally the flutes and trumpet, in unison, break loose with
the "perky, fragmented tune":

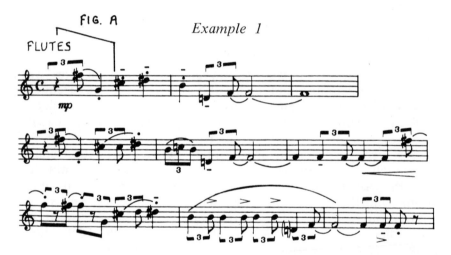

Example 1

The strings are heard in their rising figure once more,
followed by some "fancy work" for unison flutes and trumpet in
16th-note runs and motives. (All derived from Example 1, a sort of
written-out jazz improvisation.)

The sound of the vibes (vibraharp) is heard as it takes up the
16th-note passage work. What the composer calls "lazy triplets"
for single reeds and trombones with cup mutes follows. The vibes
take off again. Strings and woodwinds take over in a syncopated
passage that leads to a loud chord followed by a moment of
silence.

A variant of the blues tune, Example 1, returns in the flutes
and trumpet, once again set off against the rhythm of snare drum,

"The Twittering Machine," a water color, pen and ink drawing completed in 1922 by Paul Klee (1879-1940). This painting inspired the movement of the same name in Gunther Schuller's *Seven Studies on Themes of Paul Klee*.

suspended cymbals and a solo pizzicato string bass. Soft harmonies for the strings accompany the closing measures.

* * * *

"A *Twittering Machine (Die Zwitschermaschine)* ought to twitter. In addition, it seemed to me that a strict 'mechanical' application of latter-day serial techniques might be particularly and—I hope—humorously apt in this movement."

Schuller was so effective in capturing the comedy and spirit of Klee's painting in music, that unless one stops to think about it and analyze it, he is not conscious of listening to serial music—and, serial music that is pointillistic at that.

Softly the four horns and violas (divided three ways) set up a rumbling sound. They play four notes over and over in differing sequences, Example 2; double reeds soon join in.

Example 2

4 FRENCH HORN (STOPPED)

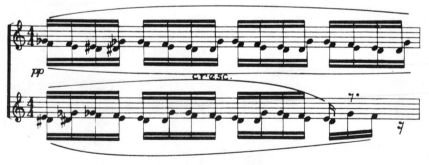

The tone-row of the "twittering" is B-flat, B-natural, E, F, G, D-sharp, F-sharp, A, A-flat, D, C-sharp and C-natural. It is presented by a variety of instruments over a span of two octaves in a pointillistic style:

Example 3

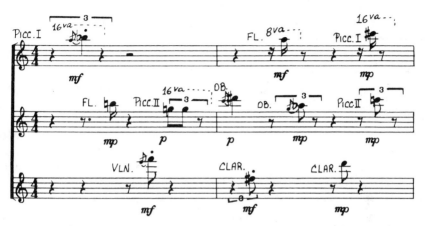

Except for a person with a completely scientific/mathematical mind and *no* imagination, there is little point in further analyzing the score. (It can be done, of course, and holds up to the strictest scrutiny.) One should simply sit back and enjoy the humorous machinations of the twittering machine.

XIX

MORTON SUBOTNICK (1933-   ) believes that the musicians of the 20th-century have searched in vain for a common musical language. "Each composer today individualizes his style, even changes that 'style' radically from one composition to another," Subotnick writes. "If he adheres to a common language, it applies only to the group he has accepted (and has been accepted by), and the group itself tends to remain in stylistic and aesthetic contrast to other groups."

One of the problems facing the contemporary composer is the challenge of "the historically accepted masters of his art." As Franz Schubert bemoaned 150 years ago, "Who ever could hope to compose again after Beethoven," so the musicians of the 20th century are forced to follow not only Beethoven's footsteps but those of Schubert himself, and Brahms, and Wagner, and Schoenberg, and countless others. The modern composer's "intense awareness of his styles and techniques as part of the musical fibre of the society he lives in—an awareness unprecedented in previous centuries—compels him to adopt new positions," states Subotnick. "He must also be aware of the discrepancy between the nature of his developing musical language (with its highly individualized form and content) and the traditional institutions within which this music functions."

Early in his career Subotnick opted for a style and musical language based on the electronic discoveries being made in reference to music. While on the faculty at Mills College in California he worked with an engineer, Donald Buchla, and a composer of like interests, Ramon Sender, to develop the kind of electronic machine that would perform the functions Subotnick wanted. "The three of us worked together for more than a year to develop an electronic music 'machine' that would satisfy our needs as composers," Subotnick later related. He then went on to say:

> The system generates sound and time configurations, which are predetermined by the composer through a series of 'patches' consisting of interconnecting various voltage-control devices. It is possible to produce a specific predetermined sound event, . . . and it is also possible to produce sound events that are predetermined only in generalities. . . . . This means that one can 'tell' the machine what kind of event you want without deciding on the specific details of the event. . . . and listen . . . and then make final decisions as to the details of the musical gesture. This gives the flexibility to score sections of the piece in the traditional sense. . . . and to mold other sections (from graphic and verbal notes) like a piece of sculpture.[75]

This "modular electronic system" (as Subotnick calls it) served him well not only at the San Francisco Tape Music Center that developed out of that tripartite partnership, it became the core of his studio when he joined the staff at New York University.

Morton Subotnick was born in Los Angeles on April 14, 1933, and grew up in the San Fernando Valley to the north of Los Angeles proper. His youth was not much different from other students at North Hollywood High School, although he played the

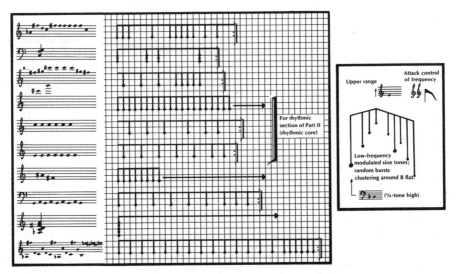

Some notes on *Silver Apples of the Moon*. Since traditional staff notation will not serve the modern electronic composer, each must devise his own notational system. At the left is Subotnick's notes for the end of Part II, — "A single silver child-angel in a glittering garden of silver star-fruit." The example at the right is for the slow section of Part I.

Subotnick in his studio with the modular electronic system.

clarinet especially well in the band and orchestra and enjoyed classes in literature.

High school was followed by matriculation at the University of Denver where he majored in literature. His familiarity with and love of poetry shows up in at least two of his electronic works. *Silver Apples of the Moon,* composed in 1967, a composition for electronic-music synthesizer, derives its title from a line of poetry by Yeats. Its sequel, *The Wild Bull,* completed in 1968, was titled after a poem by an anonymous Sumerian poet dating from around 1700 B.C. "The state of mind which the poem evoked became intimately tangled with the state of mind my own composition was evoking in me," Subotnick relates. "To title the work after the poem seemed natural."

From Denver and literature, Subotnick returned to California and music. He enrolled for graduate work in composition at Mills College and studied there with both Leon Kirchner and Darius Milhaud. At the same time he played clarinet in the San Francisco Symphony, having previously played with the Denver Symphony while in that city.

After finishing his studies at Mills College, he joined their staff as an Assistant Professor of Music. He also served simultaneously as Musical Director of Ann Halprin's Dancers Workshop Company in San Francisco across the bay. Around 1960, Subotnick began working with tape and soon helped Donald Buchla with the development of the modular electronic music system or electronic synthesizer already mentioned.

Subotnick was appointed Musical Director of the Repertory Theater at New York's Lincoln Center during its first season, and since the fall of 1966 has been involved with the Intermedia Program at the School of Arts at New York University. The purpose of this program is to bring together artists who specialize in various media—film, theater, tape, lights, etc.

Subotnick has composed music for films, including the electronic part of the recording of music from the space odyssey film, *2001.* The composer also has served as a Director of Electric Music at the Electric Circus in Greenwich Village.

In September of 1969 Subotnick became the Associate Dean of the School of Music and Director of Electronic Music at the California Institute of the Arts north of Los Angeles.

Subotnick feels that the changing nature of our times, of our media, of our music, indicates that new means for presentation are a mandate for the artist. He says:

> The need to create something to be performed spontaneously and witnessed 'live' has led me to experiment in the development of a new presentational institution—mixed media. Earlier, I thought 'music theater' to be a more valid title: the requirements become clearly defined when mixed-media becomes in this context essentially 'theatrical' and exclusively presentational. It takes many forms and is obviously different in the hands of different artists. It differs from other theatrical or dramatic forms, like ballet or opera, in that the content, whether it be the movement of lights or the movement of a body or the movement of a violin bow, is always directly interrelated with the abstract content of the musical experience related to the particular discipline of the artist, as in the case of a painter who produces a mixed-media composition. The 'theatrical' is merely a visual extension of the stuff that music is made of. The content is not easily defined, although most composers come to it with similar motivations and problems. Some compositions tend so much toward the dramatic that when the visual extensions are added, they take a form not much different from dance and sometimes opera or film. I have attempted to keep my presentational music theater compositions close to the abstract experience that motivates my musical thinking. I have also recently begun to deal with the possibility of mixed-media chamber music to be performed in a small room (a living room for instance) without an audience or, if there is an audience, with the kind of audience that would be present when string quartets are played in someone's home.[76]

Even before Subotnick turned to electronic works he was composing music that was well received. His *Serenade No. 1* (1960) is an eight-minute work for six performers: flute, clarinet, vibraphone, mandoline, cello and piano. "An air reed, a single reed, a tuned percussion instrument, a plucked string, a bowed string, and a struck string—certainly a vivid and transparent collection, at once problematic and musically suggestive," wrote a reviewer in *Perspectives of New Music*. The critic goes on to say that, "the *Serenade* is not a 12-tone composition in the usual sense, nor is there any consistent serial scheme, so far as I am able to detect. On the other hand, tonal "poles" . . . appear only very rarely." Subotnick's *Serenade No. 2* dates from 1964 and is scored for clarinet, horn, piano, and a percussionist who "plies his trade on the strings, the ribs, and the sounding board of the piano," according to the music critic of the *Musical Quarterly*. "The work brings into action a variety of more or less dense, contrapuntal, spacious, or figurated textures in opposition to alternating periods of silence or relative inactivity. It uses spectacular virtuoso effects and relies conspicuously on the performers. . . . One may wonder . . . whether new visual aspects help or hinder the work, since using mallets on the insides of a piano delight and fascinate some listeners but distress and antagonize others. Several times also the clarinet is held into the horn's bell, as both players engage in an enormous crescendo, flutter-tongue and *cuivré* respectively, on notes a semitone apart."

"There is a lyricism. . . underlying Morton Subotnick's *Serenade No. 3* [1965]" writes Elliott Schwartz in a review of the composer's third work in this genre. It is "not in the actual casting or the melodic line, or arch of a phrase, . . . but in lightness and freshness of texture, the rhythmic bounce of its pulses, and its comfortable (as opposed to *avant-garde* grim) sense of humor. The electronic tape and four instruments are integrated into a strangely surrealistic, yet well-balanced, 'quintet' of sorts, the five members of which busily toss motivic fragments back and forth, echo each other's wide vibrato, and generally respond in a true chamber style."

Subotnick feels, however, that the concert hall as it is now known is going to give way as far as contemporary music is concerned to the phonograph record. He says:

The fractionated nature of 20th-century music has invalidated the concert hall as an effective institution for its presentation. An audience, before it can understand a new composition, must have time to adjust to the language of the particular style, whether it be a group or individual style. The fact that there is so much music to be played (both past and present) and such a vast audience to reach, limits the number of times an audience can be exposed to new works. In such a situation, an audience has no opportunity to absorb the complexity of content in a new composition. Also, since the conductor knows that the audience is unfamiliar with the work he is presenting, he tends to devote too little time for its effective presentation. A few conductors are exceptions, and the gradual enlargement of this group is starting to change the dismal landscape a bit.

Luckily, the concert hall is not the only available institution. The recording industry has the potential to satisfy the needs of 20th-century music far better than the concert hall, even if the concert hall suddenly reformed. Generally, the extra time spent in preparation for a recording, and the editing done after taping, means that, more and more, recorded performances are at least accurate if not inspired. The record can be listened-to over and over again and can economically reach more people with greater ease and without having to accomodate an audience with mixed tastes. It is my opinion that the recording, although it lacks the spontaneity of live performance, satisfies so many of the joint needs and desires of the audience and composer that it is as close to an ideal medium for new music as the parlor was for chamber music. The consequences of the record becoming the primary medium for 20th-century music are not altogether pleasant, but I have come to accept the drawbacks as well as the advantages and have for some time made no attempt to deal with the concert hall as an institution.[77]

In 1967 Nonesuch Records commissioned Subotnick to write a composition specifically for reproduction via a phonograph record using his electronic music synthesizer. His previously mentioned *Silver Apples of the Moon* was the result of this commission. It received high praise from the professional critics. *High Fidelity* said "the piece is a beauty." The *San Francisco Chronicle* reported that it is "one of the finest electronic pieces in existence." *Hi Fi/Stereo Review* suggested that it "merits the attention and interest of everyone interested in the music of our time."

So successful was the venture that Nonesuch Records gave Subotnick a second such commission for which he composed *The Wild Bull* in 1968. A review in *The Musical Quarterly* said that "Subotnick is one of the few people working in this field [electronic music]—and whose work has been published—with wit and style. His compositions have personality, and personality is hard to extract from a synthesizer. . . . *The Wild Bull* . . . is its own thing: a strange, powerful lament, at times full of grief, at times wildly rebellious; in short, classically tragic."[78]

A work of an entirely different nature, one more involved with Subotnick's multi-media experiences, is *Play! No. 1* for woodwind quintet, piano, tape and film. According to Henry Leland Clarke in *The Musical Quarterly*, reporting on a concert at the University of Washington, *Play! No. 1* "beats the theater of the absurd at its own game. The players gaze now left, now right, now into the heavens, at times freezing, at times shouting questionable monosyllables, interrupted once by a film of the peripatetic composer himself back in San Francisco. The young of all ages were convulsed both in Seattle and in Portland, where this entire program was repeated the following week. But since it most completely realized the composer's intentions, *Play! No. 1* may be pronounced the most serious number on the program."

SILVER APPLES OF THE MOON

Part II

The title of Morton Subotnick's composition for electronic music synthesizer, *Silver Apples of the Moon,* is derived from the penultimate line of Irish poet William Butler Yeats' (1865-1939) "The Song of Wandering Aengus."

> *Though I am old with wandering*
> *Through hollow lands and hilly lands*
> *I will find out where she has gone,*
> *And kiss her lips and take her hands;*
> *And walk among long dappled grass,*
> *And pluck till time and times are done*
> *The silver apples of the moon,*
> *The golden apples of the sun.*

The composer tells us that the title "was chosen because it aptly reflects the unifying idea of the composition, heard in its pure form at the end of Part II."

The composition itself represents a signal event in the history of music and the phonograph: for the first time, an original, full-scale composition has been created expressly for the record medium. In his program notes Subotnick says:

The work is entirely electronic and was composed and realized at my studio in the School of the Arts at New York University. The piece, which was composed especially for .... Nonesuch [Records] is in two major sections that correspond to the two sides of the record. The idea of writing a work especially for a recording presents the composer with a rather special frame of reference ... It is not the reproduction of a work originally intended for the concert hall, ... rather it is intended to be experienced by individuals or small groups of people listening in intimate surroundings, ... a kind of chamber music 20th-century style.[79]

Part II is 15 minutes in length. The introduction—one minute and 23 seconds—consists of what sound like random beeps in the pointillistic style. Perhaps they're serial. A few faint trills are heard, then some isolated tones suggestive of the vibraphone.

Then commences an intense eight-minute segment, one long, gradual crescendo based on an incessant rhythm (á la *Bolero* of Ravel). At first the ear barely detects the faint tapping, tapping, as of someone with leather heels walking quickly down a street. The tapping changes timbre and "presence," but still continues. The random rasps and bleeps appear above it.

The tapping grows, the drumming advances; a bass-octave motor starts up in the right speaker. The great beating, zapping, rhythmic exercise goes on. ("Exercise" in the sense of muscular repetition.) At the dynamic climax, great warbles appear overhead and a skipping white-noise* cymbal pattern darts in and out of the croaking, snapping motor. There is no overlaid melody; it is *inside* the rhythm. Then suddenly, it all falls away, leaving just the low note of the octave beating, then just the original foot tapping, and then it all evaporates into random twittering again.

There are trills and pointillistic bleeps and blurbs reminiscent of the introduction, but the dynamic level is much more intense this time. As time progresses, the texture of the music grows more complex and dense.

At 12 minutes, the sound fades away. In a gentle passage, silvery tones and gongs are heard. Then silence.

> *"And pluck till time and times are done*
> *The silver apples of the moon,"*

A few faint twitterings as of birds overhead, and the music is over.

---

white noise = By analogy with light, a signal that may be considered to contain all audible frequencies, with amplitudes randomly distributed. Colored noise, analogously, is noise in which a band (or bands) or frequencies is suppressed. The audible effect of white noise is like that of escaping steam.

MORTON SUBOTNICK   CHARLES WUORINEN

XX

CHARLES WUORINEN (1938-) is reminiscent of the 18th-century musical virtuoso-of-all-trades. At an age when most composers are just finding themselves, he made his mark as composer, performer, teacher, impresario, writer on subjects musical, and musical commentator. "Composers, having gotten sick of waiting for performers to do their job correctly, have, many of them, decided to do the performing themselves," Wuorinen has said. "Thus today you will find an increasing number of us who are complete musicians in the old sense. We write the music, set up the concerts when it is to be played, perform it ourselves, and even—for we are also sick of waiting for critics and musicologists to do *their* job intelligently—write about it ourselves."

During an interview when he was but 25 years of age, Wuorinen stated unequivocally the dilemmas facing the composers of his age as opposed to those that confronted an earlier creative artist. He said:

> The present generation of young composers must concern itself more with consolidation and synthesis, with acting out the implications of the older generation's work, than with innovation.

> The young composer functions in a strange environment. On the one hand, the works of Webern (for him traditional) are still performed only on 'esoteric' concerts of 'new' music. On the other, the theatrico-musical expressions of John Cage and others of like persuasion are seriously discussed and reviewed in the press. The young composer thus finds himself largely without external standards by which he can measure his own activity. He lacks even the negative standard of revolt—for it seems today, in a musical culture which takes seriously the burning of a violin as a musical happening, there is little positive enough in existence against which to revolt.

> The young composer has a greater responsibility, perhaps, than his forebears had—all the greater because it is largely or wholly to himself. The absence of any applicable general cultural standard in our society, coupled with the removal of restraints normally imposed by taste, sensitivity, and organic convention, must necessarily drive the young composer inward, in a new way. He must define for himself—not in the 'last analysis' but from the start—the limits of his activity and the boundaries of what constitutes music. It is very hard for one to do this without reference to external standards. We are trained, if only by implication, to believe in the existence of general purposes and standards. When we face the fact that there are none, choice becomes difficult and 'freedom' meaningless. [80]

Wuorinen, like other composers of his generation, was confronted with the many divergent paths of contemporary music: post-Webern serialism and pointillism; electronic music (tape, computer, synthesizer); aleatoric music; and the *non-music* of John Cage and his school. Wuorinen himself opted for the 12-tone system, seeing in it as "flexible and profound a means of musical coherence as the tonal system had provided, and, while engaged by electronic media, never abandoning performance. Twelve-tone technique is of course the primary influence on young composers," Wuorinen relates, "but the content of this influence and the questions it raises have perhaps been insufficiently examined. . . . . Dodecaphonic organization [is] so familiar that there is today hardly a conscious decision on their part in employing it. Indeed it is the use of techniques that depart from dodecaphonic organization that requires conscious decision."

In dealing with electronic means the young composer (according to Wuorinen) "must learn new techniques and acquire new (manual) skills. He must learn new notations, or invent them, or compose without notation at all. He must face the changes in his work brought about by having the physical presence of the sound structures he is creating with him at all times during the course of composition." Wuorinen feels that "to abandon electronic media now is unthinkable." The advent of electronic music was brought about, according to the composer, partially by the fact that "the orchestra as a medium relevant to living music is passing, or indeed may have already expired." He goes on to say that, unfortunately, in the United States which boasts thousands of symphony orchestras, "the opportunities for young composers to work in this medium are to all intents and purposes nonexistent."

Wuorinen's own *Symphony No. 3*, written when he was 21 and still working with the more conventional performance mediums, was recorded—not by an American orchestra—but by the Japan Philharmonic. The symphony itself is an interesting work, "bright and cocky" according to a review in *The Musical Quarterly*. "In spite of [Wuorinen's] youth," the article continues, "he had already learned to write brilliantly for orchestra, had obviously studied a great amount of music old and new, and had absorbed all the tricks of the trade he could lay his hands on. Being 21, he was also frightfully sure of himself and bursting with energy. His symphony sounds as if nothing had as yet become stale for him or, for that matter, sacred; everything seems simply to have been overwhelmingly exciting, and so we get a roaring piece for full orchestra, which shouts and drums and rises to ecstasies, taps mysteriously, exhibits an indiscriminate but relentless procession of musical expressions, and occasionally steps rather painfully on quite a number of esthetic toes. It is a wild and disorderly piece."

Charles Wuorinen was born in New York City. His father, a historian, taught for more than 40 years at Columbia University (he passed away in 1969) and became Chairman of the History Department. The composer's mother was an amateur musician. "She told me that she stopped playing the piano when I got better than she was," Wuorinen later recalled.

The composer was interested and fascinated by music from his earliest years. At five he began to compose original fragments of music. He then started taking piano lessons. By the time he was in high school, Wuorinen was studying harmony, counterpoint and composition. At Columbia University he studied composition with Otto Luening, Jack Beeson and Vladimir Ussachevsky. He earned his baccalaureate at Columbia in 1961 and his Master's Degree in 1963.

At 16, Wuorinen won his first contest: the Philharmonic Young Composer's Award for 1954. This led to numerous other honors: the Bearns Prize in 1958, 1959 and 1961; the Lili Boulanger Memorial Award in 1961 and 1962; several fellowships including the Regents College Teaching Fellowship, the Evans Traveling Fellowship and the Festival Fellowship of the Santa Fe Opera. In 1967 he was elected to the American Academy of Arts and Letters, and a year later earned a Guggenheim Fellowship. He has received commissions from the Orchestra of America, Columbia University, the Ford Foundation, the Fromm Music Foundation and the Berkshire Music Center.

Since 1969 Wuorinen has served as an Assistant Professor of Music at Columbia University. Earlier he had been an Instructor at Columbia as well as a visiting lecturer at Princeton and the New England Conservatory. He has appeared as a soloist – usually in his own compositions – with the Buffalo Philharmonic, the Indianapolis Symphony, the Royal Philharmonic and the Lisbon Radio Orchestra.

By his 30th year, Wuorinen had to his credit more than 85 compositions. This number includes three symphonies, both a violin and a piano concerto, works for synthesizer and orchestra, and many chamber pieces, as well as choral music and a chamber opera.

PIANO CONCERTO

Charles Wuorinen's *Piano Concerto* was commissioned by the University of Iowa and was first performed there on May 4th, 1966. James Dixon conducted that premiere performance as well as the one recorded, with the composer at the piano, in 1969.

In the concerto, the orchestra is of traditional instrumentation (except for triple winds). However, the composer makes use of a nine-man percussion battery. The percussion department acts as a multi-voiced, multi-textural unit, with a thoroughly-heard musical function that is characteristic of Wuorinen's work. (This in contrast to the percussion section's usual function of "punctuating" some other section's melodic line which is of primary importance.)

Wuorinen adds: "Since the Concerto is in a single movement, the various contrasts of speed, texture and so forth, that occupy different movements in older pieces, here are all present simultaneously in a multi-layered continuity."

The Concerto is a 12-tone work which is also serial in terms of rhythm and timbre. The basic row — Example 1 — is heard at the very beginning of the work. Both melodic and rhythmic figures from it return in recognizable form throughout the Concerto.

Example 1

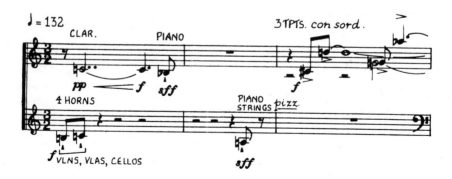

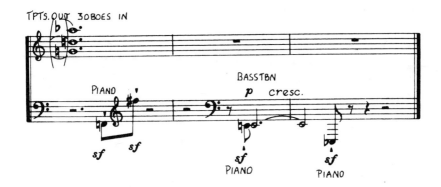

The rhythm row or series is derived from the melodic row shown in Example 1. The minor second is the equivalent of an eighth-note, since in Wuorinen's "American system" it is the interval distance between elements of the pitch set, not the elements themselves, that forms the model for extending the set-ordering to other areas. This row then becomes at the beginning, though not throughout the whole piece, as follows:

B to C is the same as one eighth-note
C to B-flat equals 10 semi-tones since one always measures upward
B-flat to A is the same as 11 eighth-notes
A to C-sharp is the same as four eighth-notes
C-sharp to D is one eighth-note
D to G is five eighth-notes
etc.

In other words, in this example, the 3/2 bar is the same pitch at the octave, and one-half the 3/2 equals an eighth-note and is the same as a semitone.

In a detailed description of the *Piano Concerto* written especially for this book, Wuorinen says:

The Concerto is in a single movement, but this movement contains — in a way typical of many recent pieces — the various contrasts of tempo and activity that used to be relegated to separate movements. The relation of soloist to orchestra is also a varying one, but there is very little of the solo/tutti duelling that used to be thought indispensable. In the main, the piano functions as the

originator of musical material which the orchestra may then
enlarge. Thus, the dichotomy between solo and orchestra exists
mainly on the structural level.

The Concerto is a 12-tone work, and as is common with many
recent pieces, the effects of the 12-tone set are not reserved solely
to the domain of pitch. Rhythm, both in the small scale (meaning
note-to-note distances) and in the large (meaning overall form), is
directly derived from the set. But here we must note a critical
difference between my procedure (typical of "American serialism"), and that of the now-defunct European "serialism." In the
Concerto, it is the *interval distances* between elements of the pitch
set, *not the elements themselves,* that form the model for extending the set-ordering to other areas. If, therefore, we speak
simply of intervals, it is clear that a succession of intervals is really
a series of proportions, and such a series may be applied, for
example, to the division of time in the large scale (sections of the
total piece) or in the small (distances between attacks, i.e.,
foreground rhythm). The same kind of extension is applied to
other areas beyond time and pitch: tone color, the density of
events at any given time, and even the degree of formal "strict-
ness," are all similarly derived. Moreover, the piece is interrupted
several times by measured silences, whose position and lengths also
owe their origin to the pitch set.[81]

"Even the general pauses," the composer said at another time,
"may be considered windows in the piece opening on the silence in
which it swims."

FOOTNOTES

1. Merriam, Alan P. "African Music," *Continuity and Change in African Cultures* (Chicago, 1959).
2. Nettl, Bruno. *Folk and Traditional Music of the Western Continents* (Englewood Cliffs, 1965).
3. Schuller, Gunther. *Early Jazz: Its Roots and Musical Developments* (New York, 1968).
4. *Ibid.*
5. Austin, William W. *Music In the 20th Century* (New York, 1966).
6. Ellington, Duke. "The Composer On His Work," *The Christian Science Monitor* (60/164; June 10, 1968).
7. Hodeir, André. *Jazz: Its Evolution and Essence.* (trans. by David Noakes) New York, 1956.
8. *Ibid.*
9. Hamilton, David. "A Synoptic View of the New Music," *High Fidelity* (18/9; Sept. 1968).
10. Mellers, Wilfrid. *Music and Society* (New York, 1950).
11. Cowell, Henry and Sidney. *Charles Ives and His Music* (New York, 1955).
12. Ives, Charles. *Essays Before a Sonata and Other Writings*, H. Boatwright, ed. (New York, 1962).
13. Bellamann, Henry. "Program Notes" quoted in the Preface to the Conductor's Score of Charles Ives *Symphony No. 4* (New York, 1965).
14. Cowell, Henry. "The Music of Edgar Varèse" *Modern Music* (V/2; Jan. 1928).
15. from a lecture given at the University of Southern California, 1939, and quoted in *Contemporary Composers on Contemporary Music,* Elliott Schwartz and Barney Childs, eds. (New York, 1967).
16 Schuller, Gunther. "Conversations with Varèse" *Perspectives of New Music* (3/2; Spring-Summer, 1965).
17. *Ibid.*
18. lecture at Sarah Lawrence College, 1959, reprinted in *Contemporary Composers on Contemporary Music.*
19. Copland, Aaron. *The New Music: 1900-1960* (New York, 1968).
20. Arvey, Verna. *Studies in Contemporary American Music: William Grant Still* (New York, 1939).
21. Hanson, Howard. "Music in Our Age" *Music Journal* (Anthology, 1965).
22. Hanson, Howard. "The Music of 1967" *Music Journal* (Anthology, 1967).
23. Copland, Aaron. *The New Music: 1900-1960* (New York, 1968).
24. Thomson, Virgil. *Virgil Thomson* (New York, 1966).
25. personal letter to Nick Rossi, 1961.
26. Thomson, Virgil. *About Four Saints* (New York, 1964).
27. Grosser, Maurice. "Scenario" printed in the vocal score *Four Saints in Three Acts* by Gertrude Stein and Virgil Thomson (New York, 1948).
28. Rosenfeld, Paul. *Discoveries of a Music Critic* (New York, 1936).
29. Brant, Henry. "Henry Cowell: Musician and Citizen" *Etude* (75/2; Feb. 1957).
30. Cowell, Henry. *New Musical Resources* (New York, 1930).
31. Cowell, Henry. *The Banshee* (Los Angeles, 1930).
32. Rushmore, Robert. *George Gershwin* (London, 1966).
33. *Ibid.*

34. Gershwin, George. "The Relation of Jazz to American Music" *American Composers on American Music*, Henry Cowell, ed. (Palo Alto, 1933).
35. Gershwin, George. "Jazz" *Revolt in the Arts*, Oliver M. Saylor, ed. (New York, 1933).
36. Rushmore, Robert. *Op. cit.*
37. Payne, Robert. *Gershwin* (London, 1962).
38. Goldberg, Isaac. *George Gershwin: A Study in American Music* (New York, 1931).
39. Copland, Aaron. *The New Music: 1900-1960* (New York, 1968).
40. *Ibid.*
41. Antheil, George. *Bad Boy of Music* (Garden City, 1945).
42. *Ibid.*
43. *Ibid.*
44. Cowell, Henry. "Current Chronicle" *The Musical Quarterly* (XL/2; Apr. 1954).
45. *Op. cit.*
46. *Ibid.*
47. Antheil, George. "Preface" *Ballet mécanique* (Delaware Water Gap, Pa., 1959).
48. Barber, Samuel. "On Waiting for a Libretto" *Opera News* (XXII/13; Jan. 27, 1958).
49. Broder, Nathan. *Samuel Barber* (New York, 1954).
50. Luening, Otto. "An Unfinished History of Electronic Music" *Music Educators Journal* (55/3; Nov. 1968).
51. *Ibid.*
52. *Ibid.*
53. Harrison, Jay. "Electronic Concert at Museum" *New York Herald-Tribune* (Oct. 29, 1952).
54. Luening, Otto. *op. cit.*
55. *Ibid.* Lester.
56. Trimble, Lester. *Program Notes* (New York, n.d.).
57. Cage, John. *Silence* (Middletown, Conn., 1961).
58. Thomson, Virgil. "Expressive Percussion" *New York Herald-Tribune* (Jan. 22, 1945) reprinted in *Music Reviewed* New York, 1967).
59. Cage, John. "Unbestimmtheit" *die Reihe* (Bryn Mawr, Pa., 1961).
60. Cage, John. *Silence* (Middletown, Conn., 1961).
61. Cage, John. "Unbestimmtheit" *die Reihe* (Bryn Mawr, Pa., 1961).
62. Cage, John, and Lejaren Hiller. "HPSCHD" *Source* (2/2; July, 1968).
63. *Ibid.*
64. *Ibid.*
65. Babbitt, Milton. "Who Cares If You Listen" *High Fidelity* (VIII/2; Feb. 1958).
66. "An Interview with Milton Babbitt," *Music Educators Journal* (55/3; Nov. 1968).
67. *Ibid.*
68. *Ibid.*
69. Babbitt, Milton. *Program Notes* (New York, n.d.).
70. Rorem, Ned. *The New York Diary* (New York, 1967).
71. Rorem, Ned. *Music From Inside Out* (New York, 1967).
72. Schuller, Gunther. "The Future of Form in Jazz" originally in *The Saturday Review* (1956); reprinted in *The American Composer Speaks*, Gilbert Chase, ed. (Baton Rouge, 1966).
73. Salzman, Eric. "The Music of Gunther Schuller" *New York Times* (Jan. 21, 1962).
74. Schuller, Gunther. *Program Notes* (New York, 1966).
75. Subotnick, Morton. *Program Notes* (New York, n.d.).
76. Subotnick, Morton. "Extending the Stuff Music is Made of" *Music Educators Journal* (55/3; Nov. 1968).

77. *Ibid.*
78. Dockstader, Tod. "The Wild Bull" *The Musical Quarterly* (LV/1; Jan. 1969).
79. Subotnick, Morton. *Program Notes* (New York, n.d.).
80. Wuorinen, Charles. "The Outlook for Young Composers" *Perspectives of New Music* (1/2; Spring, 1963).
81. Wuorinen, Charles, in a letter addressed to Nick Rossi dated May 20, 1969.

BIBLIOGRAPHY

(Arranged According to the Table of Contents)

MUSIC OF EUROPE AND LATIN AMERICA

Austin, William W. *Music In the 20th-Century: From Debussy Through Stravinsky.* New York: W.W. Norton & Co., Inc., 1966.

Hartog, Howard (ed.). *European Music in the Twentieth Century.* New York: Frederick A. Praeger, Publishers, 1957.

Hodier, André. *Since Debussy: A View of Contemporary Music* (trans. by Noel Burch) New York: Grove Press, Inc., 1961.

Machlis, Joseph. *Introduction to Contemporary Music.* New York: W.W. Norton & Co., Inc., 1961.

Salzman, Eric. *Twentieth-Century Music: An Introduction.* Englewood Cliffs (N.J.) Prentice-Hall, Inc. 1967.

Schwartz, Elliott, and Barney Childs (eds.). *Contemporary Composers on Contemporary Music.* New York: Holt. Rinehart & Winston, 1967.

Yates, Peter. *Twentieth Century Music: Its Evolution from the End of the Harmonic Era to the Present Era of Sound.* New York: Funk & Wagnalls, 1968.

CLAUDE DEBUSSY

Lockspeiser, Edward. *Debussy: His Life and Mind* (2 vols.). London: The Macmillan Co., 1962.

Thompson, Oscar. *Debussy: Man and Artist.* New York: Tudor Publishing Co., 1940.

Vallas, Léon. *Claude Debussy: His Life and Works* (trans. by Maire and Grace O'Brien). London: Oxford University Press, 1929.

ERIK SATIE

Austin, William W. "Satie Before and After Cocteau" in *The Musical Quarterly.* XLVIII/2; April, 1962.

Myers, Rollo H. *Erik Satie.* New York: Dover Publications, Inc., 1968.

ARNOLD SCHOENBERG

Schoenberg, Arnold. *Fundamentals of Musical Composition* (ed. Gerald Strang). London: Faber, 1967.

Stuckenschmidt, Hans Heinz. *Arnold Schönberg* (Trans. by E.T. Roberts & H. Searle). New York: Grove Press, Inc., 1960.

Wellesz, Egon. *Arnold Schönberg* (trans. by W.H. Kerridge). London: Dutton, 1925.

BÉLA BARTÓK

Stevens, Halsey. *The Life and Music of Béla Bartók.* New York: Oxford University Press, 1964.

Szabolsci, Bence. *Béla Bartók: His Life in Pictures with Introductory Study* (trans. by S. Karig & L. Halápy) London: Boosey & Hawkes, 1964.

IGOR STRAVINSKY

Siohan, Robert. *Stravinsky* (trans. by E.W. White). London: Calder & Boyars Ltd., 1965.
Stravinsky, Igor. *An Autobiography.* New York: N. & J. Stever, 1958.
Stravinsky, Igor, and Robert Craft. *Conversations.* Garden City: Doubleday, 1959.
————*Expositions and Developments.* Garden City: Doubleday, 1962.
————*Dialogues and a Diary.* Garden City: Doubleday, 1963.
————*Memories and Commentaries.* Garden City: Doubleday, 1960.
Vlad, Roman. *Stravinsky.* (trans. by F. & A. Fuller). London: Oxford University Press, 1967.
White, Eric Walter. *Stravinsky: The Composer and His Works:* Berkeley: University of California Press, 1966.

ANTON VON WEBERN

Kolneder, Walter. *Anton Webern: An Introduction to His Works* (trans. by H. Searle). Berkeley: University of California Press, 1968..
Moldenhauer, Hans (comp). *Anton von Webern Perspectives* (ed. D. Irvine). Seattle: University of Washington Press, 1966.
————*The Death of Anton Webern.* New York: Philosophical Library, 1961.
Webern, Anton. *The Path to New Music* (ed. Willi Reich; trans. Leo Black). Bryn Mawr: Theodore Presser Co., 1963.
Wildgans, Friedrich. *Anton Webern* (trans. E.T. Robert & H. Searle). London: Calder & Boyars, 1966.

ALBAN BERG

Redlich, Hans Ferdinand. *Alban Berg: The Man and His Music.* London: John Calder Publishers, Ltd., 1957.
Reich, Willi. *The Life and Works of Alban Berg* (trans. C. Cardew). London: Thames & Hudson, 1965.

HEITOR VILLA–LOBOS

Helm, Everett. "The Many-Sided Villa" in *High Fidelity.* XII/7; July, 1962.
Mariz, Vasco. *Heitor Villa-Lobos: Brazilian Composer.* Gainesville: University of Florida Press, 1963.

SERGE PROKOFIEV

Hanson, Lawrence and Elisabeth. *Prokofiev: The Prodigal Son.* London: Cassell & Co., Ltd., 1964.
Nestyev, Izrael. *Prokofiev* (trans. F. Jones) Palo Alto: University of Stanford Press, 1960.
Prokofiev, Serge. *S. Prokofiev: Autobiography, Articles, Reminiscences* (ed. S. Shlifstein; trans. R. Prokofiev). Moscow: Foreign Languages Publishing House, 1961.

DARIUS MILHAUD

Milhaud, Darius, *Notes Without Music* (trans. D. Evans). London: Dennis Dobson, Ltd., 1952.

CARL ORFF

Helm, Everett. "Carl Orff" in *The Musical Quarterly*. XLI/2; April, 1955.
Liess, Andress. *Carl Orff: His Life and His Music* (trans. A. & H. Parkin). London: Calder & Boyers, Ltd., 1966.

PAUL HINDEMITH

Hindemith, Paul. *A Composer's World: Horizons and Limitations*. New York: Doubleday & Co., 1961.
Strobel, Heinrich. *Paul Hindemith: Testimony in Pictures* (trans. E. Helm). Mainz: B. Schott's Söhne, 1963.

CARLOS CHÁVEZ

Chávez, Carlos. *Musical Thought*. Cambridge: Harvard University Press, 1961.
Weinstock, Herbert. "About Carlos Chávez: Some Notes" in *Tempo*. 51; Spring, 1959

DMITRI SHOSTAKOVICH

Brown, Royal S. "Shostakovich's Symphonies" *High Fidelity*. 19/4; April, 1969.
Martynov, Ivan. *Dmitri Shostakovich: The Man and His Work* (trans. T. Guralsky). New York: Philosophical Library, 1947.
Rabinovich, Dmitri. *Dmitri Shostakovich* (trans. G. Hanna). London: Lawrence & Wishart, 1959.
Shostakovich, Dmitri. *The Power of Music*. New York: The Music Journal, 1968.

BENJAMIN BRITTEN

Holst, Imogen. *Britten*. New York: Thomas Y. Crowell Co., 1965.
White, Eric Walter. *Benjamin Britten: A Sketch of His Life and Works*. London: Boosey & Hawkes, Ltd., 1954.
Young, Percy Marshall. *Britten*. London: Benn, 1966.

ALBERTO GINASTERA

Chase, Gilbert. "Alberto Ginastera: Argentine Composer" in *The Musical Quarterly*. XLIII/4; October, 1957.
————"Alberto Ginastera: Portrait of an Argentine Composer" in *Tempo*. 44; Spring, 1957.

PIERRE BOULEZ

Boulez, Pierre. *Notes of an Apprenticeship* (trans. H. Weinstock). New York: Alfred A. Knopf, 1968.
Bradshaw, Susan, and Richard Rodney Bennett. "In Search of Boulez" in *Music and Musicians*. XI/5; January, 1963.

LUCIANO BERIO

Beckwith, John, and Udo Kasemets (eds.). *The Modern Composer and His World.* Toronto: University of Toronto Press, 1961.
Berio, Luciano. "The Composer on His Work" in *The Christian Science Monitor.* 60/195; July 15, 1968.

HANS WERNER HENZE

Henze, Hans Werner. "The Composer on His Work" in *The Christian Science Monitor.* 60/188; July 8, 1968.
Kay, Norman. "Henze: Present Day Romantic" in *Music and Musician.* XIII/5; January, 1965.

KARLHEINZ STOCKHAUSEN

Stockhausen, Karlheinz. "The Composer on His Work" (trans. H. Davies). in *The Christian Science Monitor.* 60/201; July 22, 1968.
––––"Two Lectures" (trans. R. Koenig). *die Reihe.* No. 5, 1961.

ELECTRONIC MUSIC

Cross, Lowell M. (comp.). *A Bibliography of Electronic Music.* Toronto: University of Toronto Press, 1967.
Dorf, Richard H. *Electronic Musical Instruments.* New York: Radiofile, 1968.
Judd, F. C. *Electronic Music and Musique Concrète.* London: Neville Spearman, 1961.

MUSIC OF THE UNITED STATES

Barzun, Jacques. *Music in American Life.* Bloomington: Indiana University Press, 1956.
Chase, Gilbert. *America's Music: From the Pilgrims to the Present.* New York: McGraw-Hill, 1966.
Chase, Gilbert (ed.). *The American Composer Speaks: A Historical Anthology, 1770-1965.* Baton Rouge: Louisiana State University Press, 1966.
Copland, Aaron. *The New Music: 1900-1960.* New York: W. W. Norton & Co., Inc., 1968.
Cowell, Henry (ed.). *American Composers on American Music.* Palo Alto: Stanford University Press, 1933.
Edwards, Arthur C., and W. Thomas Morrocco. *Music in the United States.* Dubuque: W.C. Brown Co., 1968.
Fisher, Miles Mark. *Negro Slave Songs in the United States.* New York: Russell & Russell, 1968.
Howard, John Tasker, and George Kent Bellows. *A Short History of Music in America.* New York: Thomas Y. Crowell Co., 1967.

JAZZ

Hodier, André. *Jazz: Its Evolution and Essence* (trans. D. Noakes). New York: Grove Press, 1956.
Schuller, Gunther. *Early Jazz: Its Roots and Musical Developments.* New York: Oxford University Press, 1968.

BIBLIOGRAPHY

CHARLES IVES

Cowell, Henry and Sydney. *Charles Ives and His Music.* New York: Oxford University Press, 1955.
Ives, Charles. "Essays Before a Sonata" in *Three Classics in the Aesthetics of Music.* New York: Dover, 1962.

EDGAR VARÈSE

Chou Wen-Chung. "Varèse: A Sketch of the Man and His Music" in *The Musical Quarterly.* LII/2; April, 1966.
Ouellette, Ferdinand. *Edgar Varèse* (trans. D. Coltman) New York: The Orion Press, 1968.

WALTER PISTON

Carter, Elliott. "Walter Piston" *The Musical Quarterly.* XXXII/3; October, 1946.
Taylor, Clifford. "Walter Piston: For His Seventieth Birthday" in *Perspectives of New Music* 3/1; Fall-Winter, 1964.

WILLIAM GRANT STILL

Arvey, Verna. *Studies of Contemporary American Composers: William Grant Still.* New York: J. Fischer & Bros., 1939.

HOWARD HANSON

Ashley, Patricia. "Howard Hanson." in *Hi Fi / Stereo Review.* 20/6; June, 1968.
Hanson, Howard. "Music In Our Age" in *Music Journal.* Anthology—1965.
————"Strange Gods for Young Composers" in *Music Journal.* 25th Anniversary Issue; 1967.

VIRGIL THOMSON

Hoover, Kathleen, and John Cage. *Virgil Thomson: His Life and Music.* New York: Thomas Yoseloff, 1959.
Thomson, Virgil. *The Art of Judging Music.* New York: Alfred A. Knopf, 1948.
————*Music Reviewed: 1940-1954.* New York: Vintage Books, 1967.
————*The State of Music.* New York: Vintage Books, 1962.
————*Virgil Thomson.* New York: Alfred A. Knopf, 1966.

HENRY COWELL

Brant, Henry. "Henry Cowell: Musician and Citizen" in *The Etude.* LXXV/2; February, 1957 – LXXV/3; March, 1957 – LXXV/4; April, 1957.
Cowell, Henry. *New Musical Resources.* New York: Alfred A. Knopf, 1958.

ROY HARRIS

Ashley, Patricia. "Roy Harris" in *Stereo Review.* 21/6; December, 1968.
Harris, Roy. "The Composer Speaks" in *The New Book of Modern Composers* (ed. D. Ewen). New York: Alfred A. Knopf, 1961.
Sloniminsky, Nicolas. "Roy Harris" in *The Musical Quarterly.* XXXIII/1; January, 1947.

GEORGE GERSHWIN

Goldberg, Issac. *George Gershwin: A Study in American Music.* New York: Simon & Schuster, 1931.
Payne, Robert. *Gershwin.* London: Robert Hale Ltd., 1962.
Rushmore, Robert. *The Life of George Gershwin.* New York: Crowell-Collier Press, 1966.

AARON COPLAND

Berger, Arthur. *Aaron Copland.* New York: Oxford University Press, 1953.
Copland, Aaron. *Copland on Music.* New York: W. W. Norton & Co., Inc., 1963.
————*Music and Imagination.* New York: The New Library of World Literature, Inc., 1959.
————*What to Listen For In Music.* New York: McGraw Hill Book Co., Inc., 1957.
Dobrin, Arnold. *Aaron Copland: His Life and Times.* New York: Thomas Y. Crowell Co., 1967.

GEORGE ANTHEIL

Antheil, George. *Bad Boy of Music.* Garden City: Doubleday, Doran & Co., Inc., 1945.
Pound, Ezra. *Antheil and the Treatise on Harmony.* Chicago: University of Chicago Press. 1927.
Schuller, Gunther. "Conversation with Varèse" in *Perspectives of New Music.* 3/2; Spring-Summer, 1965.

SAMUEL BARBER

Broder, Nathan. *Samuel Barber.* New York: G. Schirmer, Inc., 1954.
Salzman, Eric. "Samuel Barber" in *Hi Fi / Stereo Review.* 17/4; October, 1966.

OTTO LUENING

Ewen, David. "Otto Lueinng" in *American Composers Today: A Biographical and Critical Guide.* New York: The H. W. Wilson Company, 1949.
Luening, Otto. "An Unfinished History of Music" in *Music Educators Journal.* 55/3; November, 1968.

VLADIMIR USSACHEVSKY

Ussachevsky, Vladimir. "The Making of Four Miniatures: An Analysis" in *Music Educators Journal.* 55/3; November, 1968.

JOHN CAGE

Cage, John. *Silence: Lectures and Writings.* Middletown (Conn.) Wesleyan University Press, 1961.
————*Notations.* New York: Something Else Press, 1969.
Cage, John, and Lejaren Hiller. "HPSCHD" in *Source.* 2/2; July, 1968.
Hollander, John. *"Silence* by John Cage" in *Perspectives of New Music.* 1/2; Spring, 1963.

MILTON BABBITT

Babbitt, Milton. "An Introduction to the RCA Synthesizer" in *Journal of Music Theory.* Vol. VIII; 1964.
————"Who Cares If You Listen?" in *High Fidelity.* VIII/1; January, 1958.
————"The Use of Computers in Musicological Research" in *Perspectives of New Music.* 3/2; Spring-Summer, 1965.
Kostelanetz, Richard, "The American Avant-Grade: Part I – Milton Babbitt" *Stereo Review.* 22/4; April, 1969.

NED ROREM

Rorem, Ned. "Four Questions Answered" in *Music Journal.* XXIV/5; May, 1966.
————*Music and People.* New York: George Braziller, 1968.
————*Music from Inside Out.* New York: George Braziller, 1967.

GUNTHER SCHULLER

Schuller, Gunther. "American Performance and New Music" in *Perspectives of New Music.* 1/2; Spring, 1963.
————"The Future of Form in Jazz" in *The American Composer Speaks: A Historical Anthology, 1770-1965* (ed. Gilbert Chase). Baton Rouge: Louisiana State University Press, 1966.
————"What and Why Is A Conservatory" in *Music Journal.* XXVI/8; October, 1968.

MORTON SUBOTNICK

Carlos, Walter. *"Silver Apples of the Moon* by Morton Subotnick" in *Electronic Music.* No. 7; July, 1968.
Subotnick, Morton. "Extending the Stuff Music Is Made Of," in *Music Educators Journal* 55/3; November, 1968.

CHARLES WUORINEN

Wuorinen, Charles. "An Interview With Barney Childs, 1962" in *Contemporary Composers on Contemporary Music* (eds. E. Schwartz & B. Childs). New York: Holt, Rinehart and Winston, 1967.
————"Notes On the Performance of Contemporary Music" in *Perspectives of New Music.* 3/1; Fall-Winter, 1964.

INDEX